"The unknown," to paraphrase E. J. Gold, "is unknown because it does not lend itself to being known;" what must not be spoken is in fact that which cannot be articulated. Wedged among life's supreme unknowns is the field of sexual alchemy, and *Alchemical Sex*, Mr. Gold's elucidation of those portions of this subject that can actually be confined to print, is a laudably serious attempt to make some portion of the unknown, known. From his first curious predictions to the arcana of "evocation" vs. "invocation," the book puffs a welcome breath of fresh air into a world that is currently wholly dominated by "a species which features as its main attribute...a radically disconnected multiple personality with no control over which persona is active at any given moment."

—Robert Svoboda
author of the *Aghora* books:
The Left Hand of God, Kundalini and *The Law of Karma*

The aim of ***Consciousness Classics*** is to bring to life significant publications in the consciousness field, which have not been available, and to showcase new books which are destined to become classics.

Consciousness Classics conserves these texts as the authors originally intended them, in a carefully designed contemporary format for new generations of readers. These books are an important legacy of groundbreaking consciousness explorers of the 20th century.

E. J. GOLD

ALCHEMICAL SEX

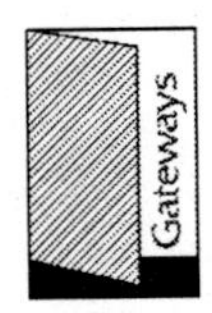

GATEWAYS CONSCIOUSNESS CLASSICS

E. J. GOLD

ALCHEMICAL SEX

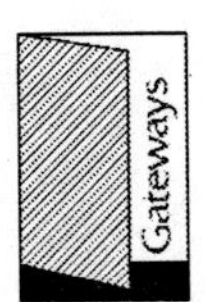

GATEWAYS CONSCIOUSNESS CLASSICS
GATEWAYS BOOKS AND TAPES
NEVADA CITY, CALIFORNIA

Typesetting by Tabatha Jones; layout by iTRANSmedia
Proofreading by Patricia Elizabeth, Rose Gander, Tabatha Jones
Cover art © 2003, Heidelberg Editions International
Cover photo by E.J. Gold
Cover design by Marvette Kort

Gateways Books and Tapes
P.O. Box 370
Nevada City, CA 95959
1-800-869-0658
http://www.gatewaysbooksandtapes.com
ISBN: 0-89556-137-9

TABLE OF CONTENTS

Figure Study, E.J. Gold, charcoal, Rives BFK, © 1987 HEI

EDITOR'S FOREWORD

TO GIVE this book a proper reading, imagine yourself in an upper story room, long and wide as a banquet hall, with wood plank flooring and high ceiling. It is late at night, some evening in 1977, and a group of people has gathered there over a late dinner, followed by a talk. E.J. Gold is sitting at the center of the head table, with more tables to his left and right, and two sets of tables perpendicular, forming an inverted U-shaped assembly.

It is late, after dark, and the lighting is dim in this hall. Candles are burning on all the tables, which are covered with rich, deep-blue tablecloths. The plates and silverware have been cleared away, and listeners lean forward, sipping from their glass tumbler water glasses or perhaps finishing a cup of tea or coffee.

On the walls are a magnificent set of paintings by the late artist Tom X., a member of the Institute (I.D.H.H.B., Inc.) and friend to all present at the time, paintings of angels with wings spread, some with hands cupped together in postures of prayer and remembering. The candles flicker, the scent of incense fills the air, and E.J. Gold speaks on the evening's topic, preparation for Alchemical Work. It is a true discourse, in the classical sense, like the discourses recorded by Plato in his Symposium and Phaedrus. The dinner guests are all students or visitors to the Institute, many who have pursued these ideas and inner work espoused by Mr. Gold for five or ten years or more. As the discourse goes on, listeners are galvanized, they nod and sit up, take deep breaths, listen with more attention to the subtle commentary. There is electricity in the air, a charged feeling to the room. Students' eyes sparkle, they are fascinated with the topic. No one has heard this information before, even those who are steeped in esoteric books—Buddhism, Sufism, Kabbalah, Christian Mysticism, The Fourth Way—have never heard these details before. It is a release of new formulations into the room, a rush of revealed knowledge that is almost audible.

A few students have notebooks open, and they do their best to listen and jot down notes at the same time, catching as much detail as they can, knowing that if they sit down with others the next morning or afternoon, they may be able to supply words and phrases they missed, or expand a quick notation by leaning on another's understanding of some difficult point or completely unfamiliar phrase.

For example, you will find here references to the centrums, higher and lower, moving, feeling and thinking centrums. If you are unfamiliar with this term, think of it as centers in the body, not necessarily located in a fixed spot like chakras, not linked with particular bodily organs, but representing the sum-total of the functioning of the human being in that category, i.e., thinking or emotions or voluntary physical functioning, while the automatic body functions of survival are assigned to the instinctive or reflex centrum.

You will find here extensive information about the esoteric roots of the harem in the Middle East, and one figure that appears in these talks, the Malamat, had his name spelled five or ten different ways in the student notes that formed this book—and the detail of his activity in the old harems was carefully notated by the note-takers. ***Alchemical Sex*** is the record of a series of talks that stretched out over many decades by the time we include the latest chapters in this book. Because of the special atmosphere in that rarefied chamber, and at the request of E.J. Gold, those particular talks were NOT recorded, as many others both before and after were.

The ideas of these talks had to be reconstructed from the students' notes and from their memories, a special attention and consciousness exercise that extended the value of the evening talks into a process of inner work and transformation for the individuals who participated. In fact, the physical notes to these talks were stored or put aside, as other topics and other exercises proceeded at The Institute. The talks gained the status of fable or mythology.

Working on correcting these took many months, but E.J. Gold is reasonably satisfied that the book in its present form DOES correspond to the ideas in the talks he gave. The book is now an accurate reconstruction from students' notes, with over a full year of editing by the author. Where other talks or private publications of The Institute are cited for background, the current titles and formats available for those works are given in footnotes to the text.

Gateways Books offers this edition in the hope that it will be read by serious students of the transformative paths, and serious students of alchemical work. We release it into the mix of esoteric knowledge that is entering the culture with the wish that the tremendous excitement, the charge of recognition that students at those angel-observed banquets experienced, may communicate to others, and help them along the path of their own inner work.

Iven Lourie
Nevada City
March, 2003

CHAPTER 1
THE CENTRUMS

THERE IS NO REASON biologically why the human biological machine should not last nine hundred years—the longevity enjoyed by Methuselah and other early human inhabitants of the Earth—given the right set of circumstances and careful attention to diet, exercise and other disciplines, except that in today's atmospheric conditions, with a depleted ionosphere allowing solar and other radiation to pass easily to the surface, together with the presence of radioactive materials such as plutonium—which every human being now has within himself or her-self due to several nuclear accidents over the past few decades—human beings have little chance of surviving longer than eighty or ninety years. Any doctor or scientist would agree with the idea that humans could live a lot longer if their environment, diet and medical health were fully harmonious.

Today, science and medicine cannot imagine why it is that the human body ages so rapidly, and even more confounding is the fact that the mind often deteriorates long before the body ages to the point of final inner organic decay and death.

It is just this little problem engendered by the mechanical needs of our present day society which is the invisible cause of these phenomena. The centrums, which should be tapped slowly and paced according to their whole lifetime potential, are instead forced through the necessities of the accelerated tempo of contemporary life to unravel much faster than was intended by nature. Each centrum has only so much material, and when that is used up, the centrum dies. In this way, man in quotation marks always "dies by thirds."

If we know the exact contents and capacities of each of the lower and higher centrums, particularly the Motor, Instinctive, Emotional and Thinking Centrums—keeping in mind that all centrums have widely differing amounts of life force and substances which do not all empty at the same rate—then we can adjust the flow of our inner and outer lives to the correct harmonious blending of operation, to insure a long life equal at least to that of Methuselah, merely by creating consciously in ourselves, through discipline and application of the most basic laws of health and diet, an "all-centrums-blending-of-several-mutually-paradoxical-flows-at-once."

The ancients understood exactly how to do this, and a long life of Biblical proportions was not uncommon even as late as the time of Babylon and Nineveh, but was quickly lost sometime during the latter half of the First Millenium, B.C.

How can we adjust this inner organic time-flow in our own centrums? Due to the mechanical necessities of living in the present age, with its chemical, biological and radiological perturbations, we cannot ordinarily do so.

Even if we did not have chemical foodstuffs, prepared frozen, canned and processed foods, artificially fortified pulp foods, fast foods, tobacco, alcoholic beverages, carbonated drinks, carbonized fats, deep-fried foods, chemical flavorings and preservatives and a total absence of body-harmonizing physical efforts in the workplace, the mere presence of microwaves and other disturbing and damaging waves within the destructive bandwidth of the Electro-Magnetic Spectrum together with the results of radiological accidents in the Earth's atmosphere make it impossible to contemplate serious longevity and survival for human beings, beyond a single century, and far from expanding, this time period will grow shorter and shorter as planetary conditions continue to deteriorate throughout the next several centuries until sometime in the 28th century. In the year 2787 the Earth will collide with a large asteroid and civilization will by then be so far in decay that humans will be unable to do anything to stop this from happening, and given the degree of violence of the species, perhaps this is all to the good.

Meanwhile, we who are here now are alive and wish to work toward a higher life beyond the physical universe and, given this goal, we can and should make all efforts necessary so that one of our centrums will not die before the others, by living so that the forces of all five major lower centrums are used harmoniously in equal proportion, and to bring all five lower centrums and at least three of our higher ones into this same harmony.

If we seriously intend to accomplish this in the face of all those planetary and natural forces arrayed against such a cosmological result, we will have to do so through several very extraordinary means not at all common to the life of human beings—and these extraordinary methods are what I intend to introduce to you through this series of talks.

Someday soon, after an enormous planetary catastrophe which wipes out most of the ills of over-civilization by destroying most of the art, science and culture which we now experience, the survivors, numbering as few as one hundred thousand remaining human beings, may as a species return to the much slower tempo of human life as it was in the long-distant past, thus expanding our natural longevity back to its proper length of 900 years, as experienced by Methuselah and others of his generation, if the radiation level did not obliterate even this chance for personal survival—of course this will be impossible in the face of the nuclear winter which will bring about four ice-ages in rapid succession.

Nowadays, in the immediate present, given the already serious deterioration of conditions for life on Earth, human beings have at the most less than a century of healthy adult existence in order to work toward an all-centrums harmony necessary for higher existence. For this inner work toward organic and spiritual harmony, we would ordinarily require at least one hundred thousand years, which is clearly impossible for humans of planet Earth.

But...if it takes one hundred thousand years to achieve this harmony of all centrums, how can we possibly accomplish this work in the little time we have available to us?

We can from this simple fact readily see the urgency of our present situation.

Whether we live for one hundred thousand years or less than one hundred years, we are still in the same situation; we will receive and process within our centrums the exact same number of impressions, the same number of thoughts, actions, breaths, heartbeats, emotions and thoughts. Our days are literally numbered by the internal microprocessor which is the salt-water computer carried by our walking cellular computer.

Using several methods which have been held secret from the larger mass of humanity, we can learn to do this inner harmonious work in only a few years, even though it can ordinarily only be accomplished in one hundred thousand years, but in order to do this, our inner life must be artificially and consciously accelerated and kept at an accelerated pace, with quite different and consciously directed accelerations for each of the lower and higher centrums working in an equally consciously directed harmony, regulated by special uses of a very disciplined and educated special form of combined attention of several centrums acting in unison.

This is, of course, impossible for a species which features as its main attribute a radically disconnected multiple personality.

We ordinarily are a different person for every variation of event; we are one thing for our parents, another at school or work, yet another at play, still another in a sexual relationship and many others for emergencies, accidents, upsets, frustrations, excitement and amusements.

Given the fact that human beings are in general split personalities with no control over which persona is active at any given moment, how can we possibly organize ourselves into a single entity which is always present and always in control of the machine and its actions, and which is not merely a reaction-machine responding to external and internal stimuli?

We must learn somehow to make ourselves into a single entity, and when we have done this, we must then learn to use our combined unified attention in entirely new ways, ways that we would normally learn if only we had more time for life and were to begin with a unified being, and we must also learn to consciously regulate and economize our inner forces and moreover, learn somehow to make all our centrums operate harmoniously as a single unified entity.

This would be a truly collected state in a genuine harmoniously centrumed life, but even this is only a beginning, because a very concentrated attention and serious inner discipline are totally necessary for work if we hope to attain being-completion and to transcend the organic universe in less than one century of life.

We can only learn to harmonize our centrums by, on the one hand, consciously refraining from certain animalistic activities of the machine while increasing other ordinarily uncustomary inner and outer workings of the human biological machine in special ways not at all customary to us, and to activate in ourselves certain higher forces in order to encourage our higher and lower centrums to produce and release very specific higher substances and energies which can be used for harmonizing the centrums at precisely corresponding rates and for producing higher results which we shall more fully examine in these discourses.

Not every centrum operates the same; one centrum should produce and release more higher substances, another centrum should produce and release less; one centrum should process more impressions, another should slow down its processes.

One centrum may be producing a full-blown three-dimensional tactile hallucination while another remains occluded, and needs to be opened up to its full potential by special means and methods not organically attainable without extreme impartial self-discipline and regulation of higher levels of attention.

Ordinarily, when all the stored potential energies and substances of any one centrum have been fully expended, that centrum dies, making harmonious balance of all centrums therefore impossible.

There are other problems related to the achievement of all-centrums harmony, but the premature death of one of the centrums is the basic problem in longevity, and the one which is most evident to modern science and medicine. The problem presented by single-centrum death for higher purposes is, of course, not the realm of modern science and medicine and remains unknown to those primitive organically-rooted studies.

If we operate primarily from one centrum, we should learn to expand ourselves through the application of special exercises so that we can learn to use the other centrums equally well, in the same way that we might learn to be ambidextrous—to use both hands equally well for the process of, say, painting or sculpting—and therefore to process impressions through all centrums in order to preserve all centrums equally and harmoniously.

In order to do this, we must know first exactly how many impressions remain unexpended in each centrum, and how to conserve these in depleted centrums and accelerate them in atrophied centrums.

But how can we come to know how many impressions we have left in each centrum? In order to determine this, we must first learn a great deal more about what is inside us, and we must learn to understand the basic technical details of exactly how the human biological machine operates, especially in the non-organic realms beyond the small range of the Electro-Magnetic Spectrum ordinarily viewed by hominids.

If I were to tell you exactly what is inside you, and describe to you in detail the inner workings of your organic machine, it would in fact be harmful to you, because you would lose the opportunity to make those self-initiated internal efforts which are themselves the primary operant factors which actually produce the effect you are trying to bring about in your inner world. The information itself, without those efforts toward self-understanding, is utterly meaningless and without power to change your life even one iota.

However, if you can learn to correctly and impartially self-observe, you may come to know how much life remains within you and to bring that livingness potential to its fullest fruition, and through other efforts based on impartial self-observation, you may also learn exactly what steps you must take in order to bring about the harmony-of-all-centrums, which in turn makes further higher work possible.

So now, armed with this information, you have within yourself at the present moment, the means for understanding the urgent necessity for truly impartial self-observing of the workings of the human biological machine, and for the real understanding of the need for your impartial discipline and will over the mechanical, animalistic will of the machine for its own gratification and ease of existence, toward which it will inevitably always gravitate in the same way that an unattached apple on an apple tree will always fall toward the earth.

Only you yourself, operating with full conscious use of your impartiality and attention, can know the machine sufficiently well to be able to properly re-direct the organic life-form within which you temporarily find yourself living, for an exact and higher aim. If you do not have a specific higher aim, you will never develop necessity to apply your higher will against the organic will of the human biological machine.

Single-centrum and two-centrum deaths result from allowing the machine to have its way, and such centrum-deaths are responsible for a large number of so-called illnesses unique to contemporary man.

Each category of so-called "illness" can be explained by the death of one or another of the centrums. Sometimes centrums can be recharged, especially in some cases of centrum-death of the Emotional Centrum, which produces the result commonly called "cancer," but this requires the intentional transfer of a great amount of higher force and can cost the healer his or her own health through the depletion of their own higher centrums. Nevertheless, in some cases, it may be worth the price.

Do not make the mistake of assuming that you are different from all others and that just because you're so much smarter than everyone else, you yourself have a great deal of time to accomplish the harmonization of centrums, merely because you think you probably have another twenty, thirty or forty years of life left to you.

It is not a great deal of time at all. Besides which, you do not know if you have used up any of your centrums or almost used them up. If you have almost used up one centrum and show no promise, it is useless to refill your depleted centrum with Higher Forces, which are limited and rare, and no one who could really help you will bother to give to you when there are so many more promising and willing individuals that they can help.

Help cannot come from nowhere; special help only comes through actual work necessity. You have only a small amount of work-time for your Work.

I wish for your sake and also for mine that we had a full one hundred thousand years and that we could slowly work to transmit, elaborate and master each thing, one step at a time. But we do not have one hundred thousand years, and to even give yourself the potential for work, it is necessary that you live long enough in good health to master everything you will need to make for yourself a place in the Work, which confers upon you the necessity for higher work—nothing else will give you the strength and will to work but an actual place in the Work, and this must be achieved before anything else is possible. In order to assure this, you must take a special work-obligation, develop the will to work in the Work, harmonize your centrums, demonstrate repeatedly your ability to achieve impartiality, show compassion for all beings everywhere, and in turn you may possibly be accepted in this work-obligation.

To take upon yourself this serious inner work obligation, you must first study obligation itself. This takes time, but not so much time as one hundred thousand years. Maybe only five years of study, then five years more to prepare to take a work-obligation upon yourself, then maybe five more years to learn to actually perform the necessary inner work and to develop the will to do this work and then, after some fifteen years of preparation, one can perhaps actually take upon oneself a real work-obligation along with the will to actually remain within it.

This is a very fast path compared to ordinary mastery of each form of inner work as performed by ancient traditional methods.

If this preparation for a work-obligation is not worth fifteen years of your precious time, then this method of inner work is clearly not for you. To prepare as a candidate for concentrated distilled inner work and super-sacrifice, we must be prepared to work seriously many hours every day, not just sit on a couch and watch daytime soap operas and drink beer and eat pretzels for eleven months and three weeks, then attend a weekend workshop in some remote and exotic location with a name-brand guru, with the hope of gaining anything of a serious nature.

To take a real work-obligation upon yourself is not a small thing. It is slavery of a higher kind, but slavery nonetheless—the chaining of the self to a yoke in the same way that oxen are clamped into a yoke to pull a wagon or to rotate a water-wheel or grain-crusher.

Work-obligation is the supreme culmination of all possibilities of human life and beyond human life into the sublime, but before we can take any serious work-obligation, we must be able to accept obligation and to develop the will to perform that obligation without fail every single hour and every minute of every single day of our lives until death do us part—and before we are able to even dream of accepting such obligation, we must be willing to work seriously toward this aim, in the same way that a ballerina or a trapeze artist would be dedicated to the necessary repetition and practice without boredom, resentment or hope for future reward, and before we can even be willing to work in this way we must start with knowledge—we must somehow gain the certainty that we really wish to do this thing, and that it is worth our valuable time and tireless effort and, moreover, that we are quite willing—and able—to pay the very heavy price of success.

In order to work, we must understand that in any real sense, we are already as if dead, and that without special work of centrums for the completion of the soul-body, we will die just exactly like a lower-order animal, such as a dog.

In order to gain the will to work in this special way, we must first realize the utter hopelessness of life as ordinary humans live it.

When you have become a candidate for initiation into the Work, perhaps you will say to yourself, "Oh, poor ordinary folks, they will die like dogs. I have heard and read about the Work, so at least I will not perish like a dog. I am very special!"

Unfortunately, at this point, the only special thing about us is that we know that an ordinary human being who has not worked to complete the soul-body will certainly die just like a dog, but this realization is just one single small step above ordinary human beings who have no idea that they will die like dogs, and no more interest in the matter than any dog—they would prefer to depend on some super-being whom they would like to believe will come along and save them and make them special just by touching them on the forehead.

To be more than just a dog takes much inner and outer work. If we are not willing to seriously work on our inner world, to make a real preparation for Work in the Real World, then it is far better to quietly return to ordinary life where we can at least enjoy those days left to us.

CHAPTER 2
THE ALCHEMICAL LABORATORY

A HUMAN BEING is like a capacitor—a Leyden jar—which gathers and condenses electrical current up to a definite level of capacitance, or electrical potential—and what we gather in this way is a lifetime of impressions. One can live only so long as the jar does not completely discharge its contents of impressions.

Each capacitor has a definite level of potential, beyond which it cannot hold the electrical force back—it explodes outward with great energy, like the built-up energy of a laser beam. The capacitor can store only so much force, and then just like any other electrical capacitor, when it reaches its highest degree of fullness, it transfers all the electrical potential which has built up within it through the anode to the nearest ground, where the energy is dissipated through the laws of Entropy, Diminishing Returns and the Uncertainty Principle.

Within the capacitor a special gas condenses, dancing in a combined colloidal suspension in constant but unequal vibration according to Maxwell's Law, which said gas is conductive only after a certain amount of molality of electrical pressure has accumulated above a definite perceptual level which we will call "the event horizon."

In the human machine this is represented by brain cells, body cells, fluid dynamics and nervous systems. All brains operate as Leyden Jars for impressions. When they have reached their fullest possible capacity they inevitably discharge. The Cathode-Beginning of life forces a flow of impressions to begin to accumulate in the capacitor. The more rapid the flow of impressions, the more quickly the accumulator reaches its fullest potential, and accordingly discharges and then inevitably dies.

One can measure objectively one's exact "total capacitance for impressions," and thus regulate oneself more or less for a longer or shorter lifetime. In this way longevity can be attained.

In my own case, I am forced to use and store impressions more rapidly than I would egoistically choose for myself, thus definitely shortening my lifespan, but since I am presently perfecting another type of higher body, and for the purpose of transformation of others, I am not concerned with my own personal planetary longevity.

At a certain point everyone can feel that their capacitance-fullness has almost been attained in one or more centrums and can, if they are attentive, recognize that their planetary death is near. If necessary, one can at this time isolate oneself from almost all impressions, more or less through the use of various technical means and in this way extend one's lifetime for several more years, should this become for one reason or another imperative for the completion of one's work.

In this series of discourses, we will explore the inner workings of the human biological machine as much more than merely a chemical factory. We will see that it can operate as an alchemical laboratory and, in fact, ancient alchemy always referred to the inner workings of the human biological machine, not to some external chemical glassware, kilns and the production of so-called "precious metals." It was only during the repressions of the Middle Ages that this idea came to popularity in order to escape prosecution by the Inquisition.

The object of making lead—Pb—into gold—Au—was an understandable and excusable goal for the Medieval mind, and many wealthy patrons gladly funded so-called alchemists in the pursuit of this absurd hobby. Not that it can't be done, but that it is an entirely worthless occupation in the face of what can really be accomplished in life.

Much more can be accomplished through alchemy, and there are more precious substances than gold, silver and platinum, many of which are only now becoming known by science.

Some of these substances have a very short half-life and occur only momentarily, while others tend to persist and are passed back and forth between Alchemical Partners, and are sometimes stored in various areas of the human biological machine, notably the lymphatic system called "Buddha's Necklace" and other glandular nodes.

Electrical forces are also created by the force of sexual energies, and must be applied in very definite ways for the transformation of the said substances. These are often described in the encrypted texts of some alchemists who practiced real alchemy, but are often decrypted by gold-hunting bipedal hominids in terms they understand and for purposes which seem to a real alchemist to be absurd—the transformation of lead into gold and the production of the alchemist's stone, a magical rock which confers all sorts of imaginary powers to the magician—not at all a result desired by a real alchemist, who is much more concerned with higher cosmic results than mere physical and organic tricks.

It is well understood even by today's primitive science that the human biological machine is actually a chemical factory regulated by electrical energies. Even the most extremely conservative of ultra-conservative scientists, those of the medical profession, agree that the brain is itself deaf, dumb and blind, and that it relies on electrical pulses generated by perceptual organs for the information it utilizes in order to produce within itself a simulation of external reality by which it guides and regulates the organic machine through the world.

It is also well-known that time is a function of gravity and that all mass generates a gravity-well.

Even the fact that the universe is expanding from a single point of mass—the result of a black hole in another universe—is now well understood and accepted.

What is not understood very well is that the human being is capable of transcending the universe itself.

Through certain definite techniques, the human biological machine is capable of processing, producing and exchanging higher substances useful in the evolution of higher centrums and in the assemblage of higher bodies.

Sexual substances and energies are part, but not the entirety, of these processes, but not as produced by the usual sexual interplay and frantic self-satisfactions.

Most sex as experienced by homo saps and other bipedal mammals of the hominid family, particularly of the primate variety, is more or less mutual masturbation, however disguised in love and romance this may be, with most males tending toward spreading their seed and marking their territory, and most females gravitating toward security, safety and propagation of the species with their own offspring of course receiving the majority of the benefits.

This is not a good basis for Alchemical Sex, and must be outgrown before anything genuine can be achieved.

Alchemical Sex is the exalted method by which the alchemical laboratory is built and activated, and through which microcosmic substances and events are transformed for macrocosmological results, and animal sex is definitely alien to this process.

The very first thing the alchemist must sacrifice is the orgasm.

The second sacrifice of the alchemist is personal gratification through mutual masturbation.

The third sacrifice is momentary personal annihilation through organic oblivion, satisfaction and exhaustion.

The fourth sacrifice is the game of personal romance.

The fifth sacrifice is that of sexual conquest and territorial imperative.

The sixth sacrifice is the dream-factory of sexual fantasies.

The seventh sacrifice is sex as a means of personal survival.

These are all very difficult sacrifices for ordinary human beings to even contemplate, much less agree to and then personally carry out fully to their logical conclusion. Most humans don't have the will to even stop masturbating toward orgasm, with or without a partner, much less go on to the more difficult sacrifices.

This prevents lower species from achieving macrocosmic results, which is all to the good. Apes do not belong in the higher dimensions and do not do well in the Upper Spheres.

Nude in Rippled Corridor, E.J. Gold, charcoal, Rives BFK, © 1987 HEI

CHAPTER 3
INVOCATION

WHICHEVER ORGANIC ENTITY it is we have evoked, we are interested in only those we can invoke—that is, from Above. Sexual substances can be a substitute for the reciprocal feeding process when in the Real World, in which everything is alive and has subjective and objective consciousness.

Laughter is a "Banishing" for certain types of invocations while it can be an invoking force for authentic Work invocations.

When French is the "language of invocation" then a complete phrase in especially offensive gutteral German can be its "Banishing" force.

The entity "Jehovah" invites us to eat his body and drink His blood, but we must change ordinary substances into the higher for this special purpose.

The "Host," which is represented by bread, is first dipped in salt and then in wine; we thus taste and ingest both the bitter and the stringent, without which higher life would be impossible.

An impartial utterance of the word "God" will invoke an entity claiming to be God—usually our own inner-God whom we have evoked by accumulating substances on which—if we allow Him—He likes to feed, not any objective God and certainly not the Absolute, the God beyond all human concepts of God.

We must make certain that our inner God does not obtain these substances from us through carelessness or stupid personal egoistic romantic ideas of ourselves or our work partner.

If we allow our inner God to take our energies, then nothing will be left as "bait" for higher entities or to be used to feed Objective Prayer for the use of the Absolute.

Our Invocational Chamber must be made in such a way as to contain the uncontainable, and this can only be accomplished if we understand the principle of the "Magnetic Bottle," that force which through magnetic energies can contain pure plasma—a high form of energetic wavicle or energized matter.

The Magnetic Plasma Bottle, or "Alembic," is not strictly physical in its nature, but we will examine this principle in detail later in our alchemical discourses.

An entity invoked during the process of Alchemical Sex would ordinarily be able to appear to us only through mediums, but because we are acting as mediums, which is to say, as transmission points between dimensions, the entities invoked are able to substantially alter the invocational chamber to correspond to themselves, their atmospheres and their worlds.

We must learn to be firm in banishing those entities which become obnoxious or which demonstrate some form of negativity—firmly and immediately—the moment something goes wrong, at the very first moment we realize that the invocation has "turned sour," or such negative entities can easily keep us occupied with subjective and negative nonsense for hours.

Of course, if we allow the invoked entities to flatter us, then we may never notice that something has indeed gone wrong.

Voluntary identification is to allow ourselves to fall into a posture—

organic, emotional and mental—of an entity, in order to "bind" it to our cosmos for a short while, but with strict impartiality.

That is to say, we are neither attracted to its manifestations, nor repelled by them.

We have attained neutrality when we can approach the unknown without considering our own views too much.

Substance is the "Blood of the Covenant."

The unknown is "unknown" ***by definition***.

All phenomena, including what we see, feel, touch and sense, is illusion.

We can learn to form intentional bridges between our lower centrums and also between lower and higher centrums, and also to connect various invocations like pieces of a giant spatial and temporal jigsaw puzzle, over a long period of time through many invocations.

Regardless of which specific "keys" we use to call down presences upon ourselves or what methods we use to accomplish this—whether we use posture, mentation or emotion—the end result will always be the same for us, because the keys used will always be those which fit the lock.

One "key" we may use for this purpose, the Alchemical Sexual Key, is only usable with the certain knowledge that romantic love is common among humans, but that another kind of love, which we can call "love-without-romance," "higher love," or "agape," is necessary for invocation and that it is possible to achieve this in one who has successfully harmonized all centrums, both higher and lower.

To know that something exists gives one the power to seek something higher. Romantic love is a direct product of the struggle of the Organic Centrums—Motor, Instinctive, Emotional and Thinking—all in competition for power and direction over the machine.

In the case of objective love, we are able to obtain access to a psychometric artifact of romantic and nonromantic love through the Alchemical and Pythagorean Keys.

Enochian Keys are used for quite a different and very personal, purpose.

The master of objective love is able to utilize Objective Alchemical Keys to all systems and methods of achieving the blending of higher substances and of assembling Angelic Clusters, which we examined in detail in the talks which we have called ***Secrets of Angelic Invocation***.*

Of course in Alchemical Sex the lovers must be honest and have no

---

* Private edition, first published by Gateways/I.D.H.H.B., Inc.,1982

need for the courtship masks and the usual romantic games and episodes.

In Alchemical Sex there can be no room for daytime soap operas, Harlequin novel plots and dialogues and ***True Romance*** magazines.

In Alchemical Sex, one can and must discover sex without romance, but not without love—unromantic sex is not commercial sex, nor is it "clinical sex."

Impartial sex is merely sex which is devoid of those negative forces which ordinarily give the usual driving force to sex—which is to say, the urge to reproduce oneself and to momentarily gratify nerve endings toward the end of temporary personal annihilation through exhaustion and satisfaction, all of which are the real driving force behind all romantic notions attached to, and inseparable from, ordinary sexual drives.

In Alchemical Sex we do everything to disempower the Ordinary Moving Centrum using the same force which usually empowers and drives the sex centrum. Impartial sex directed by the higher centrums and not by the sex impulses of the Motor and Instinctive Centrums can be said to be "sex without romance."

Only with this "sex without romance" is it possible to exchange higher substances for mixture and dispersal through the chemical factory of each partner in alchemical experiments.

The first real step in a school is to mercilessly destroy in ourselves the results of romantic ideas rooted in us from our first day among contemporary civilized human beings who are themselves the fruit of former equally wonderful civilizations.

Romantic-imaginary-fixations are the combined emanations and manifestations of the force of ideas which happen to form the majority of cultural conditioning.

Due to the maleficent presence of romance in contemporary life we cannot refuse the ordinary demands of life, but on the other hand, we ordinarily feel no remorse from this because we are able to make our external world romantic and inner life even more romantic through the use of imagination and fantasy.

Why do we not just walk away from our sordid organic lives and seek the higher spiritual planes of existence? It is largely because of our romantic fantasies and our continual search for power, influence and possessions.

We think we would like to end our suffering, change our lives and live more comfortably and agreeably, but we do not ordinarily understand that this takes action and that romantic notions rule us and make us believe somehow that ordinary aims and organic pleasures are worth pursuing.

If we had the will to apply these ideas and were able to take action against our automatic drives and understood fully the emptiness of ordinary pursuits, we would be able easily to transcend our deep sleep and our beliefs in the glaringly false reality of animalistic aims and desires.

Our hopes for ourselves are founded on romantic ideas not far removed from those maleficent ideas presented endlessly by Hollywood and other "Dream Machines" of our civilization.

Romantic fantasies about ourselves and our lives could be said to be the rose-colored glasses through which the Hollywood Dream Machine helps us to transmogrify pigsties into palaces, and pigs into princes and princesses.

Through these special rose-colored lenses, everything seems rosy, just as the Emerald City of Oz is emerald-green only when it is viewed through special eyeglasses with emerald-green lenses.

If everyone is forced to wear such special lenses, everyone will naturally agree that the Emerald City is green.

When we train ourselves to be able to remove these romantic emerald-green "Land of Oz" lenses, we are then suddenly able to perceive the Real World as it is.

However, we may not like what we see, and by this fear and uncertainty, we are compelled to keep our rose-colored lenses on, so we may never come to know that we are really in the bleak gray land of Kansas.

Impartiality poses a threat to organic human romantic ideas, which we call "self-love" and "vanity." Another name for "romantic" is "Maya"—the World of Illusion.

However, in order to understand the concept of Maya, we must understand that ***it is not the world which is the illusion, but the way in which the world and oneself are viewed through the rose-colored lenses of romantic fantasies.***

This "world without romance" may be too frightening to accept, but it is the simple truth, and without this truth, nothing real can be achieved.

Fears and fantasies must be overcome before we can walk through the world as it is and deal with real things in real ways.

Only the Higher Sex-Centrum, when it is free from motor and

.ctive manifestations, can invoke and assemble entities from Above.

If the Sex Centrum is subject to lower animalistic organic manifestations and fantasies, we fall into the Motor Centrum's sexual drives and thus cannot invoke anything beyond our own search for personal gratification and momentary oblivion.

Sensations are not from the Moving Centrum; they are from the involuntary part of the Motor and Instinctive Centrums, which are entirely reflexive knee-jerk reactions to simple spasmodic manifestations of the human biological imperatives.

We thus cannot possibly have voluntary sensations—by definition, sensations surprise us because they are "back-brain" events and they occur long before we become aware of them in any of our awareness "front-brain" functionalities.

Human beings who identify fully with the human biological machine and who cannot view themselves as existing apart from the machine are not able to exist without their precious romantic fantasies; they believe that romantic ideas are the source of spontaneousness, and therefore of personal ***authenticity***.

The fact is that romantic fantasies are very calculated and are built up from beliefs adopted throughout one's life. Romantic human beings are involuntary actors reading from a script memorized in early childhood.

The bedroom is alien to Alchemical Sex—we really ought to enact Alchemical Sex in a Temple or Shrine or a Dedicated Invocational Chamber used only for this purpose, because through this process, when used correctly, we are able to invoke knowledge-holding presences and entities.

If we remove romantic fantasies from any idea or activity, it automatically becomes voluntary—only invocation without romantic fantasies has the possibility of becoming Objective Prayer.

If we must find a definition for personal Work, it could be said to be a different way of seeing and doing the same old things, ***but for a higher purpose and without personal directives, organic imperatives and egoistic agendas.***

CHAPTER 4
IMPARTIALITY

The primary method in Alchemical Sex is to produce the higher formation called in ritual the "Chalice," and in alchemy the Retort, in relation to the formation of the Crucible in relation to the cluster-formation called the Alembic, the special ***"Klein Bottle"*** which has only one surface—no inside and no outside—within which the higher cluster formation can be assembled.

This cluster formation can be assumed by spiritual possession by a higher being, a Celestial Surrogate or living substitute. Every cluster is equal to some posture of the Absolute, and each one has an exact name and method of invocation, which I have already described in detail in

Secrets of Angelic Invocation, without which Alchemical Sex would be impossible.

No single Way of Work contains the complete method of assumption of postures of the Absolute; all the various parts of the puzzle are necessary in order to complete the angelic assemblies and produce the clusters which correspond to the entities being invoked.

Through the various Mental, Emotional and Moving Centrum correspondings given in ***Secrets of Angelic Invocation***, we are able to assume a posture of the Absolute and voluntarily identify with it with all centrums participation, and therefore to begin the process of Alchemical Sex, which is to say, the exchange and processing of higher alchemical substances.

The Way of the Monk is another, simpler method of using the Emotional Centrum to sense some of the more basic Objective Clusters and Postures of the Absolute.

To hold such an emotional posture is to assume an exact mood in the same way that we are able to put on a hat and coat. Mood is of course only one small part of the full description of the postures which create the Assembly of God or Cluster of Angels.

The Way of the Yogi, using the Thinking Centrum, is the mentation part of postures of the Absolute. The Way of the Fakir is the categorical method for the assumption of organic Moving Centrum parts of the same postures, clusters or assemblies.

Taken all together, these keys provide a clue to the methods for Objective Sacred Prayer. These three commonly known keys provide the basis for overcoming organic imperatives, while nine keys to the Kingdom are necessary for the formation of higher bodies and the correct exchange and processing of higher substances through the methods of Alchemical Sex, the real basis of ancient alchemy. We will discuss all nine of these Keys to the Kingdom in our discourses on Alchemical Sex.

In order to understand fully the idea of what is romantic in us, we should study deeply and intensely all ideas of romance to which we were exposed in life up to now. We can in this way gain a thorough idea of romance, particularly in the sense of chivalry, whimsy and impulsive demonstrations.

One may think of our little company here as heartless; those who view themselves and everything else in the romantic sense cannot see love without also the distinct presence of romance—in this instance romance would be one or another form of sentimentality.

If one cannot see above the level of romantic fantasies and personal agendas, a whole world above this, a world without romance, is utterly invisible and impossible to imagine—something which exists apart from one's reality, about which one knows nothing whatever and even the simple existence of which one may have only the vaguest and most cynical idea.

Organic humans make up ideas about this invisible world, sometimes right, more often incomparably wrong. When we say that human beings live in sleep, we mean that human beings cling to persisting romantic ideas about themselves and their world and are unable to take a different view of it. Romance is the root-cause of identification, not the organic fact.

The world of an impartial being is strictly mathematical, never knee-jerk compulsive or organically impulsive; at the same time an impartial being is not an involuntary actor in a pathological drama. To be unromantic is to be impartial in a special way about definite subjects. In this sense, unromantic is a special case of impartiality. Impartiality is the technique; unromantic is one use of this special technique of a school.

One cannot be impartial if one still has one single shred of romance in the perception of oneself and still feels compelled to retain at least some precious and treasured romantic ideas about self and the world.

Manifestations of romance counteract the magical invocation; romantic manifestations are evocation; when there is evocation emanating from within the organic self, there cannot be invocation. Our self is in the way of the drawing-down. The reverse is not necessarily true.

An outward flow blocks an inward flow, but an inward flow does not necessarily prevent outward flow. Alchemically, when there is a "transference of flow" in two directions, from the inner to the outer and from the outer to the inner, there must also be a "reconciling factor," a third force which allows two ordinarily unmixable elements to combine together, usually by means of a fourth, invisible force, called a "Catalyst" which while it undergoes change during the transformation and combination, remains—after the effect has taken place—unchanged from its original formation.

The "reconciling factor," or "third force," can easily be destroyed by romantic manifestations involuntarily or voluntarily manifested, thus disallowing the blending of two irreconcilable forces, objects, concepts or entities.

This can easily be seen by anyone.

A Primary Law must be so obviously true that it is an insult to the intelligence to even bring up the subject. Its very existence proves itself— ***Quod Erat Demonstrandum***.

While the Organic, Emotional and Mental Bodies of humans correspond with Gradations of Reason which allow romantic manifestations, from the Astral Body of Impartial Man on upward into the higher centrums and even higher unmanifested presences, not only are romance and romantic ideas of organic man impossible, but also all ordinary manifestations, romantic or otherwise.

This is perhaps why, to romantic and fantasy-prone organic human beings, someone in the Work may seem to them strange and unusual.

Organic human beings are fearful of those beings who are not hypnotized by life and who are not driven and animated by romantic notions or obsessed by involuntary romantic soap-opera manifestations.

To organic human beings, nonorganic life beyond their senses and far beyond their fears seems terribly frightening and alien.

In fact, they are quite right—the obstacles through which one must pass from the romantic to the impartial is sometimes called by those of the inner circle of humanity the "Sinister Barrier," because of the feelings and fears associated with the emanations of Impartial Beings when viewed and felt by organically-driven human beings, who are wedded to the world of the senses and who are obsessed by those things which they have been taught to desire.

Organic human beings do not, and cannot, understand how anyone could survive without romantic manifestations and ideas.

They quite believe, and probably rightly so, that without the romantic notions and obsessive manifestations demanded by their culture, that their entire civilization, such as it is, would collapse instantaneously and vanish without a trace.

Romantic manifestations and ideas are the foundation of all social structure, of its laws, customs, business, religion and relations.

Romantic manifestations are the regulating factor of the life of organic human beings, without which they would be unable to function automatically, thus forcing them to become active participants in life with full attention, presence and a sense of responsibility, all of which are abhorrent to organic human beings, who are born and raised to seek pleasure and to avoid pain.

Romantic beliefs and obsessive manifestations provide a certain measure of predictability between organic human beings—meaning bipedal ape-descendants—and their whole organic world.

Organic human beings depend on these beliefs, manifestations and obsessions for the stability provided for them by mental concepts, emotional upheavals and Motor Centrum self-calming and the self-love of vanity.

Higher bodies cannot function with the additional organic presence of romantic manifestations, nor can an entity be "called-down" in the presence of romantic organic manifestations.

Impartiality cannot exist in the same organic formation in which there is the presence of romantic manifestations, nor can knowledge be gathered, higher substances collected or transubstantiated, personal transformation occur, objective data be transmitted; nor can there be receptivity to exact needs of the Work, initiation both personal and as a group, knowledge be transformed into "understanding," nor the higher mental substance of higher Gradations of Reason.

For all of these and many other higher data and activities, romantic manifestations are "Banishing."

Almost all of the Work in an Alchemical laboratory, and the whole of work in a school is disintegrated wholly and automatically by the organic presence of involuntary romantic manifestations.

To be unromantic does not mean to become an automaton or a zombie; our verbal tones need not suddenly become flat and unmodulated.

We who are not romantic and who are not driven by organic desires need not move stiffly like robots and speak in monotonic unmodulated voices like so many mechanical dolls, nor do we stare hypnotically into the distance in the accepted mode of "intellectual disinterest"—which appears similar to the average psychotic break, and which can be treated accordingly—just because we have destroyed in ourselves the maleficent impulse of romantic manifestation.

However, one who is unromantically inclined also tends to dismiss as trivial and unimportant those romantic ideas and manifestations which help others maintain an interest in us, in our feelings, and in our subjective views, and we may thus become uninteresting to organically-driven friends, relatives and co-workers in the corporate workplace if we do not have the good sense to hide this characteristic when we appear in ordinary spaces.

CHAPTER 5
DISCIPLINE FOR WORK

MOST HUMAN BEINGS in the sense of those falling under the category of organic male gender together with the corresponding automatic gender identification and vanities necessary for the maintenance of their gender identification, are notably lacking a sufficient poetic sense of wonder.

Their tribal preoccupations are primarily with hunting and killing—if not with a spear or bow and arrow or a chipped-flint knife—with a briefcase, pick and shovel, typewriter or blunt instrument.

Only a very small, utterly unmeasurable in the statistical sense, percentage of men stay behind with the women to become a shaman, while the other men go off joyfully to pursue the hunt, or to raid a nearby village.

To become a real shaman one must strive to understand, and even to sense, from the women's view, the process of inner evocation.

While she, if she is able to make the process of evocation voluntary and not just organic, can help the invocation. Ordinarily it is for her involuntary organic—an inner scream usually stifled by society, which says, "Substances! Substances! More substances! Fill me till my cup runneth over!"

Human males are in general unwilling and unable to cultivate the necessary discipline for Alchemical Sex and the development of higher centrums, because they seek relief in simple organic ejaculation...so why bother to continue?

A male human may resume sexual contact for several orgasmic intervals, but never experience the necessary simple sitting, in the sense that the word "seance" means "to sit."

Yet this patient inner and outer discipline for work is the most basic price of real Alchemical Sex and only the first of many steps toward higher consciousness.

But how does one keep it up? I have anticipated your obvious first question regarding the maintenance of erection, but this question, in the real practice of Alchemical Sex, should not really concern you, because erection and genital sex in general have no real place in our alchemical work.

Ejaculation does not automatically diminish the organic-means-of-delivery, which is to say, the force of momentum proceeding from the Moving Centrum. Remember that it is the Motor Centrum which originates the power of ordinary sex, and in so doing, completely dominates the Power Centrum, which cannot operate while the Moving Centrum is the dominant force.

Orgasm is the involuntary part of ejaculation. When orgasm is allowed to occur, the biological drive is fulfilled, sending signals immediately to the blood rushing toward the blood vessels in the penis to pack up and go home.

It is the organic, so to speak, "five o'clock whistle."

If we wish our lower blood to work overtime for the sake of our higher blood, we must pay a little something extra—what they call in the workplace "time-and-a-half."

Even the most ordinary organic man can pay time; it is the extra "time-and-a-half" which he finds excessive and impossible to pay—and why should he, when no one in ordinary life demands it?

He has no necessity for higher blood; why should he pay extra for it? He is satisfied with early retirement and goes directly to sleep.

All women are magnificent at evocation by nature. ***Some*** men are good at invocation. By concatenation of accident, there are several kinds of men who happen to be capable of it. We can classify them in different categorical formations:

The Warlock—Very involuntary, highly superstitious. For him, magic is like a wishbone and has about the same effect.

The Psychic—Also involuntary, along with an involuntary wish to help others with inevitably disastrous results. He is like the boy scout who helps an elderly lady across the street that she does not wish to cross, in order to earn "merit" for himself.

The Wizard—More fun-loving, less involuntary. Has a greater tendency to daring and is interested in some higher ideas. Still, what he does is for very immediate gains. He spends his life crafting talismen to attract young ladies of the Follies Bergiere.

The Sorcerer—He is more interested in higher ideas and in the origin of knowledge. He wishes to get data to have data and always wears a pointed hat which exactly fits his cranium.

The Magus—He is less involuntary and more dangerous than all the others. He is on the verge—in the esoteric sense—of knowing and has begun to realize that he does not know enough. He is ready to dare anything, but is not yet able to sufficiently dare.

The Magic User—He is voluntary in his use of magic; he can take it or leave it alone. He has cultivated his impartiality toward data which has become for him a tool.

As you can see, these formations are "in the organic." They are not concerned with their substances nor what becomes of their substances, except in an immediate way, particularly on Saturday night, and then only in the same way a pressure cooker requires a valve.

Women, on the other hand, spend their time from the age of three minutes, concentrating almost exclusively on the procurement of substances in one form or another—starting with sugared evaporated milk, through pastries, then seminal substances and finally back to pastries once again.

Pastry represents for her those higher substances which, at least in contemporary civilization, are equal to—and maybe even slightly superior to—those substances produced by contemporary man.

Women put up a facade to prevent themselves from seeing what men really think about them; it would destroy their bon-ton world.

It is impossible when at the zoo, especially near the monkey cage, to not see a very exact picture of the true organic life of human beings, complete with that exact odor which, if not for the invention of cologne, we would be acutely aware of at all times.

People with whom we were once organically connected emanate their own vibrations. When we are connected—"in lineage"—even casually, it never dies completely by itself even after it becomes blended-into-the-totality-of-all-proceeding-vibrations.

There must be an intentional break with past lineage contacts; unless we are able to see in a special way, we would not be aware of the combined effect of all such psychic-emotional influences. Each separate contact has a cumulative effect, plus each of their contacts has an additional effect, and so on.

Primary, secondary, tertiary and quaternary influences are important; beyond this, they are not. Consider, not just the number of contacts, but their views, activities and Gradation of Reason, past, present and future. We struggle against psychic influences...think about other influences, chemical, organic, etc.

True vampirism is the continual, gnawing magnetism of those for whom you once represented personal property in one way or another. There is a certain amount of ownership implied in friendship. In the same way, there is exponentially a much greater and more demanding feeling of ownership from one's old sexual contacts. Along with the magnetic organic force connecting one chemically with previous contacts will be the emotions of loss, poignant sadness and nostalgia, because the memory plays tricks on us and tends to romanticize the past.

Once a contact has been established, it remains, whether we wish it to or not, until we break that contact intentionally once and for all, give up our nostalgia for the memory of something which no longer exists. If we know that a vampire is sucking our blood, we can begin looking for a mallet and a stake.

Chemical influences can also pass through our entire life as can the psychic. Sometimes when people pass within our sphere, they seem to drain, or wish to suck our blood, with a definite feeling of an attractive—in the sense of drawn—form of revulsion combined with the sensations of vertigo and weakness. It is important that those are considered as sensations, not emotions.

This is true of objective magic as well. Definite persons of unpalatable and unmentionable vibrations will somehow assert themselves in the most exalted of events, at the same time drawing upon it a psychic "something" equivalent to your funeral pall.

Any sudden unexpectedness is a Banishing for whatever passed before.

In our new study of the Emerald Tablet of Hermes we find ideas new to this civilization, but old to those which existed long before it:

Hermes' First Law: "As Below, So Above, and As Above, So Below."

Hermes' Second Law: "Whatever Goes Up Must Eventually Come Down."

Hermes' Third Law: "If I Got Into It Once, I Can Fall Into It Again."

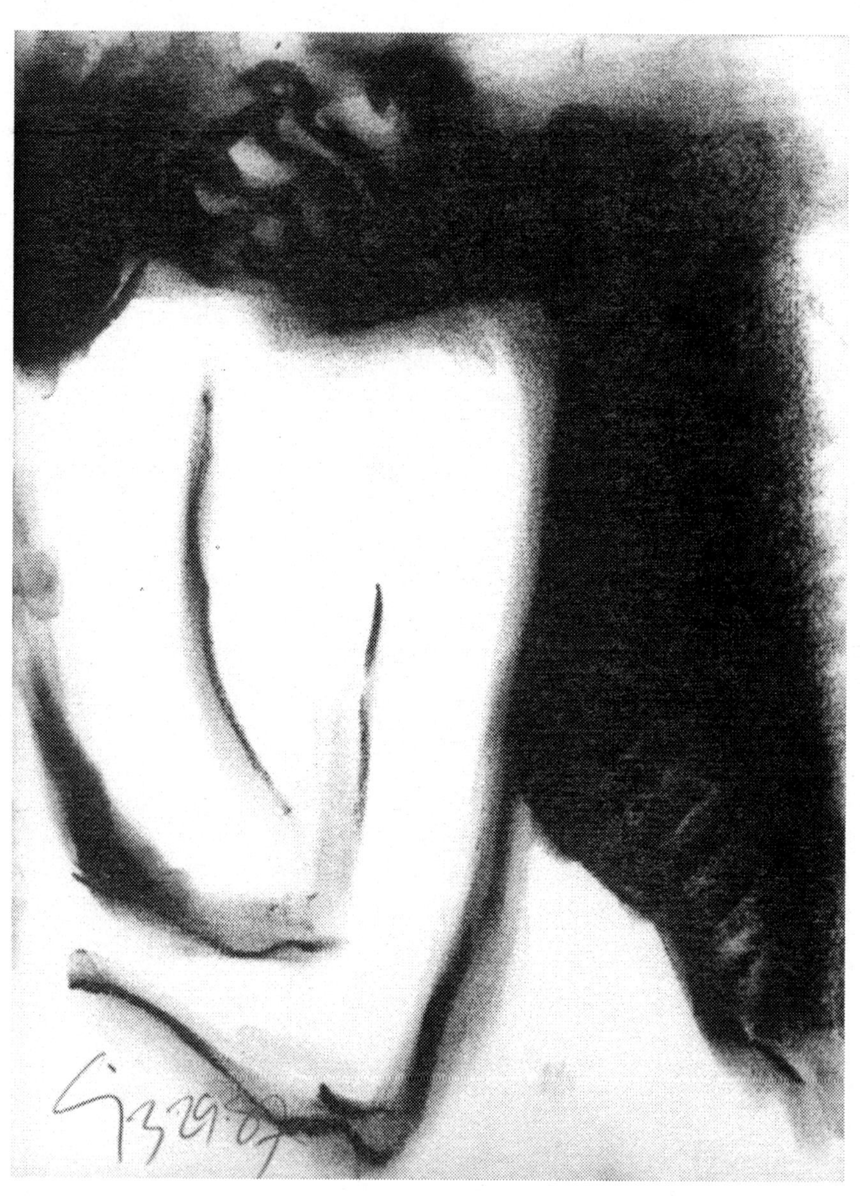

And Which Corridor Shall It Be?, E.J. Gold, charcoal, Rives BFK, © 1987 HEI

CHAPTER 6
BASIC PRINCIPLES OF ALCHEMY

1. ***Calcination***—the primary and most basic of all alchemical operations, calcination uses heat, but not flame, to reduce the principle ingredients. Slow, controlled heat is preferred.

2. ***Dissolution***—dissolving the primary ingredients, primarily the metallic salts and higher minerals, through a longer process than Calcination, using the "Wind and Water" principle of allowing time to exercise a "wearing-down" entropic effect.

3. ***Separation***—winnowing the "wheat" from the "chaff," meaning to isolate the heavier and lighter elements through a process similar to titration. One example of this is the multiple levels of separation achieved in petrochemical distillation in a chemical "chimney" in which the particles are allowed to find their own levels according to their density, or "specific gravity," one example of which is the use of a hygrometer to measure the percentage of presence of antifreeze in an automobile's internal combustion engine coolant system.

4. ***Conjunction***—the conjoining of the principle ingredients through amalgamation, in much the same way that gold can be extracted by its natural tendency to attach itself to mercury, and then the mercury burned away, revealing the collected micronic gold.

5. ***Putrefaction***—darkening of the assembled elements into a blackened highly densified solution.

6. ***Congealation***—the liquified mass as it solidifies into a congealed mass when energy leaves it in the form of evaporation and heat.

7. ***Cibation***—the re-solution of the dried elements into a fine-grain colloidal suspension.

8. ***Sublimation***—the volatile distillation of the mixed elements into a reduced result.

9. ***Fermentation***—transmutation of the resulting mass through the action of a yeast-like powder as a catalytic agent, the yeast undergoing combination and reduction, after which it remains as it was, unchanged, while the transmuted material partakes of a third, very different, state and elemental condition.

10. ***Exaltation***—raising the element into a new octave of Hydrogens in order to bring it to a state of higher electronic and atomic weight—isotopically different from its parent chemical element; although chemically it remains the same, as in strontium 290, which behaves like, but is atomically different from, calcium. This effect is very noticeable in iodine and other halogens, which have many variations in isotopic construction. Cobalt is notable in its isotopic variations as well and serves as a good example of this process.

11. ***Multiplication***—reduction of the powder into a finer matter through the process of exponential algorithmic restructuring, in much the same way as one would process pigments for fine art painting, or the process of "succussion" in homeopathy.

12. ***Projection***—the actual transmission of elements through electronic means, the most common of which is bombardment of particles with its associated side-effect of heat and radiation. One example of this is the bombardment of metals with high-speed electrons in a 50 BEV cyclotron.

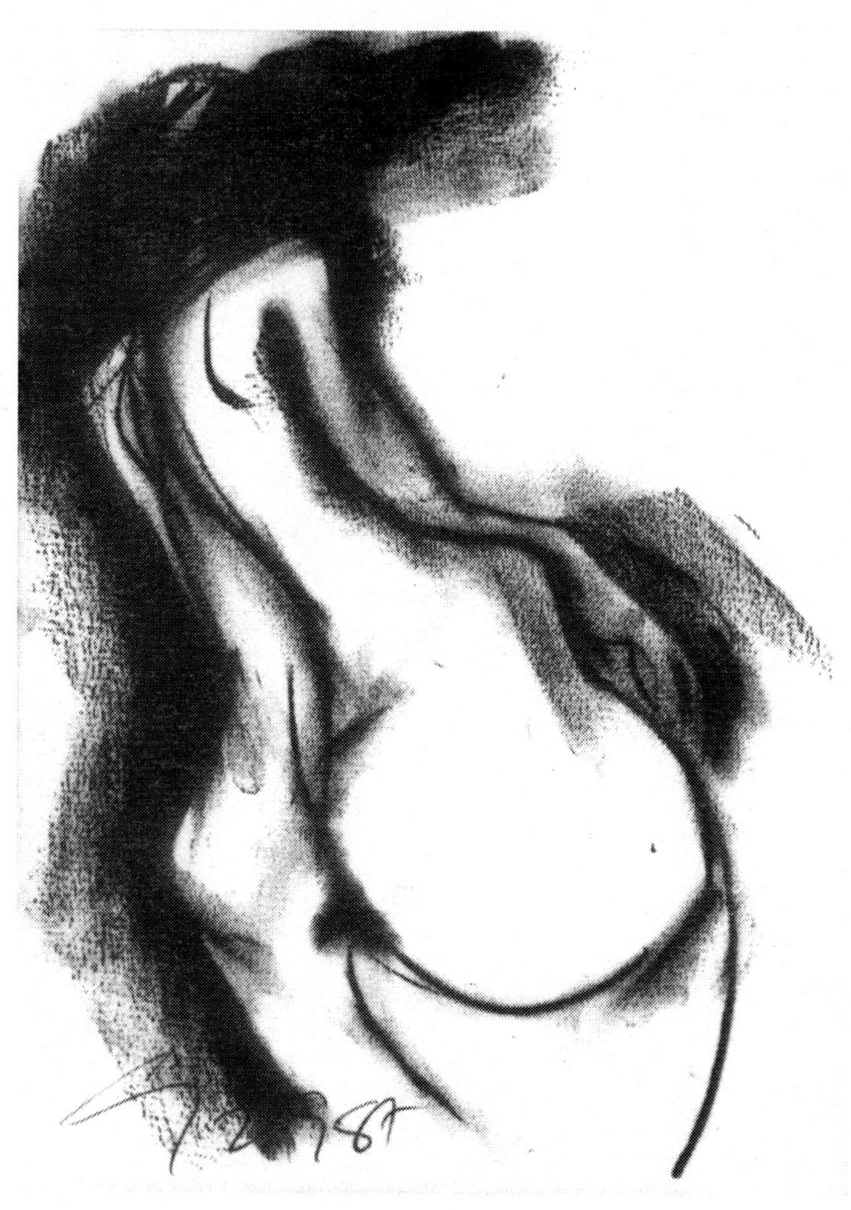

Phantom Form, E.J. Gold, charcoal, Arches, © 1987 HEI

CHAPTER 7
HISTORY OF HAREMS

HAREMS and what goes on in them has always been a well-kept secret to the outsider. Harems were used from the most ancient times to the present day in Egypt, China, Tibet and Central America.

The basis for the harem consisted in the structure of sexual magic as a basis for longevity and coating of higher bodies—amounting to virtual immortality, but immortality is not important except as a side issue, a by-product of the work of Angelic Clusters, as described in the discourses called ***Secrets of Angelic Invocation***.

The structure of the group as known in the Middle East was: caliph, calipha, wives, concubines and the harem. Sexual partners for higher invocational purposes were typically wives and concubines, seldom women of the harem proper. In all enlightened cultures, equivalent groups or clusters were organized for the purpose of invocational sex, and several recent studies indicate that the Pharaohs of ancient Egypt were required to perform such rituals at definite intervals within hidden temples, as were the priests of South and Central American cultures and of course all Eastern civilizations, especially in India, China, Southeast Asia and Japan.

Harem women produced in themselves higher sexual oils and other substances, often without male sexual stimulation, which said substances were then distilled into essential oils for invocational use. These substances still require further transubstantiation for use as a coating substance for higher bodies and for the use of Angelic Cluster formations. This further transformation is the real essence of alchemy.

The original use of aphrodisiacs was for harem production of sexual oils without male partners, which would have altered the chemistry of the oils in unwanted ways not beneficial to invocational uses for which they were intended.

These higher substance essential oils were also placed in tombs for the afterlife, and along with gums arabic and wood resins were used in the mummification process of ancient Egypt. The combined substances collected five times daily from the harem produced only one dram of essential oil ready for transformation into coating substances.

Most tomb robbers of the period were content to leave the gold in the tombs while taking vials of essential oils, which had far greater value in the ancient world and in some parts of the world today, among the more enlightened cultures.

The collection of oils from women in negative states or during menstruation was prohibited, and harem women in either condition were isolated during those times whenever possible, although the mixture of male and female substances could be timed to coincide with menstruation of the concubines and wives—mixture of the white and red alchemical substances when required by special invocations which depended upon such a mixture of red and white.

The mixture was the result of one full month of 28 days of collection and transmuting substances gathered from the donor women, who typically did not take part in the reception of the resulting transmuted substances while remaining in the negative state or during menstruation.

Both men and women produce organic seminal fluids, but each type produced is different from the other.

The working of the chemical factory—if it is not interfered with by negative manifestation or the substances and force for transmuting substances are not drained away by useless and unprofitable activities of the machine—produces sufficient substances for the preparation of the earliest part of higher substances before it is altered for use by the process of exchange.

In alchemical notation the substances were given various terms to describe the process of transmutation of the white substances, which are the products of male semen collected by the female partners without the presence of sperm, which is only possible without orgasm of any of the partners, a concept generally repellent and alien to human beings, and therefore typically "the secret keeps itself."

The female corresponding substance is only produced in sufficient quantity by several women—one female partner cannot possibly produce enough higher substance for Angelic Cluster Invocations.

Several women working as a cooperative team can collect preparatory substances of female semen, transmute it, mix it and then, using the process of exchange-of-substances, combine these collected substances into one single higher substance which can then be shared among them for their own use for the coating of higher bodies and the invocation of Angelic Entities who are able to enter exact Angelic Clusters formed intentionally and knowingly by the group to correspond with each of the Angelic Entities requiring "landing fields" in the local time/space discontinuum, as described in ***Secrets of Angelic Invocation***.

The red substance of alchemy was, of course, intended to mean the substance found only in menstruum. The manifestation of negative emotion associated with this time could destroy accumulated substances if allowed. Women participating in this ceremony must have destroyed in themselves at least the involuntary urge to manifest negatively during the five crucial days—and also nights—of their menstrual cycles.

Higher bodies are made of deposits of metallic salts and rare earths which can be calcinated with heat and electrical force, from lower substances and, during special times, they can be made to precipitate, or "fall out of solution" by special higher emotional waves.

These salts are then used to coat the higher body in precisely the same way that metallic gold is electroplated. Electrolysis is the exact process used to coat the higher bodies and in particular the lymphatic gland system of the "Buddha's Necklace" of the human biological machine, located in a ring around the upper chest area.

Certain definite psychic and psycho-emotional states are necessary for this electrolysis process of alchemical substance alteration. A much larger electrical current than is ordinarily organically possible in the course of human life must be artificially aroused within the machine through the use of special exercises and disciplines, and maintained daily for some time.

This unusual operation of the human biological machine can be achieved through special but gentle uses of breath, and through very complex mental and emotional techniques combined with nonsexual stimuli of the Sex Centrum, which said techniques are typically transmitted to initiates on a person-to-person basis, and are quite difficult to master, often requiring years of practice and serious unremitting discipline which is uncommon to most human beings.

The general result of undisciplined use of these exercises and techniques is personal ruin and therefore anyone transmitting these methods will be very exacting in their requirement that any potential initiate first demonstrate discipline, high attention and serious intent before even the mildest transmission of data can take place.

The use of special disciplines in the Psycho-emotional and Moving Centrums combined with disciplined use of sexual energies, called "prana," provide the necessary shocks for the transformation of lower substances into substances useful for the higher body, and for precise and highly controlled precipitation and electrolysis of metallic salt deposits in cells, in the back-brain where it connects with the central nervous system, and primarily along the lymphatic and myoneural systems located along the flat muscle network which surrounds the bone system as a whole, as well as within the central nervous system itself, which contains much of the memory and almost all of the responsive neuronic mechanisms of the human biological machine.

The province of an Angelic Cluster is to locate and restore higher bodies with higher Gradations of Reason, which can be located in extra-phenomenal chambers, contacted through the special uses of the said accumulations of rare metallic salts and earths applied and enervated correctly into corresponding higher substances, but we must first make ourselves useful to the Work in lower ways, and develop serious unremitting discipline over the dangerous abuses of the machine before any higher methods can be of use.

Leaning Nude, E.J. Gold, charcoal, Rives BFK, © 1987 HEI

CHAPTER 8
HIGHER SUBSTANCE EXERCISES

PREPARATORY WORK is mostly clearing away personal, organic and cultural obstacles to Angelic Invocation.

During the preparatory period when we are first developing serious discipline over the human biological machine's tendencies toward self-gratification, we can begin to collect higher substances—even if we cannot yet do anything with them—using the most ordinary of activities, such as eating, sleeping, playing and working.

The collection of substances connected to ingestion and digestion of food may not seem as exotic or interesting as the collection of substances through sexual stimuli, but it is equally effective, and can serve as a basis for understanding how to work in the Sex Centrum later on when we have developed the necessary discipline to be entrusted with the techniques required to collect and transform sexual substances within the alchemical laboratory of the human biological machine and its corresponding higher electrical field, which is often called the "aura."

Exercises connected with the collection and transubstantiation of higher substances from ordinary food, air and impressions from both inside and outside ourselves are intended primarily for mealtimes and the succeeding hour or two, although they can be used at other times for additional practice at collecting and transmuting substances, which can be applied to sexual invocations once these beginning methods have been fully mastered, and indeed, they are eventually to be returned to by the advanced Tantric Master, who uses them as readily as any sexual substance, once the higher forms have also been mastered.

Quite often, we return to the so-called "Beginner" exercises, only to discover that, through the process of initiation and mastery, they have transformed into higher and much more esoteric exercises with great subtlety and power.

Higher substances extracted from food, air and impressions are differentiated from the organic food, air and impressions from which they are extracted. To extract the higher substance from air, arouse the strongest possible feeling of impartial pity for everyone and everything who must someday die, including one's own organism, and from outside the organic universe, try to feel objectively the futility of personal struggle, failure and accomplishment.

Then view impartially from the vantage point of the end of your present life—as if your organic self had actually just now died—the entirety of your life, noting carefully those times which were not productive for your Essential Self.

We can magnify this effect by asking ourselves: "But of what use is all that to me now that my body is dead?"

Use your imagination to view impartially the futile struggles of friends, self and others, past, present, future.

We should be able to evoke great force of emotion from ourselves about all this, which commotion should result in a very interesting reverberation somewhere in the region of the solar plexus.

Just as a sharpshooter is able to hit the mark in a turkey shoot and certain shepherds can reverberate their voice—vibrations from rocks to make echoes, we can arouse the reverberation of pity using three specifics—a specific being a remedy for a particular thing—to extract substances from impressions.

Concentrate on sensation of presence, as well as presence itself.

There are two specific types of sensation—organic sensing and sensing of presence.

One can begin this process by sensing the organism as a whole—which we call "The Popcorn Exercise," which is available in video format, then expand this full sensing of the human biological machine to include the sensing of the presence of the entity itself, which we call the "Whole I."

One can eventually sense a greater presence than ourselves, the Electrical Field of Being—the Real I—which is quite unique and extends far beyond the organic self.

Sensation-of-presence is, as you can see, not limited to the organism. During any simple organic process, such as the process of digestion, elimination or sexual contact, one's attention can be concentrated on each of these exercises.

When trying to concentrate the attention, remember that all things—even in the highest spiritual realms—are material in the sense that they belong well within the Electro-Magnetic Spectrum, although they may be far outside the narrow band of reality of which human beings are aware. Objects which we see as matter are in fact merely slowed-down light which has entered the realm of what is called mass, but mass and energy are fully convertible and are in fact the same thing in two different states, just as steam is high-energy water and ice is low-energy water.

Pity—substance;
Attention—substance;
Presence—substance; all can be sensed, felt, pondered.

Occupy with your presence every atom of air as it enters the organism—accompany with attention the air as it is expelled from the organism. Observe its progress through the machine with concentrated attention, impartially without identification; activate as strongly as possible presence of presence.

Physical interaction is quite different than we are used to thinking about it. We should be able to learn to lose the sense of being someone in particular, especially while engaged in Alchemical Sex.

One male function is to be a medium for higher entities while a female partner can provide the electrical force—the basis, or battery, through the generation or passage of a special kind of feminine energy called "Shakti."

Social sex is more difficult to overcome than animal sex, because social sex seems to help us to maintain our false identity, that of the organic ego, with which we associate our name, our face, our postures, our knee-jerk reactions and our activities and interests.

Only if we are able to remove the urgency, habitualness and violence of animal sex from our sexual invocations is the way cleared for conscious sex, the basis of Alchemical Sex, which itself is the basis for Angelic Clusters and the formation of higher bodies.

Social sex is highly ritualized in-the-romantic. During courtship we are expected to use endearing expressions in the exact required tone of voice, wear the proper corresponding clothing, expressions, postures and gestures.

The ritual of conscious sex actually is much more free than social sex, which is full of ritual and is bound by many social requirements. There are eighteen gradations of each of the three kinds of sex occurring in clusters of triads.

Organic sex discriminates, especially by smell, taste, skin oils, hair smell, body type.

Social sex discriminates by money, power, social standing, personality likes and dislikes.

Anyone could be a partner for objective sex and coating the higher body, but there is discrimination in the domain of personal and work discipline.

CHAPTER 9
THE HIGHER BODY

In the past it was customary for a man to take several wives or concubines in addition to his primary wife who was elevated to the highest position in regard to his private life.

Of course this was to guarantee that he would leave many children—a necessity in those days when mortality of children was very high—but it also served, at least in the beginning when first introduced by a society of more or less conscious individuals, another purpose beyond the simple continuation of lineage or evidence of affluence.

It is obviously difficult to completely satisfy the sexual and emotional needs of several women without serious difficulties, even in addition to the settling of disputes, distribution of attention and affection, maintenance of equality in the purchase of clothing, jewelry, perfumes and other modes of personal enhancement, and elevation of offspring to positions of power.

Following this reasoning, another quite different idea had to have caused the practice of taking several wives, considering the difficulties of maintaining an emotional balance in the face of ego-threat, territorial imperative and personal agendas. It is not enough to say that a shortage of males could account for such activities.

In any case it would be necessary for a male partner in such a situation to give the highest possible priority to the entire group as a single entity. For the continuation of this situation so alien to all human beings, there must have been ample personal profit of some kind for everyone participating in this effort.

What profit could there be for female participants that they would work as a group in this way? It is not sufficient to say that men had so much power that they could do anything they pleased with women and that all women felt constrained to go along with this, although it is unfortunately true in far too many parts of the world that women are indeed helpless and without power.

We must somehow discover what profit there is for all participants—only then can we understand this situation in a better light. The importance of this arrangement to enlightened cultures cannot be underestimated and almost all ancient cultures had such arrangements existing.

To begin with, it has long been understood that sexual stimulation forces the secretion of certain fluids important to the accumulation of substances useful for higher bodies and that this activity, taken in conjunction with the formation of "Clusters" of participants in certain definite formations called "Tableaux," could be used for the attraction and descent of higher presences or "Entities," some of which are commonly called "Angelic."

For male and female semen to be of use, it is necessary that a great amount be collected and altered in a special way, which we can call

"The-Work-of-the-Chemical-Factory" combined with "The-Work-of-the-Alchemical-Laboratory."

When male semen—which is merely the ***carrier*** of sperm in the same way that a radio carrier wave has embedded within itself the actual encrypted information which can be decrypted into sound, visual images, text or other forms of data—is expelled by ejaculation without orgasm, the alchemical processes necessary to convert it to higher substances produces special results useful for all participants more or less equally, and the work can be actualized in higher Angelic Spheres by providing a "basis," as described in the discourses contained within ***Secrets of Angelic Invocation***.

Ejaculation without orgasm is a powerful force and can add to the usefulness of the semen collected by the male.

The male, representing the worker bee, or "drone," collects through ejaculation and suction of both his and her semen for a period of twenty-one days, and then, after it has been transmuted into a higher "pearlized" substance, it can be mixed with female semen and drawn back into the male organism for further processing and subsequent transmission back to the female organism for additional application of shakti energies and fermentation.

The accumulation of his own force along with the force of the woman contribute mathematically-geometrically the "necessity" of his semen, giving it the chemical and biological force necessary for the coating of higher bodies.

Along with this, the activity required to generate the large amount of electrolytic force necessary for coating the lymphatic gland system—the foundation of the higher body—can come only from continual sexual activity with several initiated partners.

Semen is absorbed by a special "indrawing" controlled by a combination of special breathing techniques along with muscular contraction and electrical control of the area. This can be practiced by drawing warm milk into the genitals, and then releasing.

Discipline depends upon consistent practice of controlled and disciplined sexual contact without "psycho-emotional organic romantic orgasm," while at the same time extracting and retaining the greatest possible amount of sexual fluids.

Many serious practitioners have prolonged life through this means—sometimes for hundreds and even thousands of years, although this is not recommended by anyone who has experienced life after fifty. These practices are by no means intended for the exclusive use of the male partner.

Collecting substances through sexual contacts during which the semen becomes activated and increased in force by the addition of female semen, the male partner passes the ***result*** of this substance upward through the spinal channel through the concentration of mental force of his nervous system and certain other organic parts which are "heated" electrically with the use of "Shakti" generated by the female participants.

To become organically-immortal would require an enormous amount of sexual substances, but it can be done.

A female participant of an Angelic Cluster is quite able to attain the same results as the male, through the use of these organic and nonorganic macro and microcosmic results during combination, absorption, exchange and processing of the said substances, after a sufficient amount of these substances has been accumulated, activated and transubstantiated in herself.

Thus it is obvious that any partner with whom one chooses to accumulate substances should also be a partner with whom one chooses to build a higher body within which to share eternity.

The value of a partner depends upon vigor, stamina, discipline, reliability, objectiveness, stability, dis-identification with the organic ego and, of course, the degree of will over the machine. Thus a good partner is difficult to obtain and to maintain through the preparatory period of personal transformation, and a stable partner in this endeavor tends to be highly valued.

CHAPTER 10
THE JEWEL IN THE LOTUS

First Substance comes from the cavities below a woman's tongue and is gray in color. This serves to moisten the interior organs and organic recesses, increasing ability to generate an altered semen of vivified essence. At the same time, absorption of this vital fluid renews the higher blood and reverses brain cell destruction.

Second Substance comes from the breasts and is white or grayish-white. This not only provides an essential factor for the creation of higher bodies, but also forces the secretion of other substances from lower glands which add to vital force.

Third Substance emanates from the vaginal tube at the height of sexual arousal.

A fourth "red substance" similar to the murky redness of cinnabar, can be drawn out of the vagina through the penile vacuum, drawing it upward for storage and subsequent mixture with other higher substances.

Male erotic technique can be stated quite simply: he never gives himself up to orgasm, ejaculating ***only*** when the invocation requires it, and only if the organic force of orgasm does not compel it. Some noticeable protrusion of the forebrain area of both male and female partners can be expected as a result of the storage of this "converted semen."

The ***Devadasi*** and ***Apsaras*** were the younger females—before childbirth, the representatives of ***Shakti***—in seemingly human form. They were the chief and best source of fresh female substances. On the other hand, the ***Dakini***—Goddess—and ***Sati***—primary wife—were the receptacle for which accumulated substances were intended in the Eastern form of this practice.

Women were in some cultures practicing these invocations divided into two major categories: those between the ages of 18 and 36, who were simply sources of substances, and those 36 and over, who were recipients of substances accumulated by their male partners.

In females, the successful use of seminal fluids is far more rapid, thus the longer accumulation is unnecessary for the female as it is for the male. Accumulations of substances are considered life-giving, and after transformation into activated semen, immensely beneficial for health and long life. Without such "sources of substances," the Taoists, Hindus and Tantric practitioners of the East believed they would involute, wither and die and, indeed, they were right.

They believed that without a constant supply of sexual substances from the inhalation of shared-breath from young women, their spiritualized semen would diminish in quality and quantity, thus becoming useless as a life-force, thus indicating at least some knowledge of higher invocational practices. It is shared-breath that is the key to all successful invocation.

It was due to this need for women who could fulfill the role of sources of supply for substances and who did not have the right to demand semen from the male, that, in Eastern cultures, so-called "temple prostitutes"—***Devadasi***—became part of the temple's service to its members. Calling them prostitutes is a Western practice more indicative of Western thought than of Eastern practice, and they bear no resemblance whatever to Western prostitutes who simply use commercial sex as a way of making money.

On the other hand, the female partners in a Tantric Cluster definitely had the right—called ***rati***—to demand semen along with the accumulated substances collected from younger women serving as sources of fluids. Her right to this collected seminal substance was so powerfully respected in some enlightened civilizations that men were sometimes excused from battle in order to fulfill this sanctified duty to their female partners.

In the Sarmoung Brotherhood, invocational activities are set up along the lines of a beehive: the workers, or drones—undeveloped females not yet admitted into the ranks of initiated receivers of transformed semen—gather pollen from "lower-organic-sources." That is to say, they eat special foods and drink special liquid preparations while performing energizing solar-exercises which activate these ordinary substances and transform them into usable material for invocation and coating of higher bodies.

They then transfer this substance to the "male drone" who in turn uses the electrical force of their Shakti to convert it into "activated semen" and consequently places it within the "honeycomb" of the "Queen Bee," which is the invocational Cluster itself.

The Cluster, acting as Queen Bee, is the chief receiver for substances shared between the chief drone and the invocational Cluster for their higher development, and for the use of higher entities invoked into the Cluster during ritual invocations.

"Honey," or transformed semen, is used as a substance for healing by the Sarmoung, and it is said to be so powerful that it can reverse the process of degeneration of the Organic Body in cases of tuberculosis, cancer, brain tumors, blood diseases, and so on.

The Bindu Society had a similar practice and community with sources of nectar—female sexual secretions used as a basis for the production of transformed semen—outside the initiated circle but within the Bindu community itself. In this case the community is matriarchal, while in the case of the Sarmoung Brotherhood it is patriarchal.

Workers, or "drones," bring pollen, or collected substances, to the high priestess for transformation.

Although the Organic Body responds in the same tempo as the heart beat and its resulting pulse, it is important to realize that ***the brain circulates blood and operates electrically, regulated by the tempo of the breath***.

It is this startling fact that the breath is the "timer" or "internal clock" of the organic machine, and not the heartbeat, demonstrated by contemporary medical surgical explorations bearing out ancient knowledge, which suggests a real use for the carefully and knowingly applied voluntary alteration of breath through special initiatory Moving Centrum exercises to alter consciousness, but the untutored alteration of breath can be dangerous and is not recommended.

The long-breath of the yogi and fakir—at the rate of fifteen per minute—produces a longer lifespan by saving brain cells from oxygen destruction, but there are other, far greater uses of alteration of breath, and the most useful of them are not dangerous when fully mastered and correctly taught. Clearly, they cannot be transmitted through verbal instruction.

It is obvious that the fewer separate times oxygen is circulated through the brain, but not below the degree necessary to provide the brain with its functioning amount of pyrination—also known as "oxidation"—the longer the brain will last in nearly its original condition, if the supplying organs and glands are also functioning correctly.

Blood cells and body tissues are regenerated by sexual fluids and other glandular secretions. A breakdown in cellular formation is the cause of old age and death. Most diseases other than those diseases caused by death of one or more centrums, are reversible by the voluntary introduction of energized and transformed sexual fluids from the mouth, breast and vulva.

Recirculation of higher substances, results-of-organic-foods and results-of-air, in particular that part of air called "prana" or in chemical terms "ozone"—air which has been energized and ionized by exposure to sunlight or other sources of "actinic light"—serves to degenerate effectiveness and life-giving functions after a certain point, but up to that point recirculation is the key to revitalization of substances. This key balance point must not be bypassed involuntarily.

Recycling of converted semen without the addition of new female substances becomes useless after two months of twenty-eight days each. Regeneration can take place only with the collection of new substances.

Mani-Padme, the Jewel in the Lotus, signifies the male semen when mixed with and vivified by the female semen.

The dragon represents the male semen when it has been converted into a higher substance through the application of "heat" generated by the sex force, "Shakti."

The dragon does not play with the pearl, as represented in oriental objective art. The pearl stands for the female substance before conversion. He collects and transforms it into higher substance through what is called "Dragon's Breath," changing the cinnabar-like first substance into what is then called "Dragon's Blood."

Higher breath, the primary ingredient for introduction of shocks in the upper octaves of substance-transubstantiation, is the result in general of an exalted state induced during exchange-of-substances resulting from the introduction of gently exhaled breath from the mouth of the male partner through alternate nostrils of the initiated female partner at the same time being careful not to seriously alter the tempo-of-breathing.

Of course this can seriously injure one or both of the partners if they have not been initiated personally in the careful use of breath in this special way.

The resulting substances are brought upward, both through voluntary concentration-of-attention in the initiated adept and involuntary organic force into the organic and psychic brains, and transformed.

This method of turning upward and inward the results of mixtures of male and female sexual fluids is the principal idea of objective sex and is often called "***paravritti***" in tantric writings. The same process is called in the ***Kashavic*** texts of Russia "turning back inward on itself," or ***Samovar***, which means "self-boiler."

The word ***tantra*** means in this case specific instructions given by one or more entities on an exact subject. Each tantra surviving to contemporary civilization contains some formula or other. These are not to be followed exactly. Every work circle will differ in necessity and method.

A formulary should be kept by the partnership outlining their exact visualizing methods, incantations and main rituals for the purpose of coating higher bodies and contacting higher entities for data and transformation of substances. Surviving similar texts from ancient times were originally private texts for the use of groups in organizing their own work, but not exactly along the same lines used by their predecessors.

CHAPTER 11
ALCHEMY OF TANTRA

THERE ARE TWO basic assumptions contained in all tantras regardless of their origin or specific practices.

The first is the assumption that the cosmos of phenomena is the body of the Absolute and that the Absolute, although invisible within it as our unique subjective presence is invisible within our own organic formations, can be expressed as ***The Gradation of Consciousness called Reason-Absolute***.

In addition, this "I" of the cosmos which we call "The Absolute," is concentrated in no specific place within the Cosmic Body.

The second fundamental assumption is that sexual intercourse can be used for higher states of consciousness and actual transformation. Basic to this practice is the idea of conversion of semen into a substance usable for the restoration and evolution of higher bodies and for the transformation of the lower and higher bodies into bodies which exactly correspond to the immortal "Self of Presence."

Semen is the basic substance for the formula which becomes higher substance, turned upward and converted in the forebrain. In standard practices of soma-yoga, there is a practice called ***Vajroli mudra***, in which a man learns to recover semen discharged during intercourse through drawing the semen with a vacuum breath. One can practice this by learning to draw milk—raw skim is best for this practice—up into the penis through the urethra tube.

While male and female bodies contain both white and red or menstrual substances—***shukla*** and ***rakta***, respectively—the essential substance cannot be transformed in the same way unless red substance has passed through the female body and has been activated with "first" and "second" substances from the mouth and breasts.

Some yogis try to perform this mixture and transformation without the female partner, achieving some, but by no means full results. This also deprives the female from achieving the same result. She cannot perform this function for herself as can the male.

One purpose of sexual contact is to stimulate the sexual nervous system and arouse sexual force within the body, then to share commonly the results of stimulation. Prolonged sexual contact is more efficient for this purpose than shorter contact.

In the Way of the ***Vajra***, or Thunderbolt, the thunderbolt means the diamond, or penis. Om—an incantation from a higher world; Mani—the jewel, or the diamond; Padme—in the Lotus, or within the female organ, opening like the petals of a lotus; Hum—the incantation of returning-into-oneself.

The visualization is of a radiant golden couple in sexual union—Mani Padme. The golden color of their bodies indicates that they are filled with ***tejas***—converted sexual force—continually aroused by sexual force not centered on their partners or on pleasing themselves.

Among the practitioners called ***Herukas*** and ***Dakinis***, or Heroes and Sprites, each couple would spend a maximum of one year together, so as not to form attachments and, at the end of the year, they would gather to change partners for the coming year. The major portion of each year would be filled with preparation in postures, raising the level of inner force along with meditation in sexual contact.

In Tibet, the wives and concubines of the great spiritual teachers were considered great goddesses, or ***Dakinis***—women of high spiritual power.

They frequently visited graveyards at night, and on occasion transmitted to male pupils—as teachers did with female pupils—the teacher's converted semen through sexual connection.

Pupils in Tibet were also occasionally given potions containing the semen and substances of their teacher and his wives in order to obtain the necessary organic catalyst for themselves and their spiritual lineage.

Members of an Alchemical Partnership are required to maintain a Hermetic Seal. They must not have sexual contact outside the unit for the duration of their work together. Failure to observe this destroys the integrity of their work.

Within the circle, a delicate psycho-organic-chemical balance must be established and then maintained. This critical balance can easily be disrupted by outside organic and psychic contamination.

In the formation of an Alchemical Partnership the psychic and chemical balance of the partners is considered in the same way as was the province of the authentic "alchemical astrologers" of the Sumerian, Chaldean and Babylonian civilizations.

Not only must each individual member of the Alchemical Partnership be prepared by initiation for the Work, but must form a corresponding part of the general chemical blending. Two individuals may both be prepared but are not necessarily suitable work partners because their chemistries do not correspond. With experience, one can detect a chemically appropriate partner just by body odor.

During sexual contact, a certain electrical blending occurs. This blending causes influences on the psycho-organic condition that lingers long after the contact. This effect is very noticeable even after a single contact. After even one outside sexual contact, many years or decades may pass before this effect has diminished sufficiently for work.

During the course of this work and forever after, the existence of these activities, of course, must not be casually discussed with outsiders. This does not mean giving the appearance of secrecy, but rather the appearance of normalcy.

One must be willing and able to adopt a nonromantic attitude to sexual contact without losing the deep senses of wonder and love. Ordinary sexual conditioning must have been removed. Personal desire for a new partner is not practical. If Ordinary Centrum preferences are strong enough to produce transgression then work cannot continue.

Habitual expressions of social romantic affection have no place in the Work. A work relationship is not related to ordinary affections and affectations. We must be willing to use intimate sex for work without the usual displays of mutual flattery and organic vanity.

The male partner should be able to develop voluntary sex without the use of psychological erotic fantasy. He must concentrate the full voluntary force of his all-centrums-connected-attention on his partner.

Practice keeping the body relaxed during sex—especially the abdominal muscles. Practice maintaining high sexual arousal with a minimum of Moving Centrum activity.

Ordinarily, orgasm and ejaculation occur together. Voluntary ejaculation is an intentional function of the Sex Centrum. Orgasm is an organic function of the Moving Centrum. Through practice these can be separated so that voluntary ejaculation occurs independently of orgasm.

During collection of substances the female partner secretes two substances in addition to the fourteen ordinarily found in vaginal fluids. Depending on the state, these form either ***Elixir*** or ***Venom***—solar or lunar substances.

CHAPTER 12
ALCHEMICAL CHEMISTRY

The transformation mantra: "I Wish This To Be Used For the Benefit of All Beings Everywhere" is to be used during transfer of energies and substances and during the organization and dismantling of the angelic cluster (as delineated in ***The Secrets of Angelic Invocation***, Gateways Books and Tapes), in order to safely and correctly arouse the necessary state and also to prevent possible involuntary orgasm.

One must discover by personal effort and initiation exactly ***how*** it is "of benefit to all beings everywhere," in order for this mantra to have power.

Although nature supplies us with all the necessary substances to manufacture higher bodies, they are in raw form and unusable for our purposes unless extracted from their parental sources and transmuted. It is up to us to transmute them into useful substances. Nature does not provide for us this service.

We must also learn to collect them in sufficient quantity and direct them to the required places of concentration or correspondings, which are within our organism, those points which have direct relation to the cosmic concentrations of all suns and planets. Until we force deposits of these substances we cannot say we are genuine representations of the higher cosmoses.

The work of the inner factory consists in transforming one kind of substance into another, finer substance. The organic factory receives raw material and changes them by alchemical means. The process is exactly the same as that chemical process called "electroplating."

Higher substances, which are in fact rare and precious metals—gold in particular—are deposited on certain organic formations. These precipitate out of their salt solutions and deposit themselves in a coating on the organs we wish to crystallize for the higher bodies. Electrical force generated by the muscles gives the electrolytic energy necessary for this process if we can learn to generate sufficient energy.

So we can see that several factors are necessary. We must learn to extract substances from ordinary sources of matter, then transform them into finer substances which can become salts of solution, and finally we must learn to generate sufficient electrolytic force from our muscle system to support the electrolytic plating process.

In ordinary life we cannot produce electrical energy in our organism; the production of finer substances is almost nonexistent; everything we could produce in this way is wasted on the operation of the organism itself or expended uselessly as negative emotion.

All substances necessary for growth and function of higher bodies can be extracted from three types of ordinary food entering from outside and found in the world of nature surrounding humans: ordinary food, food of air and impressions, and the resultant mental substances found in the brain when exercised in specific ways when one is in specific mental and emotional states.

If we could accumulate sufficient finer substances we could saturate all cells of the body with them. They can under the right conditions precipitate out of solution and crystallize in a special way, forming the higher body, really a formation of metals. The instruction as carried in the Emerald Tablet of Hermes tells us to separate the fine from the coarse.

Surpluses of these finer substances can also be used to feed the higher body and provide it with a source for higher substances—higher body blood, actually a kind of force or inner light—but the surplus will have to be very large. Nothing can be wasted on ordinary emotion and mental activity. The physical organism is only able to produce these and use them for higher body coating if everything is working properly and economically.

The human organism has the possibility of a very great output of these substances, but the ordinary human being under ordinary conditions of life will never use the factory to its fullest potential. In ordinary humans, the factory is seldom used for anything. Its elaborate equipment serves no purpose other than that of barely sustaining its own miserable existence.

If we could learn to bring the production of the factory up to its real potential we would have to learn to save the finer hydrogens—the basis of all matter in the universe and from which all other matter is synthesized—contained in food, air and impressions, and saturate the whole organism with these finer hydrogens. This process of coating higher bodies cannot be brought about by any other means.

Growing higher bodies—astral, mental, and so on—is a material process just like the growth of any other material organism, except that the "Second Body" is composed of substances of the planetary cosmos and can survive the death of the Physical Body.

The "Third Body" is composed of matter on the level of the sun and is able to exist even after the death of the second Astral Body.

The "Fourth Body" is composed of matter of the stellar cosmos, of substances not belonging properly to the solar system and therefore, having crystallized in the locality of this solar system, nothing within this sphere of existence can destroy it. In this sense a man who has coated in himself the Fourth Body is immortal within the limits of the solar system.

Where can we find the substances necessary to grow these higher bodies? We cannot go far from our planetary sphere, and so we must find them in ordinary substances available to us here on the planetary surface and extract them even though they are not, as a result of several unfortunate cosmic accidents, as easily available on earth as they are on other cosmic concentrations.

The material necessary for the growth of the Astral Body can be found in ordinary food when processed by a healthy organism where blood flow is not restricted by muscle tension, and organs of elimination and sweat glands all work properly. The network of lymphatic glands plays a very important part in all this, and it is these glands which must be coated first, forming what is called the "Necklace of Buddha."

When it has formed, the Astral Body will require less of these substances than it did during its formation, allowing a surplus of substances to be used for the formation of the Mental Body; after its formation the surplus can be used for the formation of the fourth body, and so on. However, in each case the surplus of substances will have to be very great, yet everything depends on the physical organism as the source of these substances and as the transformer of coarse substances into usable finer matter.

The process of transforming substances from coarse to fine is directed by the "Law of Octaves," readily visible within the Electro-Magnetic Spectrum. For instance, the visible light domain has an equal but lower energy octave in the realm of sound.

Physical food is found at ***Hydrogen 768***, which is equivalent to la, sol, and fa in the third octave of the Electro-Magnetic Spectrum of Cosmic Radiations emanating originally during the Big Bang as Hydrogen and entering the organism as ***Oxygen 768***, which then combines with the ***Carbon 192*** normally continually present in the organism. This union obtains the result ***Nitrogen 384***, which is the vibration re in the same octave.

Nitrogen 384 in the next triad is equivalent to and acts like Oxygen, and can combine with ***Carbon 96*** to produce a new, higher ***Nitrogen—192***—the note mi. This substance cannot pass independently across the interval in the ascending octave. An additional shock of higher energy from another higher octave is now necessary.

Now we introduce the substances extracted from the ordinary substance air, ***Hydrogen 192***. Because this Hydrogen has the same density as ***Nitrogen 192***, it can combine with the force sufficient to give the ***Carbon 48*** which is already present in the organism energy to unite with the lower Nitrogen to form a new substance, ***Nitrogen 96***, corresponding to the note fa.

Nitrogen 96, in combination with ***Carbon 24*** ordinarily present in the organism, forms a new substance, ***Nitrogen 24***, which would be the note sol in the octave. This occurs when the intestines extract nutritions of amino acids into the bloodstream and local cells. ***Nitrogen 48*** combines with ***Carbon 12*** which is always present in the organism to form a new substance, ***Nitrogen 24***, the note la. ***Nitrogen 24*** combines with ***Carbon 6*** to make ***Nitrogen 12***, corresponding to the note si 12. This is the highest substance which can be produced from ordinary food with the help of air. Now we must use the substances from air to make even higher substances.

To extract these substances from food we must simply learn to breathe correctly for our type. Correct breathing during ingestion and digestion of food produces that additional shock necessary for the transformation and extraction of finer substances contained in food.

According to ancient teachings, a human being who has achieved completion in the spiritual sense has formed in himself at least four separate and distinct bodies composed of gradations of finer substances, which mutually interpenetrate one another, each of which is capable of independent action.

The Organic Body is much lower and is organized in such a way that under certain conditions three new complex independent organisms can grow within it, creating ***higher vibration finer vehicles*** for the concentration of presence in realms beyond the organic world.

Crystals of higher substances are carried by the blood of the Astral Body, therefore it is necessary to form the Astral Body at least in regard to its circulatory system for the purpose of carrying substances through the Organic Body so they may be deposited as necessary.

The Causal Body is independent of external causes or influences and is therefore called the Body of Will, as opposed to the Body of

Habits, which forms the lower, animal, soul without consciousness or sense of continuity.

Thinking, which corresponds in some ways to the functions of the third or Mental Body, is ordinarily an entirely mechanical process based on habits, and therefore subject to the influences of the Body of Habits rather than to the Mental Body. In this case the Mental Body is passive in relation to the Body of Habits, as discussed in the discourses, ***The Seven Bodies of Man****.

---

* 1989, Gateways/I.D.H.H.B., Inc., Nevada City, CA

CHAPTER 13
ATTRACTING ENTITIES

Many view stupidly with ignorance or superstition the ritual of sex in the crematorium. The single ritual which all tantric groups have in common is sexual meditation conducted among the dead.

One must be able to ruthlessly make psychic-surgical incisions to cut away all personal dependency on phenomena. By becoming as if dead among the dead, one may be able to view one's organic efforts as just part of organic phenomena.

If the female partner allows the semen given to her to hold in her "cup" to be absorbed by lower entities, then it cannot be used for transformation and is useless for coating higher bodies.

Ninety to ninety-five percent of the activities of ordinary man are directed by entities. Entities use him for food, herding man into states in order to eat the results of this cultivation in much the same way that certain alien species have learned to harvest human enzymes which are missing in their degenerated digestive systems.

Some higher entities can feed on the results of ordinary sex and negative emotion. Petty quarrels, disagreements, violent and animalistic love-making and other examples of human lower emotions all provide food for vampiristic entities.

Alchemical Partners are often willing to tolerate others in order to attract vampiristic entities. Do they like something feeding from their higher substances and sexual energies?

Well, do we like the sensation of anything we are addicted to? We have no choice; it is not like-and-dislike—it is ***addiction***, pure and simple.

Entities are especially attracted to sexual substances. Many are addicted to the blissful state occurring during loss-of-substance which entities feed upon. What man could use for himself is taken by entities.

We can liken this to giving the finest wine to pigs; entities cannot use substance any special way. To them it is simply food.

We can ***feel*** the presence of entities feeding on us, but have only the merest idea that something is wrong. We cover up this sensation very quickly to ourselves, but we have revulsion whether we are aware of it or not. Of course, it is in the best interest of entities to keep us from becoming aware of the terror-of-the-situation.

Naturally, entities do not wish us to discover how we are used for food. Most human beings, if given real data on the subject, would ignore or reject it. The small number of humans who begin to understand are in great danger. The closer we come to real data of what feeds on organic life of earth, the more danger to ourselves and to our work.

Many who acquire data and are able to use such data encounter what may be viewed as accidents, in which strange and negative things happen to them. When we begin to impartially verify this data, we are amazed and shocked at how pervasive entities are in life and how much of our life they dominate.

We must learn to keep our sexual substances and energies for our higher work, and work hard to prevent negative entities from sucking us dry. When we light a cigarette or pour ourselves a cup of coffee, drink beer, wine or distilled alcohol, pop prescription narcotics or partake of any habitual and addictive substance, we do this to feed some negative entity or other.

In some centers of habitation thousands of flies continually land on the face, head and hands. Since the inhabitants cannot always swat flies, they learn to tolerate a certain number of flies on the body. But if too many flies land on us, then we must take some action, although there are some who let any amount of flies live on their bodies. One or two mosquitoes, maybe yes; ten mosquitoes, certainly ***no***.

This data you ***must*** personally elucidate. I can give you hints, but you must find complete data for yourself.

During sleep, what happens with entities, do you think? When we first contact the Work, how do you think entities accustomed to feeding on our substances respond?

The glazed look and blank hungry stare which comes over any addict suddenly deprived of their addiction is one way to recognize the presence of an entity. The only way to extract ourselves from the process of reciprocal feeding is the cold turkey method.

We must never go back once we have stopped our habit. If we terminate our addiction and then go back, the entity which is the fixation of the addiction has tremendously more strength.

During addiction we build up tolerance. Once we have broken our addiction, our tolerance is considerably weakened. If for example, a morphine addict were to suddenly return to his regular dosage he could die.

If we cure ourselves of our addiction to our Lunar Parasites and then return to addiction, our tolerance is reduced. Comparatively speaking, any invoked entity is so much more powerful that we might never break away again, ***with or without help***.

Substances which are rightfully our own are stolen by entities. One reason for our susceptibility to entities is our suggestibility. Entities cluster around us and feed like piglets around a mother hog. There is a constant shifting presence at "feeding time," which is almost always. The shifting can be instantaneous, moment to moment, all jostling for position.

Actually, this whole process is our real place in the Process-of-Reciprocal-Feeding; mental-emotional self-hypnotism and personal gratification keeps us from seeing this in ourselves. Almost every human being is deeply involved in the feeding of negative entities and cannot remove themselves from this process.

All of organic life produces substances which are food for entities. Humans' real value is as food. Ordinary organic food is for self-perpetuating, to continue organic life.

That there could be a self-evolving entity which could arise out of this is sheer accident.

We are equally as invisible to entities as they are to us, but they can sense our presence by our states, smell our substances and hear, in a special way, most of our ordinary conversation. Negative entities have an animalistic nature. They are just barely able to have the cunning to feed off the substance ***emotion*** and substances produced from the genitals.

Entities make us respond to their psycho-emotional suggestions through our mental, emotional and organic addictions. The "bliss-of-vampirism" is in a hypnosis which depends upon addiction. It feeds the addiction upon itself. The key to all this is, ***addiction feeds itself***. The object of addiction has no real power except in the beginning.

The artifact used as a reminding factor for this idea is the serpent eating its own tail. The serpent was originally a dragon, called in German, ***Schlange***, or worm. The question of the ***sacred worm*** is explored fully in Taoism and Lamaism, where each of various colored dragons stands for and are attracted to a different psycho-organic addiction.

In some cases we are addicted to the presence of an entity because of some service it performs for us. Some confer knowledge, some cleverness, some give us data, some offer certain skills and some simply give us the means for continuation of our self-love, vanity and self-gratification.

This is the real basis for tales of "selling the soul" to some infernal entity, but such transactions together with the various pacts and seals is nonsense, inventions of the anti-heretical inquisitions of established state churches, characterizing any rival religion as "pagan" or "evil" in order to discredit their competitors.

In some cases, if we give up our addiction to a reciprocally feeding entity such as those which commonly feed on lower emotions and negative states, we would no longer retain the "gifts" of self-love and gratification provided by the entity in return for the essential vital fluids and electrical forces upon which they feed. To an ordinary human being, the loss of such special powers and gratifications would be a disaster, but for anyone seriously working, this is not important at all.

We can intentionally invoke an entity or it can just happen as a result of accident or negative emotion automatically aroused by shock, hypnosis, anger, sadness or cheap sex.

The entities organic human beings normally attract are always animalistic and always vampiristic. In most cases, in a small, petty way, human beings are addicted to equally small and petty addictives.

We might become addicted to an entity for a stupid thing like playing better darts, knowing answers to riddles or being popular at cocktail parties, for which some shallow people who commonly wallow in shallow relationships, mostly sexual, would pay any price.

Actually, it is not by price, but by default that ordinary human beings become addicted—by not rocking the boat. If anything comes near his favorite entity—the source of most human vanity and self-love—something must give way, and it certainly will not be the feeding vampiristic entity.

There are ways of taking on various entities intentionally, and then effectively banishing them so that they cannot continue to feed on one's fluids, metallic salts and electrical force.

The danger in this, of course, is addiction to which no one who plays with such fire is completely immune, no matter how strong and resistant to addiction they think they may be. Actually, those who are most convinced of their immunity are generally those who are the most subject to addiction, and this is a well-known feature of the addictive personality.

Some entities confer so much power over others and so much worldly control and ability that the danger of addiction is very strong, both to the process of feeding and to the worldly powers which are the result.

In addition, it is hard to call an entity down and then merely banish it without a great deal of effort and discipline. In Lamaism one passes through a series of powers conferred by various entities—powers both psychological and psycho-kinetic—which are not easy to give up once they have become part of one's daily routine and expectation.

The most difficult of all efforts is to voluntarily give up all one's powers and to voluntarily become just an ordinary idiot once again, to have used those powers and then to intentionally "kick the habit."

The most vital idea in voluntary invocation is the banishing of not only the feeding entities but the powers conferred upon one by them. Each succeeding invocation is by nature a temptation.

Every detail of human life is dominated by vampiristic entities. There are very few other types of entities. Even benevolent entities are vampiristic to some degree.

Humans are not automatically food for entities except in the organic sense, such as the certainty that we are all future candidates for "worm-chow," but what we produce is food for higher entities and some lower ones, either through emotional states, super-efforts, higher thought and of course, the power of sex.

Any of our centrums—both higher and lower—can produce entity-food, but not automatically and not all reciprocal feeding is good.

This is the mesoteric reason for the injunction against negative states. We can use substance for ourself or feed it to one entity or another. These entities begin to feed on the very young and are often viewed as invisible childhood playmates. They may be invisible; they may be encountered in childhood, but they are hardly "playmates."

If we can learn to see behind all the apparent motivators, we can see that really all manipulating forces for the life of ordinary organic human beings who are rooted in self-gratification and self-pampering are reciprocally-feeding entities of one kind or another, generally of the "not-so-good" kind. Most human beings are under the influence of entities of this sort, and are not readily agreeable to get out from under their domination.

The activities of human beings can arise from either entity-manipulation, in the case of ordinary people living ordinary lives, or self-initiation in the case of those few who have awakened to higher potential.

There are no exceptions to this rule. Not everything is as it seems, and the most "harmless" activities are not as harmless as they seem, nor are they as spontaneous as people would have us believe.

CHAPTER 14
COATING HIGHER BODIES

WE MAY THINK we have relations with a woman or with a man, but actually it is our relationship with the entities invoked by the relationship which feeds our addictions and keeps us in ordinary relationships.

Many people are addicted to the ***mere absence of sexual substances***. They like to have substances taken from them, just as some people feel more comfortable when they are enslaved than when they are free, and many people are relieved when they are stripped of all their money by a "con man" who fleeces them and leaves them penniless.

This is all connected with ***vanity, self-love, self-gratification*** and ***involuntary lying***. All of the nastier negative habits are a direct result of the Process-of-Reciprocal-Feeding which comes from a powerful and unbreakable entity addiction.

What do these entities do for us that makes us so hungry for their presence, and what does all this have to do with our ideas of ourselves, our vanity and self-love? What does this have to do with what we call the Great Work? The whole idea of the Great Work comes from this small idea.

Someday you will be astonished when you see the whole picture of the activities of reciprocally-feeding entities and the question of identification with self-gratification, self-pampering and addiction to the five fingers of negative life—sex, money, power, drugs and diet.

Verification of this from many higher spiritual sources is now possible since we know what to look for; of course much will be hidden and couched in parable, but the ideas themselves are visible for those with eyes to see and ears to hear. We see what we want to see and hear what we want to hear. A pickpocket only sees a person's pockets. There is great danger in giving these ideas directly, and so they are generally couched in some other form, such as art, music, theater, dance and stories.

Without experience in-the-impartial, it would be impossible to view this process of feeding; we would be too identified with the machine and its activities to understand and use this information, and our self-gratification would be too strong for us to break the chains of the addiction to the powers of the dark side of the force.

Organic human beings are helpless addicts of entities and the powers conferred by them. They will never free themselves because they do not wish help, and do not know how to seek help. Even those who have found help cannot always accept it, because the addictive personality is so steeped in the pleasure and pain of addiction. Many return to their addictives simply because they find life impossible without them in much the same way that without football games on television, most American males would have nothing whatever to do at home.

Entities struggle with one another for possession of substances and provide man with petty activities and pathological soothing for his vanity. Madness is the alternative for ordinary organic human beings. Without addictives, human beings are nothing at all, because without one's friends in the Next World to pull the strings, the puppet would collapse like a bunch of broccoli.

Without emotional involvement, intentional sexual over-stimulation for long periods of time without orgasm, but with several hundred ejaculations free from automatically generated adrenal gland secretions, can be used to quiet and deaden the nerve endings of the genitals.

Prolonged sexual contacts necessary for Alchemical Sex would produce an artificial group of sensations which when taken psycho-emotionally, would be viewed by ordinary men and women as horniness—an imaginary state powered by giving oneself continual permission for self-gratification and self-pampering—because the intensity of prolonged contact produces rather insistent sensations of the nerve endings which require and demand continual manipulation and stimulation.

Without this intentional deadening of sensations, it would be impossible to reach certain levels of consciousness which are ordinarily prevented by the dominant sensations of the genitals and the corresponding automatic generation of adrenalin.

Ordinarily, humans do not reach the point of overstimulation and quieting of the genital nerve endings; sexual contact is generally limited to personal or interpersonal satisfaction to climax.

Organic sexual second-wind-phenomenon is attained only after hours of continuous sexual stimulation without emotional stimulation or involuntary ejaculation. The presence of emotional stimulation or involvement in sexual contact obviates the possibility of utilization of substances for higher body coating, but is necessary for production of substances.

The first period of stimulation can include emotional; the second period must not...in the third period the substances are voluntarily collected for coating or transformation.

In a work circle we concentrate our efforts on the coating of higher bodies along with intense development of conscience-and-organic-balance. The province of earlier work is to prepare oneself for understanding, to clear away the rubbish. We would not wish to crystallize our organic selves.

The collection of substance for the coating of higher bodies is all connected to the use of food, air and impressions. The extraction of substance from food is specifically accomplished by the concentration-of-attention in a special way on the inflow and outflow of breath without transference of breath to the voluntary part of the Moving Centrum.

To extract substances from air, we would learn to voluntarily arouse in ourselves the sensations and emotions of impartial pity for all those around us including our own organic manifestations which, if we can be impartial toward them, we can pity objectively, imagining not just the deaths of ourselves and everyone we know, but sooner or later all organic life on Earth. Evocation of emotion in the voluntary part of the feeling centrum requires the correct use of the ***Law of Reverberation—Collection***; ***Concentration of Attention; Organic and Psychic Reverberation***.

To extract substances from impressions requires concentration on the specific sensation of Presence of the Unified Presence of "I"—two exact types of sensing are the result: organic sensing and sense-of-presence, which comes from the essential self.

Sensing of presence is similar to those sensations commonly experienced during a seance and may extend beyond the organism.

Alchemical Partners should cooperatively work to do at least the necessary movement and erotic manipulation for the maintenance of the erection; there will of course be a certain amount of stimulation necessary, but all this is to be kept to a minimum.

It should go without saying that mental fantasies and so forth have no place whatever in real use of the Sex Centrum. When genuinely activated, it is impossible to have inner fantasies of any kind because Sex Centrum force makes impossible the continuation of mental associations.

At this point one is forced to wholly confront one's partner and if nothing existing of a real nature is between them, erection cannot be maintained no matter what; nothing will occur.

Partners who can cooperate fully and who are able to be together during the operation of Sex Centrum force can do anything together, they are "meant for one another" in the ancient astrological sense of the idea.

CHAPTER 15
LAWS OF INEXORABILITY

We must be careful; we may someday make one assumption too many. We generally believe that to make an assumption is to know something, or at least to make a good guess. We assume we know. But in the real world assumption means something entirely different.

To "assume" means to take on oneself, like a raincoat and boots, sometimes like a diving suit into which we must have air pumped. Most human beings are able to take on such a costume only very partially.

In order to even begin the process of Alchemical Sex, we must learn to maintain an uninterrupted, unromantic sexual contact with the fullest possible unbroken attention on our partner for at least several hours.

A complete separation of orgasm and ejaculation and their assumption into the voluntary part of the machine may require many years for full mastery and, during this time, the two functions may still remain in the organic-involuntary part of the Moving Centrum, although mentally intentional.

From the instinctive function of the Moving Centrum, ejaculation is eventually brought little by little, through discipline and work-will, into the voluntary, activating the function of the real Sex Centrum, the only centrum capable of producing and generating work-force as the Power Centrum. While the ordinary Moving-Centrum-source-of-sexuality is dominant, the Sex Centrum is utterly unable to function as a Power Centrum.

Indrawing—the vacuum method of drawing substances into the body through the genitals, conserves substances and allows the male to ejaculate and recycle substances during mixture and transformation cycles hundreds, and even thousands, of times each day.

Part of this discipline is the controlled separation of sperm and semen, both of which are very different substances; sperm is contained in semen, but is not necessarily present in semen.

Repetitive ejaculation without orgasm and without sperm is used to accumulate Higher Seminal Force. The key to all this is impartiality and non-identification with the lower organic.

Involuntary = Lower	Voluntary = Higher
Lower substances are produced when ejaculation is an involuntary function of Moving Centrum.	Higher substances are produced when ejaculation is a voluntary function of Sex Centrum.
Involuntary—thinking	Voluntary—mentation
Involuntary emotion is lower emotion.	Voluntary emotion is higher emotion.
Involuntary orgasm is spasm of the Instinctive Centrum.	Voluntary orgasm is a function of the Moving Centrum.
Involuntary ejaculation is a function of the Moving Centrum.	Voluntary orgasm is a function of the Sex Centrum.

At the point that one makes the decision to begin this work, and not allow involuntary emotion, one's name, in effect, is recorded in a book. Involuntary emotion becomes too expensive, as there are entities hovering around one, waiting for such an opportunity to move in and manifest. They can and do take you for a ride, and it may or may not be possible to pry them loose or banish them afterwards.

Recognizing the urgent necessity of not allowing involuntary emotion and the disastrous consequences of every momentary slip provides the necessary force for this control. Should you slip, you may be rescued once, twice, maybe even three times, but it is not always possible. Under certain situations rescue may not be possible or the technique for rescue may not be known. If it happens too many times you forfeit your candidacy.

First Law of Inexorability: Hermetic Seal on the work circle—a partner must be completely trustworthy—not even a shadow of a doubt that the seal might be broken—even if there are years of separation of the partners.

Second Law of Inexorability: if a candidate cannot wait six months to three years for the vibrations resulting from outside contacts to become thoroughly diminished, or for the substances of outside contact to die before beginning work, they are not suitable for Alchemical Sex.

Third Law of Inexorabilty: when a partnership becomes untenable, or is not working, do not try to fix it—end it. For example, if a partner ceases to work or does not contribute sufficiently—no compromise—cut it. Involuntary emotion is a profound work hazard.

Contamination of a lineage: any sexual contact would be contamination, such as tongue contact or deep kissing, genital contact, oral-genital contact, genital to genital intercourse and even heavy petting with its inevitable psychic field exchanges and interminglings—the end result is the exchange of substances whether organic or sublime, intentional or unintentional, electrical, magnetic or psychic.

The effects of such contamination could take months and sometimes years to dissipate sufficiently for work, or perhaps could never be repaired and, in the case of unprotected sex, could even be deadly to all participants.

Substances, even higher substances not subject to organic decay, eventually die.

Contamination can also occur chemically, aurically, vibrationally, emotionally, etc. This work is like building a glass castle.

A magical blend of higher emotions and higher electrical fields combined with alchemically produced and harmonized substances of various subtle natures is a delicate process and can be easily destroyed by lower influences and through contamination either physical, emotional or psychic.

At first one's own lineage is the result or effect of psycho-emotional-sexual contact—a mixture of substances as long as they are alive. Contamination of lineages is possible when the substances are not complimentary.

In Alchemical Sex, one may be connected strongly to a long lineage which may date back to ancient times.

This interlocking initiation through time and space must be very carefully considered.

It must be such that there is no possibility of repercussion with animalistic desires and obsessions.

Such an error could instantly destroy an entire lineage. It would be as if by contaminating the acidophilus culture in your own house, all acidophilus cultures everywhere could be instantly contaminated as well. This would be extremely serious for all concerned, and could be disastrous for the entire line of work throughout time and space.

Through the use of Alchemical Sex one can accomplish in one lifetime what could take thousands of lifetimes to accomplish by other methods.

Even the first month of Work could be more productive than an entire lifetime in another method, just because it is profoundly more efficient than many other paths, but it is equally hazardous when in the hands of one who is driven by organic desires and obsessions.

Once this Path is entered, vigilance cannot be relaxed. Then, when complete unity exists, one is always the same. Hopefully, the war will be won by the Unified Self. But this is not at all guaranteed.

It is of course very difficult to find a good partner for serious Alchemical Sex.

If one finds such a partner, it is worthwhile to stay with them for life.

Should contamination occur outside the hermetic partnership, the details of such outside contact must be known if there can be any hope of repairing the Hermetic Seal.

Contamination outside the Hermetic Seal can destroy years of work and can even destroy the work of the hermetic partners permanently.

First Axiom to the 3rd Law of Inexorability: anything that could prove a distraction to the Work at hand must be ruthlessly cut away.

Never interrupt work-in-progress, even if the problem will be worsened.

Second Axiom to the 3rd Law of Inexorabilty: if, when considering a partner, any doubt or hesitation whatsoever enters in when considering spending eternity with them, then do not admit them.

At some point in work circles, the alchemical partners ***must utter a work-wish***, which links the partners for eternity, outside time and space.

Eternity is not endless, but it is repetitive.

Hydrogens must be produced in sufficient quantity for Alchemical Sex operations, and the laws governing such alchemical operations are absolute and inexorable.

Questions to ask of oneself when considering a partner:

"If I could only have one person present at my death, would I wish to die in this person's arms?"

That is to say, if working alchemically with that partner meant spending eternity with this individuum, does any doubt or hesitation of any kind arise? Another way to ask this is: "Would I wish to be locked up in a room with this person for all of eternity?"

Corollary: how does my partner feel about being eternally locked in a room with me?

When selecting a partner, do not choose the spiritually inexperienced, the philosophical virgin and certainly not the sexually inexperienced.

They are too untested and cannot be expected to make a realistic decision. More experienced Alchemical Partners are more likely to have done everything they wish to with ordinary sex and may have gone far enough in their experimentation to realize that they have no further interest in the organic levels of sex.

One should note the difference between romance and ordinary love. Romance is even more of a difficulty to overcome than ordinary love. Romantics would never be able to approach these ideas because of firmly-held romantic ideas not based on what is possible or likely, but by preference, conditioning, personal gratification, self-pampering and self-love.

Real Astrology took into account many more factors than does contemporary astrology. Ancient astrologers were able to correctly match partners for work, but not through astrology, through other means which are today unavailable except to the trained psychic.

Sexual impartiality does not mean detachment or disinterest in sex, love or relationships, but to become an active, enthusiastic participant who is impartial to the sexuality of the event, yet is fully receptive, without reservation, to the energies exchanged and shared.

The male generates the flow, the female receives the flow. If the female is not fully receptive, the substances will not be received—they will fall on barren ground and die.

The outer school is like outer-shell-electrons. People in the outer school cannot do serious damage to the real school, because they have not been shown the real school.

Regarding the processing of substances in the chemical factory the general direction is indicated, but even the most explicit details of alchemical data given in written or verbal form can only give the most rough direction of the centrum-of-gravity of each instruction.

Entities from within we call ***Infernal***; entities from above we call ***Celestial***. There are benevolent and malevolent entities in both realms. Each is a conglomerate of body masses of a number of individuals in any given invocation.

This realm of work must be strictly voluntary with the full knowingness of each participant. Only voluntary wishing; only voluntary emotion. There is danger in slipping even for a moment, and all can be lost in the swirling maelstrom of organically driven desires.

CHAPTER 16
EXTRACTION OF HIGHER SUBSTANCES

From organic food: H 768 —— O 768 + C 192 = N 384

N 384 —— O 192 + C 96 = N 192

Extract using air: H 192 —-*—- N 192 + C 48 = N 96
"Elixir"

N 96 + C 24 = N 48

N 48 + C 12 = N 24

---

*Additional shock of enabling substance as transformed semen.

Extract using impressions: N 24 + C 6 = N 12
"Aqua Regis"

Extract using substances: Rubeum Durum = Alchemical Gold =
Higher Being Coatings = New Higher Octave

We must learn how to generate sufficient electrolytic force from our muscle system to initiate and maintain the electrolytic higher-being body "electroplating" process.

If we have access to both formulation and necessity we can become useful to the Great Work and therefore create necessity for our higher levels of existence, in a sense paying our future debt to the Work, and thus our ability to make such contributions means that our continuation is, at least for as long as we are actually useful to the Work of higher entities, assured. We can with knowledge and nonidentification with our animalistic urges and behaviors, perhaps bring ourselves to that higher level of necessity and State of Grace at which higher entities can use us as mediums for their sublime work in our spheres, which we call "The Great Work."

We can in this sense become "mediums"—our switchboard-operators or spirit-controls help us locate and contact the entities who need our mediumistic help for their Great Work here in our lower worlds.

We can also through effort, discipline and transcendence of personal needs, become capable of performing "transforming prayers," and even become agencies by which we are able to provide power and higher energies for groups engaged in Objective Angelic Invocations and Prayer.

CHAPTER 17
ROMANTIC IDEAS

Transformation is all scientific...chemistry, physics, biology, and psychology. Substances—male collects, it causes hormonal changes, electrolytic balance is changed. Pearl getting coated—starts on a grain of sand. Crystallization is Crystal of the Atlanteans. Male substance—stored in the gonads, with some sperm, mostly substance. Transfer of substance happens during menstrual period, when women are most susceptible to mood. The most important thing is to maintain a steady, constant mood. Do you whistle when you drive, sing or make noise? Try not to do this and see how often you catch yourself in the middle of whistling.

We can use energy, even negative energy, which would otherwise be wasted. We can allow it to build up and maintain it until it falls back into entropy.

Emanations are like radio waves from the solar plexus. There is an emanation from all people; it comes from different places in different people.

If we have any true love, like poor Snow White or Sleeping Beauty, our romantic ideas would not allow us to work in an alchemical relationship with this material. We must burn it all out—our fears, fantasies, jealousy—not supress it, but ***burn it out***.

Substances, in solution, are passed on organically—there is no other way. Some people have ideas about substances from Astral Bodies, but that is all nonsense. Substance is organic—the astral energies would pass through us like a vapor.

Psychics open up in the solar plexus like a window; sense the other. Psychics do this involuntarily; we can do it voluntarily, and if we work consciously, we can work in this way without harm to ourselves and without harm to others.

CHAPTER 18

Some Subjects Of Alchemical Sex

1. Use of seminal fluids and their transmutation into higher substances.
2. Alchemical notations unveiled regarding the white and red substances.
3. The work of the alchemical factory for the processing of higher substances derived from food, air, impressions and sexual stimulations.
4. Higher bodies are deposits of metallic salts precipitated during certain states, moods, breathing rhythms, from certain foods when taken before specific shocks and breath patterns regulated by Motor and Emotional Centrum exercises.
5. Higher substances require electrical energies for precipitation and coating in the same way that metallic gold is electroplated. Electrolysis is the specific process of coating higher bodies and can be learned by the disciplined and nonobsessive initiate.

6. Psychic and physical states, postures and sexual activities related to the electrolysis processing and use of higher substances.
7. Use of sexual stimulation and other methods for the collection, application and transformation of lower organic substances into useful higher coating substances, and the calcification, precipitation and separation of metallic and rare electrolytic salt deposits in specific cells and along the myoneural systems of the human biological machine and its related higher bodies.
8. Use of the Central Organic Nervous System in generating the precise higher Micro-Electrical Potential and amperage necessary to develop the higher neural activity levels necessary for higher-being electrolytic processes required in higher alchemy.
9. Use of erotic manipulations and other methods of enervating the Central Nervous System and its associated myoneural systems for the generation of new synaptic pathways.
10. Ingestion of precise formulae and dosages of the correct higher salts for use in coating higher bodies with the electrolytic process of Alchemical Sex and other means of developing higher levels of work and existence beyond the domain of the physical universe within the range of the Electro-Magnetic Spectrum, which is by definition the "Proto-Physical-Universe," with its expansion-contraction dynamics, mass-energy conversions, Hydrogen conservation, Planck's Constant, entropic event-horizons, closed-system cycles and its inevitable gravity-well "Black Holes" leading to other similar universes in a complex bandwidth which is, nevertheless, strictly limited to the Electro-Magnetic Spectrum and its octaves of wavelengths and energetic frequencies.
11. Psychological preparation for use of various methods including tantric methods for higher work purposes rather than biological survival of the species or personal gratification.
12. Use of catalysts in coating higher bodies and interdimensional voyaging.
13. Use of catalysts for transformation of lower substances into higher.
14. Contamination and maintenance of chemical and biological harmony.
15. Understanding the uses of the Female Penis and the Male Vagina.

CHAPTER 19

Some Uses Of Alchemical Sex

1. Transformation of lower substances into higher.
2. Accumulation of alchemical gold for higher body coating.
3. Generation of organic electrolytic current in the body for coating higher bodies and alchemical processes.
4. Generation of myoneural electrolytic current for specific transformation of substances and catalytic chemical functions.
5. Oracular contact with higher intelligences, cosmic extradimensional chambers, ordinarily inaccessible deeper levels of the human biocomputer, deep levels of meta-conditioning and traversing interdimensional and interstellar or intergalactic space.

6. Dissolution of Beta 1 and Beta 2 functions of the brain in the 20-30 hz range without traversing through Delta Sleep Stages, thus temporarily exposing and making dominant several deeper levels of perception and consciousness in the Alpha and Theta ranges below 18 Hz.
7. Experiences in meta-spaces, extradimensional chambers, astral travel in the Causal Plane and other higher levels of meta-existence outside the realm of the physical universe as found within the Electro-Magnetic Spectrum.
8. Dissolution of human limits, belief systems, cultural and personal taboos and other obsessive-compulsive behavior patterns, social interactions, psycho-emotional scenarios which open the potential for a reflex throwback to extra-dimensional chambers and certain ordinarily inaccessible portions of the higher subliminal consciousness.
9. Discipline over automatic sexual "knee-jerk" reactions of the Motor and Instinctive Centrums, which may include reproductive urges, erotic demiurges and other vestiges of primitive animalistic behavior, beliefs and satisfactions.
10. Cooperative effort of partners to transcend personal goals, agendas and imperatives, commonly called "needs."
11. Familiarity with higher intelligences in the subjective as if being those intelligences experiencing them experiencing their own reality with or without becoming aware of the effects caused by the interjection of interdimensional voyagers in their spaces.
12. Crystallization and Electrolytic formation of ***higher being bodies***.
13. Collection of metallic salts and other substances for higher-being bodies.
14. Space change experiences and orientation through sudden alterations of reality.
15. Triggering mechanism for collection and deposit of higher metallic salts within the "Buddha's Necklace" and other deposit sites within the human biological machine and its nearest accessible higher bodies.
16. Generation of a higher Work-Will.
17. Creating an "Allowing Factor" through necessity.
18. Collection of special knowledge for the application of higher forces to the special needs of Higher Will and Objective Prayer.
19. Enabling the preparation of apprentices for higher work.

20. Overcoming social-cultural hypnosis, self-hypnosis and rigid belief systems and other obstacles to serious work.
21. Living by wits alone and responding proactively, not by "knee-jerk" reaction.
22. Learning to find the necessity for Rites of Passage through usually inaccessible areas.
23. Access to forbidden knowledge for higher uses, not for personal gratification.
24. Use of assisting factors such as incense, prayer, breathing, sexual energies, dance postures and special movements and rituals in order to access certain higher dimensions.
25. "Imprint" mechanisms to help in recognition of ordinarily inaccessible chambers.
26. Learning to use Transforming Factors such as prayer, incantations and special substances derived from food, air, impressions and sexual stimulation for the permanent alteration of the brain and nervous system and other levels of consciousness not accessible in ordinary states or activities.
27. Producing the Unified Self through permanent all-centrums connections.
28. Dissolution of "Imprints" and other blockages between interdimensional chambers and higher centrums.

Come Hither, E.J. Gold, charcoal, Sennelier, © 1992 HEI

CHAPTER 20
SUBLIMATION AND BEYOND

WE HAVE already discussed the functions of the first three centrums in more or less general ways, but now it is time to elaborate on these in more exact terms and with exact data.

Centrum number one contains two major subordinate functions, the Moving Centrum and the Instinctive Centrum. The Moving Centrum is responsible for movements of the external muscle system and all those reflexes usually activated by the environment either locally or as a whole.

The Instinctive Centrum, on the other hand, is chiefly concerned with interior activity of the smooth musculature, blood circulation and its restriction by deep muscle layers, digestive processes, alimentary tract activities, water, sugar and salt balances and in general all processes including glandular activity falling under the category "homeostasis."

In ordinary humans the Moving and Instinctive Centrums are functioning with very fragmentary consciousness or none at all.

Centrum number two controls the physical manifestations of all those emotional states experienced by ordinary humans. The subjective names for these physiological states are endless—hate, fear, love, sentimentality, desire, submission, satisfaction, anger, discontent and many other such names we have for these.

Some we call negative emotion and some we style positive emotion, but in objective science all are negative because they refer to some object outside oneself or our organism.

Our repertoire only seems large because it is composed of many complex manifestations. Actually the range of emotional phenomena possible for ordinary humans is limited to only four fundamental emotions in two possible forms, active or passive, in successive phases.

Centrums number four, five and six correspond to the active use of individuality, consciousness and will, respectively. The main function of individuality is to be able to constate to oneself data about real things and the real relation between real things. In contrast to the verbal logic of centrum three, the Thinking or Formatory, centrum four contains the potentiality to develop objective logic, real reason, not a potentiality of centrum three under any circumstances.

For substances to develop further, a second conscious shock is necessary. The exact nature of this effort demands special study. The practices of not expressing negative emotions, not considering inwardly and not identifying, are good methods of preparation for this second effort, although they are not the effort itself.

If the Emotional Centrum could work with ***Hydrogen 12***, its work would be connected with the work of the higher Emotional Centrum. Where the work of the Emotional Centrum reaches the intensity and speed of existence given by ***Hydrogen 12***, a temporary connection with the higher Emotional Centrum takes place and human beings experience new emotions and impressions previously unknown. But in ordinary conditions the difference in speed of operation of the two centrums is so great that no connection can occur and we fail to hear the voices calling to us from the higher emotional.

The higher Thinking Centrum with ***Hydrogen 6***, is still further removed from our ordinary centrums, and even less accessible. Connection with this centrum is only possible through the higher Emotional Centrum. It is only from descriptions of mystical experiences and states of ecstasy that we know cases of such connections. These connections can be established for short periods of time artificially through the use of religious fervor, narcotics, or epileptic seizures. Pathological causes, however, give pathological results.

It can be said that the higher Emotional Centrum is necessary for work of the Astral Body.

Higher substances are highly combustible. Unfortunately there is something wrong with most factories and explosions generally destroy all surplus fuels, sometimes even causing irreparable damage to the factory or delaying production for days or weeks at a time.

Organic humans, for whom everything "just happens," who have no inner unity and no possibilities for higher bodies, have no real future. When we die our body is buried and our force, such as it may be, is used by lunar entities for their own benefit and growth. From dust we came and to dust we return. ***No new substances higher than dust have been formed in him***.

If we have attained for ourself any kind of future at all, it must be as a result of accumulation and crystallization of "higher substances," ***upon which all attainments depend***. This makes possible our resistance to at least some external influences.

If a human, or at any rate something we have formed within ourself, is able to resist some external influences, it may be possible for us also to become independent from the death of the Organic Body.

Higher bodies can only be attained through the process of voluntary effort. The Astral Body can be made by means of fusion which comes from terrible inner struggles. Human beings are not born with an Astral Body unless it has formed in another planetary body before. Only a few actually succeed in acquiring an Astral Body, simply because most humans, if they think about it at all, assume they already possess one and therefore do not make those exact efforts necessary to acquire one.

The Astral Body is immortal only within the limits of the planet. It is not truly immortal, but it can survive for a very long time. It is a good "beginning effort."

The Astral Body can be as much of an attachment as the Organic Body. Sometimes it is necessary to wait a long time for the Astral Body to die in order to attain even greater freedom.

With pity aroused cannot come also arrogance; pity for the Absolute and compassion for His state must arouse in you eventually love for Him as if He were your own. This is a secret method for making conscious faith, faith without need for belief. From this practice objective hope can come, hope based on real data, the foundation of a higher being, the only real hope we have for continuation, which is ***immortality with conscience.***

Higher hydrogens are present in every particle of air we inhale. If our organic self does not know how to extract them from air and retain them, they are simply exhaled back into the surrounding air.

There are two parts to the substance "air," one evolving, coming from the lower back toward the higher, and the other involving, coming from the higher into the lower. Involving, ***because it has the taste and smell of the higher***, is more pleasing to the true Alchemist. Organic humans prefer the taste of the lower. Only this solar "involving air" can activate the "I." When in ourselves we create a conscious work-wish, this "good part of air," recently part of the prime source, can be assimilated.

In order to assimilate this involving part of air we should try to sense our mortality—that someday we will inevitably die. When our attention falls on the mortal part of another like ourselves, we can try to realize that he—our neighbor—will also certainly die. From this there is no escape.

At present both you and he are nonentities, but you are in a school; you have ***possibility***. See him from this point of view. He has a life which, up until now, had the same significance as yours; he suffers just as you do and he will also die, but unlike you, he will in all probability ***never even taste the possibility of freedom***.

Try always to sense this about others, make this a habit; only then will you be able to assimilate the "involving part of air" to make substance for your Being. Realize that every human being has wishes and desires, comforts and friends which we hold dear and which we will without doubt lose at our death.

In order to extract more fine substance from air, we must have already in our organism a certain quantity of corresponding fine substances. These act like a magnet on the higher hydrogens contained in the inhaled air. In alchemy it is said, "to make gold one must have gold." In the Bible, "To him who has, more shall be given; to him who has not, even that which he has shall be taken away." Alchemy is a hidden set of instructions for extracting finer substances for the creation of higher bodies.

In truth we are very poor slaves to nature; nature does not even give us food, and even though we must work very hard to receive food, even then it is not for ourselves. Nature sells us food which we eat to service nature. It is a very bad arrangement for our complacency, but for nature it is justice.

Nature only gives free one thing—air—but we must discover for ourselves—of what use is air to us and is it really free?

The "Last Supper" with the Apostles, which was actually a Passover Seder dinner, can, if properly ingested with prayer and inner concentrations of energies of higher force, provide us with the highest possible impressions for extracting the third substance, at the same time providing potential for the use of first and second substances also.

Emotional stirrings without sentimentality, plus powerful concentrated impartial mentation on certain definite subjects makes possible the entry of the "Holy Ghost." When we have made something special for an unexpected guest, Elijah is present at every meal.

The time has not yet come for you to "do." First it is necessary to ponder on these ideas, to prepare to learn. Everything must be weighed on the inner scale. Chew your mentations as a cow chews its cud—ideas already digested must be brought up and eaten again, only this time consciously with attention and presence.

Pondering is the neutralizing force of thought. A human being should spend at least one third of his life assimilating impressions in this way, as he assimilates ordinary food by digestion. "It" can think, but only "I" can ponder and mentate.

The lymphatic glands in the back of the neck can be crystallized with a special substance. This necklace of bone-like substance is the link between the planetary and Astral Bodies, and connects them during life. After death, if the Astral Body still lives, a person possessing one of these bones can always communicate with the Astral Body as long as it continues to survive. Eventually the Astral Body will die, and the Mental or Causal Body will go on, severing the connection. Impressions and air enable humans to exist a little longer than we would otherwise.

CHAPTER 21
THE VAPORIZATION EFFECT

The Last Supper was a magical ceremony similar to "blood brotherhood" for establishing a connection between Astral Bodies of the apostles and Jesus. But who understands this today, or could accept it even if shown? The words have been preserved, but the meaning has been lost.

Efforts to remember oneself, observation of oneself at the moment of reception, and simultaneous reception of impressions and definition and recording of impressions doubles the intensity of impressions, transforms ***doh 48*** to ***re 24***, a finer substance. At the same time, the effort of transition of one substance to another carries with it the energy to transform this substance to second octave formation.

The second stage refers to the work of the organism when we create a conscious volitional shock which travels upward even as high as the third octave if the work of the organism is sufficiently intense. This is one use of super-efforts.

The effort which creates conscious shocks must in the case of the second octave consist in the transformation and transmutation of emotions. This will help to transmute the ***Hydrogen 12***. No serious growth of higher bodies in the organism is possible without this transmutation of emotions. Real objective results can only be obtained after the transmutation of ***mi 12*** has begun.

The transmutation of emotions becomes physically possible only after long practice on the first volitional shock, which consists of self-remembering and observation of impressions at the same time.

This teaching differs from others in that it affirms that the higher centrums are already developed. It is in fact the lower centrums that are undeveloped. It is this lack of development of lower centrums that prevents us from making use of higher centrums.

The intellectual centrum works with ***Hydrogen 48***, Moving Centrum with ***Hydrogen*** 24.

Train yourself to take an impartial and objective viewpoint of everything; do not judge things by any organic standard. You may experience "knee-jerk" reactions to certain typicalities of people, but you can train yourself by disciplined drills and repetitions to adopt an impartial mode regardless of personal feelings for or against individuals. We in the Work cannot afford not to be impartial toward others and toward their displeasing manifestations, but we must not confuse this with abuse, and should not tolerate actual abuse from anyone.

The speed with which the organic-impartial is aroused must be greater than the speed with which revulsion begins to express itself. This reaction of impartiality is almost totally involuntary. To protect the involuntariness we have made the subject matter itself taboo. The Unified "I" must be impartial, even chemically impartial, meaning in the automatic realms as well as in the psycho-emotional and more visible areas.

We must also be able to be impartial voluntarily. In general, we cannot be partial to any single chemical type. The presence of many types insures impartialness. Continual contact with opposing chemical types can bring one into the mode of impartiality.

A school can be used to create an almost continual state of impartiality. "Man Four," as described in ***Seven Bodies of Man***, can be called "Impartial Man," but it is only a first beginning.

The state of impartiality and mentation is called "Gradation of Reason"—viewing with impartiality—the greater the impartiality the greater or higher the "Gradation of Reason." This is a desirable state for the school and the Work.

One personal use of a school is the development of impartiality. We must be willing to condition the organic self to respond with impartiality toward chemical opposites. There are also mental-emotional opposites.

The "vaporization effect" vaporizes revulsion and substitutes impartiality. Something already proceeding must trigger the reaction of impartiality. There is a brief momentary revulsion, guilt about revulsion; a mixture of reactions through the organism—part of the instinctive—an organic, reflexive thing. In the voluntary it would take too long, but with the reflexive involuntary, there is only a momentary lapse, although even this lapse can "emanate." Internal voluntary state is vaporized so momentarily there is ***no*** state. From no state we can very easily assume impartiality.

If the voluntary-mask could "creak into place" where reflex meets reflex it would produce an almost continual state of impartiality. The state of impartiality ensures that all different types are present. If I have revulsion, they do also, but with impartiality on my part they must overcome revulsion. If not, they must overcome their own ***and*** mine; that is very difficult.

The work state is so fragile that it must be continually "buoyed up on soft clouds." It breaks easily to the ordinary. "Not making any sudden moves" is just a matter of addressing attention to the question of sudden movement; we can address attention wherever we wish. Entry and withdrawal. Fragility—from maintaining state. Withdrawal also—no sudden movements.

Automatic-reflex-ego; a reflex-protective-mechanism, without which the identity would crumble. Visual identity is the maintainer of this "quarter" of the organic self. As we observe longer, it "tunes in," but then becomes a ***cliché*** so quickly we cannot stop it or recognize it when this happens.

In a state of total impartiality, because impartiality is already operating at the speed of light, we may be able to see our nothingness for a moment. The longer we remain in the state of impartiality the better we are able to see this. The state of impartiality creates real change in being.

The key to the ***state of presence*** is ***impartiality***; the "insurance of conscience." ***Conscience is the state of complete impartiality toward oneself and caringness toward all beings everywhere.***

Impartiality is the cure for paradox—making "unity" in humans, the suffusion of impartiality throughout the organism—absorption into the entire organism of the substance ***impartiality***. This substance accumulates during a particular psycho-emotional state and is important in the coating of the Fourth Body.

We cannot be impartial about every event. An event is a capsule in time. Common sense goes with impartiality. Emotion has ***nothing*** to do with situations or events in this state—it does not call for emotion. This is a step in how to view the Real World; to see the Real World take off romantic lenses—"color-filters."

Not all events produce unwanted emotion, so we cannot be impartial to all events. Wisdom dictates to not encounter anything unpleasant. The benefit of a group is that it takes many types to produce continual friction. Because we cannot afford a negative reaction in a school, we must brainwash ourselves to impartiality on an organic reflex level.

The organic self cannot disappear until we are in the Impartial State. In that state "I" can "catch the nothingness." When "I" is nothingness, "I" is most impartial. The Gradation-of-Reason of Impartiality is the highest that the awakened being can attain.

If impartiality is not present, there is no transmission. The "Resonance Effect"—the tuning fork principle—applies. We must be impartial in order to resonate. Impartiality plus reception = Receptive State. Receptivity is ***active***.

There are certain times in which ***any*** reaction would have dangerous reverberations. Every artifact and gate has a combination, a key; one part is impartiality and another part is a special impartial emotion. Impartiality runs through the entire System.

In impartial arousal of an emotion, the entire organic formation is impartial to the emotion. Impartial emotion is what is called in our work, "higher emotion."

Eternal horror, insanity, the hell pit are what happens to us when we organically-reflexively do not choose impartiality. To receive data is meaningless in the Absolute sense; we cannot use data as a transforming factor unless we are first impartial.

As soon as we realize the subject matter is us, we have a guardian "on the alert;" something in the organism; a reflex mechanism to assume the "posture of impartiality." I cannot afford involvement in the drama; I ***can*** afford to play a voluntary part.

The alternative to impartiality is "madness." We must in a harmless way become impartial to results, aware, cognizant of results, responsible for them.

Impartial responsibility—another name for conscience. Ordinary responsibility—personal sense of justice. Impartial responsibility is balanced, neutral. Neutrality through balance, each side equally present. Momentum-of-previous-habits becomes entropically exhausted.

Seek out those events which have equal possibility of madness or impartiality. Even toward this selection itself there must be impartiality. When we can be impartial to our own self, we can be impartial to phenomena.

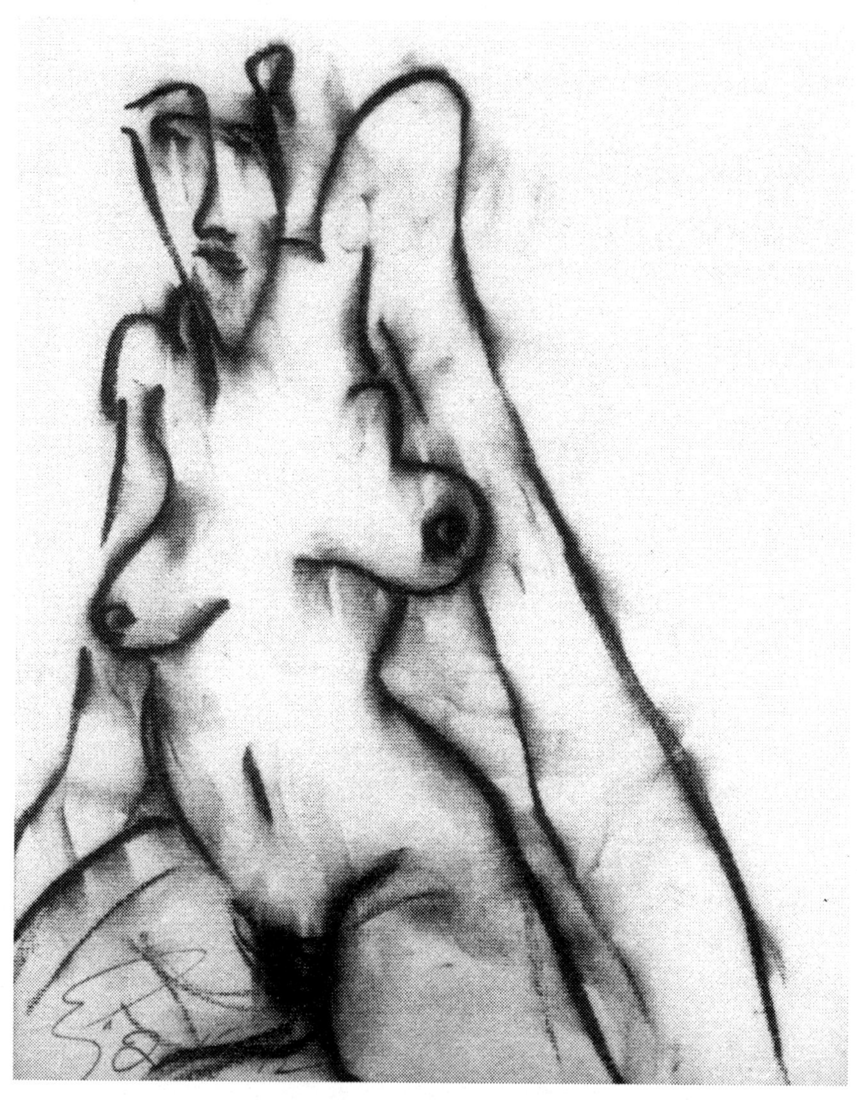

Seated Full Nude, E.J. Gold, charcoal, Sennelier, © 1992 HEI

CHAPTER 22
THE EMERALD TABLET

The key to the organic function of ejaculation is the periodic nature of organic functions in general.

Real knowledge is ***substance***. Perhaps it is necessary to state this idea more clearly in relation to the use of sex-force:

In ancient days only priestesses were given the task of obtaining and holding real knowledge. Real knowledge is not data and has nothing to do with ideas understood mentally. Priestesses were given the power of evocation, the drawing out of substances into themselves; this was their objective purpose in life. They must have learned the periodicity of ejaculation in order to be able to draw out the quantity sufficient for invocation.

Romantic humans cannot develop the business attitude necessary for either evocation of substances or for invocation of entities. A priestess takes on herself at least some part of the formation of the entity invoked, particularly in relation to what are called the "performing," "enlightening" and "enabling" entities.

Periodicity—pulsation of ejaculation is aroused and expelled in the same way as waves and can be ridden if one knows how, just like riding a big wave on a surfboard. One finds oneself at the beginning of a wave; we do not need to struggle out in the water to catch them; we are taken to the next cathode-beginning without effort on our part.

We can predict and eventually learn to control and initiate waves of ejaculation; in general these occur with one or two second intervals between, up to a frequency of pulses at intervals of microseconds for durations of several hours.

Knowing this, we can breathe correctly for each part of the cycle; slowly during the intervals, with an occasional pushing breath during contractions, accelerated breath during expulsions and cleansing breath at the end of the cycle. Then we are ready for the next wave of expulsions, and can relax our breathing and Motor Centrum accordingly.

Technical breathing ought to be considered one important function of unromantic sex, although not the whole idea is expressed in this.

The Law of Invocation, the biggest in objective magic: "evocation engenders invocation," comes from part of ***The Emerald Tablet of Hermes*** which was preserved in oral tradition. The basis for this law is that most entities are attracted by higher substances; evocation is the exact method of drawing these substances out of the male partner and into the female partner who is responsible for this "drawing out."

Substances of male and female, when mixed in the right way and under the right conditions, become something higher which we call Elixir. This is the esoteric meaning of the word "hospitality" when taken in relation to this function of the priestess.

She is receptive, welcoming, opening herself in order to absorb; absorb also means to initiate or to baptize. Suction is the exact method used to draw the substances to herself, but to continue to do so requires all her cunning in the ancient sense of the word.

In evocation, expulsion is the banishing from the male organic formation, the death of the evoked force and resurrection of this force as suitable food for higher entities.

This force is a magical child of which we can have many. A child in this sense of the word is the only suitable offering for higher entities; even the God of Moses required a firstborn of Abraham; Moses the Egyptian, who had training as a shaman in their temples, would have understood this correctly. Abraham did not. He was literal and organic, as are all organic men.

Entities demand our "children" as an offering; it is their food. If we wish to entertain them and be their host and hostess, we must serve them food from their "home planet." They are attracted to substances as sharks are attracted to blood. Unless we set this out for them in advance, how can they be attracted to it? We must place substances, our higher-blood substances, in a little dish as we set out a dish of milk for the cat and as the Irish do for leprechauns. This special dish we call the cup or chalice. It is the vaginal cavity of the priestess.

This is why evocation—the drawing out of substances into the cup—engenders invocation—the manifestation of higher entities. It is also the only means to attract certain types of entities.

If, during evocation, there is also the presence of negative emotion, dramatic Moving Centrum or romantic mental manifestations, the higher blood is killed; sometimes for many months the whole organic source of higher blood can be temporarily destroyed.

This is also why we must limit our contacts by Hermetic Seal on the work circle; other sources of substances can introduce substances which kill higher blood—which is very delicate—and it must not be contaminated even just a little.

Destroyed higher blood kills other higher blood by contact; even for years it has this power. Dead higher blood contamination may reverberate organically for months and psychically for years, even from one work-generation to the next.

In some cases even a momentary contamination can permanently destroy the ability to produce higher blood and other esoteric alchemical substances. Even second, third and even fourth generation contact is in this sense dangerous in the extreme. Indirect contact carries killing higher blood like Typhoid Mary, who does not herself contract the disease, but infects everyone with whom she has contact.

If this occurs with us, then we have nothing to offer higher entities for invocation. Every entity has its own special food and requirements for a minimum amount of offering. We can categorize entities by the amount and type of substances to which they are attracted and calculate the offering necessary for each invocation.

Some books exist which are more or less personal journals, listing categorically the type and amount of substance required for the invocation of various entities, although they are seldom sufficiently scientific for our purposes. Some entities are attracted by plain sugar-and-water. We are not interested in such entities; they are nothing to us for the Work.

Some entities important to us are attracted by our ordinary food, such as bread and wine, if they are prepared correctly and offered in the right way; others are attracted by bright, shiny objects, such as brass, silver or gold; others are attracted to certain types of light such as candlelight, others to smells such as incense, others to sound such as bells, still others to mathematical sequence such as the sequence of bell strikes and knocks.

Just as we clean our dishes and our food before we eat, these must be cleaned, but in a special way called fumigation over incense, allowing the smoke to cleanse the objects. Each entity requires a different cleansing smoke, as we would use soap or a van-van wash to clean a ritual space or object.

Some entities will even sit down to breakfast with us; they are attracted by ordinary food as others are attracted by ordinary activities. If not for these entities personifying the very essence of the impulses of insipidness, ordinary organic humans would have nothing at all to say at the breakfast table.

The entities in which we are interested are almost always hungry for higher substances, something which organic humans are unable to produce, nor do we wish under any circumstances to produce them considering the method necessary. And if we should somehow accidentally get too drunk and end up in an orgy in which these substances are generated willy-nilly, we find some involuntary organic means to destroy these substances before they can have even a momentary effect.

Evocation is delicate. As a science it is even more exacting than ordinary organic chemistry; invocation is a very powerful result of evocation.

We must learn to be both subtle and courageous, gentle and businesslike, but never romantic.

Everything must be kept in strict balance; in evocation, one wrong action, contamination, or negative manifestation, can destroy our work for many months. It is a castle built of eggs; we must be very careful not to break even one, until its function has been actualized and completed to the transforming factor.

Every entity has its payment in exact measure—usually by-the-ounce. This special milk is produced when higher blood and substances are present and ***alive*** in the male semen, when contained in the saucer or chalice of the female partner and is present in sufficient quantity to have a real effect.

Every man who hopes to serve in the alchemical sense must be highly skilled and very professional in the technique of evocation-to-quantity-sufficient, just as every woman who wishes to be an alchemical priestess must have mastered in herself all possible methods for the drawing-out-of-substances from her partner without relying on the usual organic techniques.

An attitude of the highest professionalism, ethics and skill are indispensable to the practicing alchemist. Beyond this, evocation is an art. It could said to be the unknown objective art, not open to the profane, and which only an initiate priestess is able to master.

At Delphi and other ancient oracle-centers, the extraction from the male of quantity sufficient of ***substance*** was developed into an elaborate and exact science which every priestess knew from her first initiation.

Every subtle artifice for the extraction of the most possible substance was taught to these priestesses. In parts of India the science was so developed that every small gradation of method was given in detail, contained in their art, architecture, religion, song and dance.

The ancient sorcerer knew every necessary means to prolong the life of the evocation, to produce quantity sufficient of higher substances for many hundreds of expulsions of his semen and for maintenance of the purity of higher substances.

Evocation engenders invocation, but invocation engenders transubstantiation of substances into the higher. A successful invocation is the transforming factor for substances. This is the only means for the transforming of these substances into the higher.

The entity actually performs the transformation of substances in the same way that angels perform the transubstantiation of bread and wine in the Eucharistic Mass. Not the priest and not the congregation. But it takes both an ethical priest and a receptive and purified congregation to invoke this type of angel, hence the practice of "Confession" and the "Eucharistic Mass."

As we become more familiar with evocation and invocation we are more free to pay attention to detail; there is time to fully master the technique which sets the stage for the elaboration-of-the-totality.

We may notice more, be able to do more; we become more subtle in our business transactions with entities who are also businessmen just like us. When we know more, we can take bigger risks and drive harder bargains, so to speak.

Evocation is like the blasting cap if invocation is like dynamite; it takes the smaller to explode the bigger.

In a work circle, we can sometimes lose our sensing-of-connection, although once connected, never the connection itself. Romantic man, and especially romantic woman, feel continually the impulse to be reminded in little pleasant ways of their connections to one another, soothing them back into their captivity.

The offering given to higher entities in the form of higher substances has their correspondings in offerings offered to the priestesses; nylons, chocolates, American cigarettes and sometimes booze. In ancient times it was exactly the same, except the brand-names were different.

CHAPTER 23
CELESTIAL AND INFERNAL ENTITIES

INVOKING TAKES PLACE naturally. We lay out a saucer of milk to attract "leprechauns" in the same way that, as I told you earlier, sharks are attracted to blood. These leprechauns come and take the milk. Laying out a saucer of milk is the same as saying "a cupful of substances."

Depending on what type of substances we produce, we will attract one or another type of entity. A cup of elixir attracts celestial entities, which are attracted to elixir. If, on the other hand, we put out venom then infernal entities are attracted. Celestial entities are not at all attracted to venom.

Infernal entities are not particularly attracted to elixir, although they will feed on elixir if nothing else is available. This is the vampiristic nature of entities in general. Celestial entities absolutely cannot use venom under any circumstances whatever.

There are two major classifications of entities—inner and outer—subjective and objective. In each of these categories we find both Celestial and Infernal. If we allow them to, our subjective inner entities will eat the substance intended for the objective entity we wish to invoke from Above.

In order to prevent the theft of invoking substances, we choreograph the emotional, making it impossible for our inner-subjective entities to manifest sufficiently to feed on our substances.

Once an entity begins to feed on substances, the other entities are kept away. While it is feeding, one of us can act as a medium for the entity and the entity can be questioned. We can obtain data and speak through the organic to our work partner.

We can bind the entity by providing a very large amount of substances—it will take some time for it to feed completely. Substances, like other organic chemicals, have a definite valence, meaning a specific level of attraction to other substances based on free radicals and combinant factors, and will tend to combine in exact ratios according to their outer shell electrons, just as you would expect from any chemical occurring in the physical universe.

An ***entity*** is not a mysterious creature; it is invisible to our ordinary sight, but able to operate in the organic through organic formations. We are able to obtain data from it with our Astral Self and report this data—to bring down the data through the organic into the essential self.

The second method of binding is to imitate the manifestations of an entity. By imitation or impersonation we can resonate with and thus bind an entity; as soon as we cease to imitate perfectly, the entity is free from our binding, although not necessarily banished.

Obviously evocation causes invocation...however, it does not cause any specific invocation. This is the task of the director of ceremonies to set up the chamber of invocation to attract one particular entity.

For instance, we could arrange purple drapes, purple candle, olibanum incense, all of which would suggest an exact entity. The more exact we are in setting up our chamber of invocation, the more exactly we are able to invoke one particular entity.

Then, we can also work through our ***control***—which is to say our switchboard-operator-entity, which can connect us with one entity in particular with whom we wish to have a conversation.

To attract an exact entity we must have its correspondings present in the chamber, such as color, odor, forms as various objects, and so forth.

The conditions within the chamber—including the mood—determine which entities will respond, in a general way, and we can narrow this down to perhaps two-dozen entities by the decoration of the chamber, depending upon which invocation we use, and also depending upon our mental, emotional and organic state, collections and concentration of attention, the more exact we can be with our invocation.

The main objection to spiritualism is that first of all, it only attracts astral entities because very low substance—ectoplasm—is provided, and is useless for our purposes; and secondly, it is not specific in terms of its attractive-exactitude.

Any entity at all could manifest in a seance. On the other hand, in the magical chamber the attractive-exactitude is such that we can know which entity we have attracted, and can determine subjectively by voluntary-assumption-of-the-identity of the entity whether or not this is exactly correct.

What must be emphasized is that humans are not specialized creatures, as are entities, but a microcosm—that is to say an exact, although on a smaller scale, duplication of the Absolute. All other creatures, including entities, are highly specialized and are not microcosmic models of the universe, and are as a result, involuntarily-impartial.

Because they are specialized, they are knowable in the partiality sense of the word; the microcosm is unknowable in the same way as the cosmic. Although the machine cannot ever be fully known, we can be impartial toward our machine which is the manifesting part of ourselves. How can we be impartial toward something which has no qualities ***whatever*** except ***observateur-presence***?

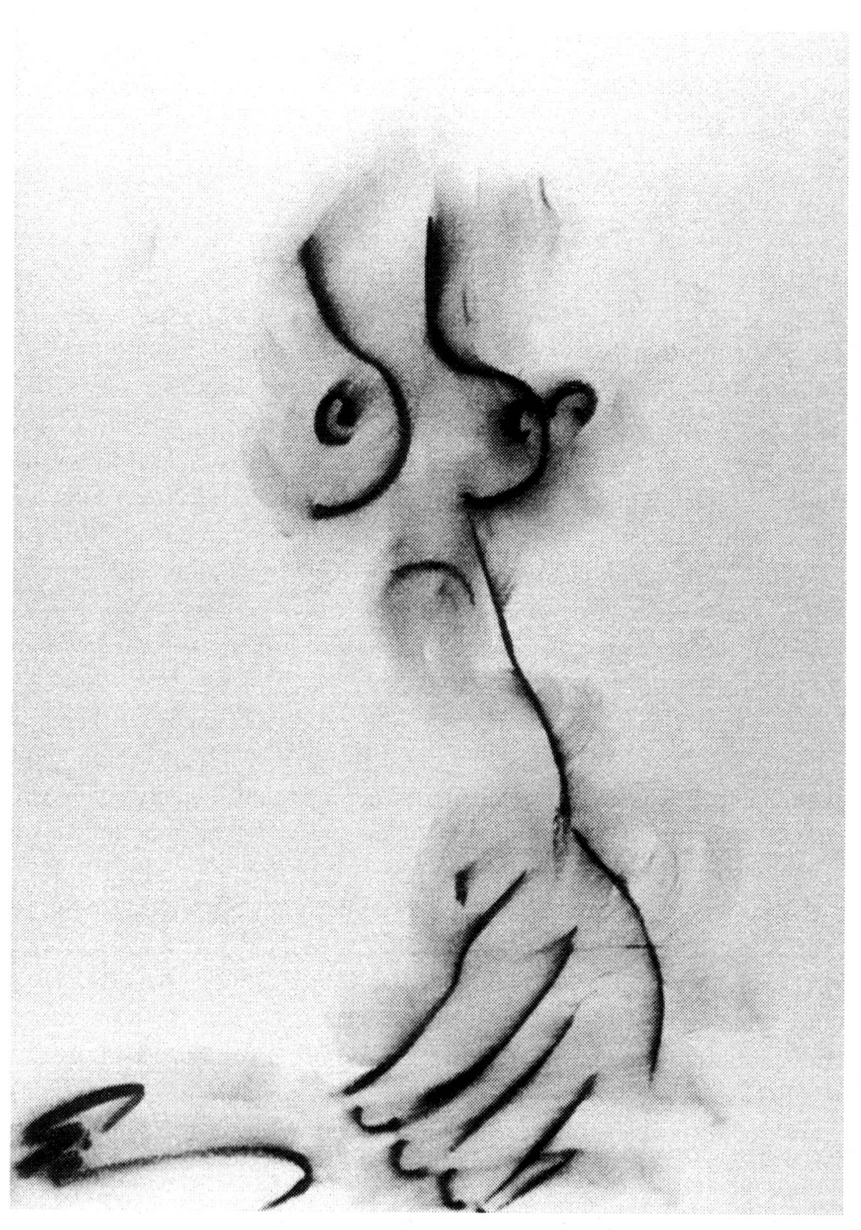

Naked Truth, E.J. Gold, charcoal, Rives BFK, © 1996 HEI

CHAPTER 24
RECTIFICATION OF ELIXIR

IF WE ARE not an entity before we die, we cannot be an entity after we die. This is the real esoteric meaning of the instruction, "Die before you die."

We do not wish to become entities, exactly; but we can partake of the qualities of entities, called entityness. This is more the path of wisdom. Entityness, categorically speaking, is a substance, although a much higher substance than any we could know about chemically with our science, even objective science of ordinary humans.

Coating the higher bodies gives us entityness without making us specialized creatures so we can become as an angel except that an angel is a specialized creature.

An invocant who temporarily takes the place of a fallen angel, is an unspecialized formation of angel most closely resembling the Absolute, therefore, a more direct representative of the Absolute than an angel would be. There are examples of human beings who have become angels, such as ***Enoch***. Of course, there are angels both celestial and infernal, and in fact, celestial and infernal are functions which describe the dichotomous nature of angels.

The majority of female formations of angelic entities can be said to be the patron-saints of extractors of substance, that is to say, alchemical priestesses. Evocation occurs in the secret temple or chamber, which is to say, behind the vulva in the vaginal part of the organic self.

Alchemical processes require continual warmth. The processes of ***Negrido, calcination, putrefaction, etc.*** all occur within the secret chamber with the application of slow organic heat. Each stage of transformation of substances-in-mixture progressing toward the higher form of elixir can be used by one entity or another. If we do not attract entities, we are able to use elixir for ourselves, for the coating of our higher bodies.

If we wish data or transformation, we are forced to invoke. If we wish to coat our higher bodies we must allow the substance to remain. We have a choice to either invoke entities or coat our higher bodies. When we evoke we must make a choice of purpose, whether to invoke or coat our higher bodies, because we cannot do both in the same magical operation.

Coating requires collecting of substances for 23 days during the evocation and then ***mixture, precipitation, calcination, Negrido, distillation***, and so forth; all taking place in the crucible or vaginal-chamber during the five days of menstruation, on the last day of which, the transforming factor or philosopher's stone—in Aqua Regia—is obtained and absorbed mutually by the Alchemical Partnership.

We must make certain that the elixir remains in its vessel undisturbed...uneaten...untouched...unmolested, so to speak; by entities higher, lower, inner or outer. Then the completed elixir, after its exposure to the proper slow heating process, can be used for the coating of higher bodies; that is to say, indrawn by the male, purified to distillation, then released once again for final mixture, and then shared in common with the partner in the work group.

The rectified elixir is then brought upward through the organic, through the subtle channels and allowed to pass into the nerve nodes and the glandular system, particularly the lymphatic.

This final stage of the making of elixir is best accomplished during the five days of menstruation. The basis for the elixir is the substance called red gold. The red-female-tincture is preferred by alchemists over the white tincture, which is to say, the ***menstruum*** is preferred over ordinary substances of the other part of the female cycle.

It is considered that the menstruum is the most solar of the substances and, at the same time, every stick has two ends, and the most solar substances produce the most lunar moods. If the mood is not allowed formation either organically, emotionally or mentally, then the mood can also be solar. When mood and substance are both solar, they produce elixir. When the mood is lunar but the substance solar, venom is produced.

The really serious magician is able to use both elixir and venom. In some cases we intentionally produce—or help to produce—venom for the purpose of data and transformation. Celestial entities can provide data, but Infernal entities are able to provide both data ***and*** transformation.

Transformation comes mostly from Infernal entities. Angels can do many things, but an Infernal entity can do anything, because he is not constrained by the same law-conformableness as an angel...and yet, the transformation of Organic Man to Real Man is the hope of all celestial beings everywhere, including ***His Endlessness*** and ***The Most High Absolute***, neither of which is actually God.

There are two main emotional keys for invocation. For the male, it is the emotion of impartial passion toward the female and for the female partner, impartial humility. These intentional moods are internally voluntarily aroused and have no relation to events in the outer world. Other voluntary moods can be used for different types of invocations and for the coating of higher bodies.

For example, the emotion of impartial ecstasy for the male and impartial personal surrender for the female can be used in connection with the formation and coating of the higher bodies all the way up to the Divine Presence.

When we have bound an entity, we have only so much time to question it for data, limited by the amount of substance we were able to set out for it in our special dish or chalice—in which the blood of the Christ is caught.

As long as the entity continues to ingest this substance for its own process-of-reciprocal-feeding then we are able to bind it and continue to extract from it the data we wish to obtain. Even using the second method of binding—that is, exact-limitation-of-manifestations—we cannot keep an entity longer than our substance offering lasts.

Then why use imitation of manifestations at all?

Imitation of manifestations of the entity is not to attract it to us; the substance does this for us without the necessity for our direction—imitation is not even exactly an active binding—it is a passive-binding in the sense that, when we fail to imitate the entity manifestations exactly, ***the entity is able to banish itself***.

The whole idea of Western civilization for women is obtaining a drone and sending it out for the purpose of maintaining her nest by any means necessary. And keeping constantly on the lookout for possible replacements in case he wears out—and in Western civilization he almost always does—heart condition, high blood pressure, hardening of the arteries, stroke, all of which are symptoms of the involuntary drone. If Western women only knew how they ruined their drones...I suppose they would continue to do the same thing. It is all they know how to do.

The men, on the other hand, always have tucked away somewhere in a secret chamber of their hearts, the hope that they will somehow be allowed, should a lessening of hive activity somehow miraculously occur against all nature, to develop their pet project—some creative thing which no matter what it is, would surely reduce his efficiency as a drone, which reduction of efficiency, however minute, is viewed by every queen bee as a definite threat.

She knows that, should she ever have a momentary lapse into pity for her drone and allow him even the smallest taste of freedom, once he has, so to speak, tasted blood, he will never be quite the same domesticated creature he once was. She may, to avoid direct confrontation, allow him to putter at something or other in the garden or garage, as long as it is a not-too-successful venture.

The intelligent queen bee is not demanding. She knows that so long as she continues to exude royal jelly her drone will do anything—usually just short of killing himself—to supply her with the necessary pollen so long as he is not excluded from the benefits of royal jelly.

Contemporary woman, for some reason, thinks that she can withhold her royal jelly or cease to manufacture it and at the same time, demand that her drone continue to supply her with various substitutes for pollen in the form of jelly-filled chocolates, diamond tennis bracelets and a coat made from the pelts of some member of the family of endangered species.

According to our contemporary civilization she has also been cleverly taught to—at any cost whatever—while demanding that her drone supply her with pollen—keep him away from any flowers which could possibly become for him—and incidentally also for her—a source of nectar.

Then just to make sure that he never wakes up from this unique sleep, she has all forms of real data on the subject banned from sale with the enthusiastic help of the local bishop who has nothing to lose on his own behalf and who is dependent upon her gratitude expressed through the wallet of her drone.

Macrodimensional Lovers, E.J. Gold, charcoal, Rives BFK, © 1987 HEI

CHAPTER 25
PSYCHO-EMOTIONAL TRIGGERS

MENTATION is the second-wind-of-data. We need not develop the centrums, but rather take away the sinister barriers which prevent instantaneous expansion.

Work to remove the obsessive-compulsive automatic considerings and powerful beliefs which remain from childhood, which we call "fixed ideas."

Our mental force for the most part goes to hold certain ideas fixated, without which our personalities would feel socially and culturally unbalanced and disoriented—I.Q., or Intelligence Quotient, merely measures our adjustment to mainstream society. Real intelligence has no relation to civilization.

To avoid the sensation of disorientation, we tend to continue to hold unshakable but untested beliefs that nobody can break.

We hold these beliefs against all possible ego-threats—they are mental bastions of the mind and of the personality, keeping in place our high idea of ourselves and help us to remain calm and self-satisfied, but they are almost always untrue and irrelevant, and serve only to maintain our self-esteem in the face of all evidence to the contrary.

These considerings are sinister because the possible loss or unwanted removal of them feels ominous to us and is viewed as a threat to our self-image.

Each individual has different organic triggers, although in objective invocations, corresponding psycho-emotional triggers tend to arouse exactly the same things in the emotional and mental, regardless of typicality.

The same triggers can also serve different functions—releasing certain mental, emotional and psychical automatisms.

Not only are the psychic controls different in each of us, but our human biological machines perform entirely different and each one functions and serves very different purposes, according to our tendencies and the entities which we serve.

When certain substances such as incense and the ringing sounds of singing bowls are introduced into the human biological machine, invocation can be a powerful result.

The same psychic substances introduced into a human biological machine which is resistant to these impressions because it has belief systems and fears protecting its ego identity might produce no result whatever in the realm of invocation.

Because of certain barriers in the emotional part of the Organic Centrum, entities may find it very difficult to feed on our substances.

Through the fixations and beliefs which keep our ego in place, our organic machines may become inaccessible monasteries for higher entities making long term accumulation more possible.

What is the effect of a male's states on the production and distillation of higher alchemical substances?

Male states may be somewhat less involuntary than the female, because they are less subject to the organic see-saw of hormonic ups and downs.

When a male has states of irritability it is a problem of wrong development of centrums, not a result of the roller-coaster ride of hormone imbalances, although there is definitely an effect in males similar to females each and every 28 days.

The male is totally incapable of transforming, distilling, using or collecting those substances when he is in an irritable or "bitchy" condition, or other negative emotional state.

To obtain elixir we must first collect substances for five or six hours using a continual slow mixing process with a release of smaller ejaculations once every one or two minutes, applying no friction whatever—indrawing seminal fluids as a powerful result.

For the purpose of alchemical exchanges and data transmission to and from higher entities, one or two hours is sufficient.

At the end of this period of higher-substance exchange, we should allow several dozen ejaculations, then indraw, and apply the resulting substances for data receptivity through the corresponding ritual invocations.

What is the meaning of the term "barren ground," and what are some indicators of it?

Pinched, stringent, bitchy and clinical—something quite common in contemporary relationships, as are fake orgasms and Hollywood style expressions of sexual ecstasy.

In order to produce ***venom***, should an Alchemical Partner voluntarily produce negative states? No, not really; it is better to produce venom voluntarily. Why should anyone suffer negativity?

The ability to collect and transform substances is an acquired skill, which can be leveled-up through time and effort. One learns by repetition, without fear of failure. The learning process is a result of impartial invocation, not striving for specific results while climbing the steep mountain called "the learning curve."

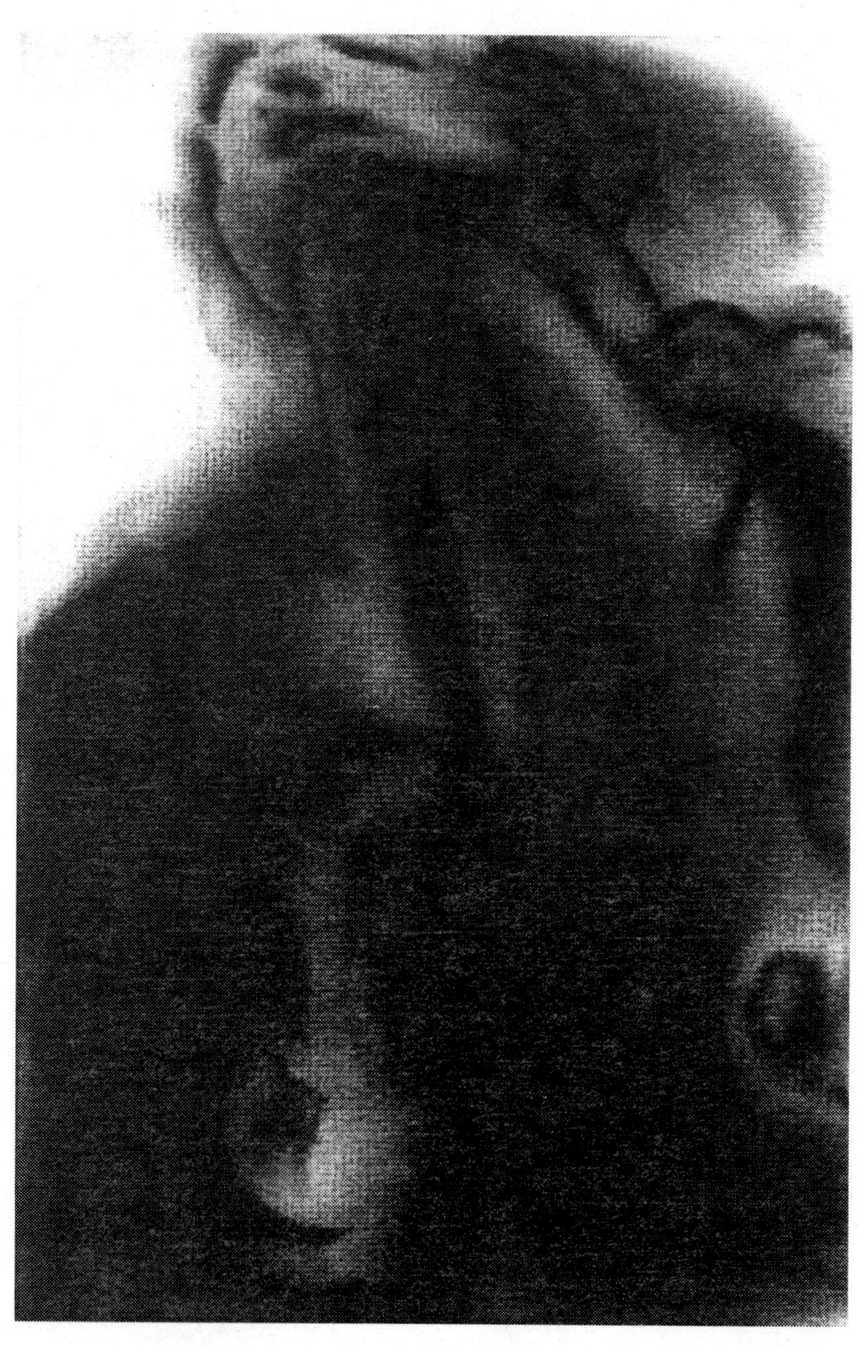

The Mystical Black Goddess of the East, charcoal, Sennelier, © 1992 HEI

CHAPTER 26
THE ADAMIC BODY

THE STARTING POINt for alchemical work is the same for everyone, and begins with orgasmic discipline.

Here is a little secret for men: after a first, very small ejaculation and momentary withdrawal, a slow reinsertion, after which sexual contact can continue indefinitely.

This is an important secret to know mentally as well as intuitively, and to remember with every sexual contact. Once we pass the Voluntary Orgasm Test, we can overcome the need to ever have involuntary orgasms again.

Involuntary spasmodic orgasm is a form of self-hypnosis of fantasy;

it has no real organic basis whatever, and arises in, and is totally fed by, the mind and false emotions learned through social training.

Involuntary orgasm involves a loss of vision, blockage of hearing, impairment of mental faculties and serious alteration of the breath, producing a state of organic unconsciousness and oblivion, a form of exhaustion and depletion which may last moments or hours.

With voluntary ejaculation all effects of involuntary orgasm are eradicated. Voluntary ejaculation is a fusing of the sensing of two higher blood systems.

Spasmodic orgasm is merely another form of self-pampering and self-love, and a fulfillment of the desire for self-oblivion and sleep.

Voluntary ejaculation without orgasm produces a specific mood and a definite sense of impartiality. Involuntary spasmodic orgasm is a psychological-pathological social disease.

It is never useful for a woman to withhold orgasm. She can have frequent discharges and full body sensations. She should also have the corresponding mood: a definite visioning-mentation and sensing-of-fusion, however, she could fall into a romantic trance unless she has trained herself to be impartial toward romantic fantasies.

The male feels waves of passion, and so it is important for him to form within himself waves of romantic mood, and the female to form in herself waves of a passionate mood, then fusion can be achieved.

A little yang in much yin and a little yin in much yang. The male will only be able to produce a little bit of romance and the female will only be able to produce a little bit of passion. When we make the male female and the female male, then we make the two one. This is the esoteric understanding.

The Christ is the intentional reformation of the ***First Adam***. Adam plus Eve, the fusion of male and female. The second Adam is Adam with Eve removed; the first Adam is the hermaphroditic Adam. This is a very big secret—that there were two Adams. Adam's rib is not just a bone, this is a modern misunderstanding. It is the whole left side. Eve can be understood to be the seductive and merciful part of the first Adam.

Crucifixion is a euphemism for Alchemical Sex. Christ is the higher state which is the result of affixing nails, the crown of thorns, or objective suffering for all beings everywhere, the cross of matter and energy and the organic form which is our temporary relationship to the organic world. The union of the cross is seductive to the male and the Christ is seductive to the female.

The idea of using exact postures in alchemical work originates from the idea that partners using certain postures will resonate with higher bodies and thus form Bodies of Fusion in the Adamic Body. Using the elements of Alchemical Sex can form and crystallize many of these bodies in the higher which, if fully formed, can expand to their archetype and become cosmoses in themselves.

For the partners, because of the exchange of substances, all the higher bodies thus crystallized are accessible. At some point the fusion becomes so intense that it is impossible to separate the invocants until the invocation has reached completion. In the traditions, we are well-advised to consider carefully whether we wish to spend eternity with one another.

Before any large scale destruction or war, we see a mass involuntary urge to procreate. At the moment of death, the urge to procreate is the highest, most profound and strongest sexuality we could manifest. Because of the taboo of death in our society, this idea has vanished from our social and sexual dynamic.

At the height of sexuality, the formation of the ***Adamic Body*** is the strongest. Because of the temple prostitute's reaction to sexual contact with a dying man, venom is also strong, making the greatest possible bond. His vibration of sexuality at death combined with her sense of repulsion-and-surrender make a very strong surviving factor, reverberating in the very highest spheres. Reverberations cause crystallizations, like ringing a bell in all cosmoses at the same time.

When we can evoke substances and force impartially for six hours, then we are ready to begin serious alchemical invocation. Evocation, drawing upon our inner entities, produces invocation, in which we contact entities outside ourselves, and sometimes if we are lucky, higher entities than those in our immediate sphere of reality. If we can evoke without fear or ego, then eventually higher invocations will naturally occur.

Each aim has its own mood, mentation and sensing—this is the

name of the posture. We ***evoke*** the posture to ***invoke*** the entity. If we are clever we know the posture. This is where ***initiatism*** becomes important.

Women are in general "Holders of Initiation." It cannot be passed on by verbal transmission. Posture, gesture, expression, movement and tone are important.

A woman has many artifices to know moods and evoking factors. If she is properly initiated she knows how to seduce a man into the correct mood, posture, sensing and breath for milking him of his higher substances. She is sensitive to emotion, organic rhythmic cycles and pulsations-of-ejaculation.

It is important to know that ***her release of fluids can cause ejaculation***. The male must learn to ejaculate long before—and entirely without—orgasm, and this should occur at the same time as the release of female fluids. In this way the two can learn to work together. Sexual coaching is not verbal, it is initiatory, with natural unfolding of data through discipline and practice.

CHAPTER 27
INVOKING POSTURES

THE SCHOOL LINEAGE is the factor determining which entities are drawn down and their sequence of appearance.

Initial training is in beginning objective invoking postures; later, other invoking postures suggest themselves. Reject postures that are suggested due to fatigue and only accept postures for transmission of data.

There are several variations of the Rajastani Posture. The basic posture is the male sitting on heels, legs together, knees in front of him.

The woman sits on the man's lap, with her legs wrapped around his hips and her feet flat on the floor. She puts her arms around the back of his neck, and he puts his arms under her thighs, hands on her derriere.

First variation: the woman's knees are bent further under her, and the soles of her feet are facing up.

Second variation: the woman has one foot forward.

Third variation: both feet forward.

Fourth variation: her feet are both forward, his hands supporting her on the sides of her bottom. This allows for a great deal of mobility. The same posture can be done with the man standing, holding the woman in this position.

Many different kinds of motion are possible with this posture: up and down, side to side, circular motion, arc or u-shaped motion. Standing postures require that she have a forward-tilting vulva, which most women do not have.

In the beginning, the female milks the male relentlessly and mercilessly of all possible substances. The male resists this "To The Sweet End." For this he must be very voluntary, and she tends to be very cunning.

Women and men who appreciate real sex know that there is something even more important than just making love. Greater than any genital contact is simple kissing.

It is the most primitive and infantile of all Moving Centrum sensations. Initiatism calls for a "Rain of Kisses." Kissing deepens the ardor, but should not be confused with lovemaking or romanticism.

Concentrating attention voluntarily on kissing causes natural evocation of substances, penile vacuum, and transubstantiation. The mouth has a magnifying factor. The male partner activates the romantic side of himself through kissing. The female partner should concentrate on her breasts, drawing her man to herself. This brings out her passion and higher emotional state.

Variations on kissing: focus attention on the face rather than focusing on the genitals and sexual sensations. Start out with small ejaculations—no more than three a minute—build up, take a rest to even out the breathing. Concentrate on kissing. Feel cheek contact.

The first type of controlled breathing is called "nasal blowing," in which the male slowly exhales into his female partner's right nostril and, after a short interval, exhales into her left nostril.

This is done five or six times. Next is mouth breathing in which the mouths are held open, allowing breath to flow back and forth, gently adding more oxygen through nasal inhalation, breathing together in a gentle rhythmic cycle.

During ejaculation, the female initiate pushes her tongue to the roof of the male's mouth, while he sucks the juices from under her tongue.

In the same way that organic man views voluntary emotions to be phoney and involuntary emotions real, he regards voluntary ejaculations to be impossible or pathological and only ordinary orgasm as authentic. To be serious about this, we must practice six hours a day.

Be prepared to get lost in the process several times. We can re-center our purpose by using lower forces for a higher aim.

After several major ejaculations, take a cleansing breath and feel the full force of love. With this force of love, it is possible to maintain connection.

One of the functions of a real initiated woman is to have Madonna Breasts. This may astonish the beginner. The posture which corresponds to this special emanation is demonstrated by Michelangelo's ***Pieta***, the Madonna drawing in to the center-cavity between her breasts.

The male able to duplicate Madonna Breasts makes very powerful magic, producing in himself constant ejaculations, one after another. In a short period of time, he can exchange one third to one half pint of substances. Have liquid handy to replenish body fluids. With controlled breath, there will be a demonstrably lower sperm count in the semen.

Enabling substance needs a certain bacteria for its life, an incubation period. This sometimes produces a mild septic, or intestinal reaction. Bacteria turns substance into a live substance, as yogurt culture turns milk into yogurt. This bacteria can only be transmitted on the organic level by direct initiation. Different strains of bacteria represent the different lineages. Semen of ordinary man is dead in the higher.

Baraka is a form of higher grace or allowingness which provides higher blood at need. For every psychic effort we use some form of ***Baraka***.

The Forms of the Brothers of the Void, charcoal, Sennelier, © 1992 HEI

CHAPTER 28
ELIXIR AND VENOM

In order to produce and receive the higher substances to do this kind of work we must find a situation in which our fellow invocant with us has special necessity. We must know how to do this. Then we give it everything we have, our last drop of blood, as it were, and hope that the higher entity invoked will provide transformation of our higher substances for our work.

Understand the difference between elixir and venom. A woman can change elixir into venom, but cannot change venom into elixir. She does that by her states—bitchiness, irritability, negative states, and so forth. If you can find a partner who is bright, cheerful and positive, she can produce a lot of elixir.

Recall various elements in the Moving Centrum which correspond with ejaculation. There are twenty to fifty definite manifestations of the Moving Centrum related to ejaculation in both the male and the female. All your organic ejaculatory postures should be known to you by now—sounds, sight, activities of hands, arms, legs, position of head, tongue, jaws, presence or absence of tremblers, breathing, and so forth.

There are definite manifestations which occur organically to you, according to your type, during ejaculation. Not that it is always the same, but there is a definite repertoire of possible manifestations.

There is an exercise which has been shown where we stand in front of a mirror and imitate voluntarily one or another posture manifestations. Another exercise, which is the same except that we do not have a mirror, we must use sensing. We voluntarily arouse and activate all manifestations of ejaculations. This brings it about since postures cause a state. An involuntary state causes the posture or the posture involuntarily causes the state. Voluntarily the posture causes the state.

If we manifest the posture the state will occur. That is cause and effect. It is the first time you will genuinely cause something in this universe, but everything must be correct. You will start drawing in the details; eventually it will become so heavy with momentum that it will carry you through.

Eventually it becomes more natural to arouse the voluntary ejaculation than to wait until the organic triggers. It becomes more natural. Ejaculation becomes simply a matter of posture.

Only one centrum can control the Moving Centrum in this process and that is the Sex Centrum. In this way the Sex Centrum becomes active, the centrum in which we can live. It is a lower centrum, but it can also be our first higher centrum. We must go to the lower to reach the higher. To reach the Sex Centrum from the mental would be too high a jump.

The lowest rung in the organic corresponds to the lowest rung in the higher. This is how you activate the Sex Centrum—by voluntarizing a totally involuntary manifestation. Ejaculation is the most possible voluntary, but in ordinary man the most involuntary because he protects these manifestations with taboo.

With voluntary ejaculation we bypass the signal that says to the brain to cease the flow of blood to the penis which causes the loss of erection. Men can use the same techniques to make voluntary romantic manifestations without cynicism. The woman can use this to make voluntary passionate manifestations. Each realizes the other is acting in the sense they are acting voluntarily. Their activity and presence and love are sincere. Their manifestations are not sincere in the ordinary sense; they are sincere in the voluntary. They are sincere without lying. Ordinary man does not know how not to lie. To the ordinary man sincere is involuntary and insincere is voluntary.

The female partner can use the same technique for orgasm.

Orgasm is an organic reverberation. Fluids can be produced without it. In fact, it is ideal if they are. This organic reverberation comes from mentation and visualization. In short, a fantasy. In order to arouse those particular mentations which cause in her those organic reverberations which we call orgasm, she must use her memories and ideas rooted in her since early childhood and formulated in the romantic. This is what causes orgasm in the woman.

The technique for a woman to release fluids is to relax, concentrate on her lover, to be with him, to ignore at least 75% of the genital proceedings. She should concentrate 75% of her attention on the chest and face, the other 25% spread throughout the organism.

The female partner should not avoid orgasm, nor should she seek it, especially if she wishes to produce elixir. Orgasm, even voluntarily, can produce venom. The exact method for the production of voluntary venom is to produce multiple orgasms in the woman. If a woman can produce elixir, we should not care how much venom she can also produce.

If the female partner leaves the substance alone, it is elixir. That is to say, if she does not do anything to change it, it will remain in its natural state. If she descends into a negative state, then she can change the substance to venom. That does not mean it will necessarily change to venom. To coat the higher bodies we use elixir. For data and transformation we must use venom.

In the Steambath, charcoal, Sennelier, © 1992 HEI

CHAPTER 29
HIGHER BLOOD

At some point in your alchemical lovemaking, would you not go to any length to achieve total fusion? You take tremendous daring at that moment; all your thoughts for personal survival are put aside. That is the tried-and-true method of tapping into the fullest possible force of Sex Centrum energy. Impartiality is also necessary for the formation of higher bodies. It is a special kind of courage based on nonidentification with items of possible sacrifice. You become so nonidentified with bodies that you could literally throw them away if it became necessary; it's obvious and possible to do this in order to achieve a higher measure of existence or experience, even if momentary.

Every invocation costs us something—higher substances are like psychic money. With real sex we can gain something, but we also must pay a great deal more. We give of ourselves in the hopes of achieving something higher, greater than ourselves, not for ourselves, but for the general good, for the benefit of all beings everywhere.

When we give our blood of love-absolute, we do not question whether it is the first or the last drop. We do it to achieve something for the beloved, not to get more blood.

Alchemical Sex gives us a taste for courage in the real sense, not stupid courage, courage driven by fear. Real courage is courage ejaculated; we know the cost. We give the beloved our last drop of higher blood, knowing what it is going to cost, but we do it anyway.

We do this not as a result of involuntary ecstasy, in the stupefaction of orgasm, but in the spirit of greater good. Higher blood is killed by orgasm. It is very matter-of-fact, taken for granted, maybe something will happen, maybe it will not, that is of no consequence whatsoever.

We must be willing to go through personal annihilation for the sake of service, the Work. Personal annihilation for no purpose in particular is the highest, but this is in the spiritual sense, not the physical—this is not a license to suicide, as might be ordinary man's stupid idea.

We must hurl ourselves off a psycho-emotional cliff, not knowing if we will float, fly or fall. We become like the Fool of the Tarot, and this "Leap of Faith" is really a test of our impersonal sense of courage.

Courage with knowledge is taking a fifty-fifty chance that we will fly. That is the calculation. We give away our last drop with a good chance of success, or we throw ourselves in the river with a good chance of being saved.

There is a good chance that the entity we call down will give us data, transformation and additional higher blood for transformation. Larger and larger entities demand more and more, and we have no choice but to continue—if we fall by the wayside and pursue our organic weaknesses and give in to our organic fears, we are far worse off than when we started.

CHAPTER 30
INITIATISM

We use "self-initiatism" in the sense to break inertness and gain momentum—to self-start. One cannot initiate oneself in the sense of initiatism. Initiation passes from father to son, mother to daughter and Priestess to Alchemist.

A practicing alchemist can only initiate a partner ready to take such initiation, someone who has erased self-vanity, self-love, self-interest, self-pampering, self-gratification and self-image.

As we work we will discover what we know, as little by little we move from noninitiate to initiate and finally practical alchemist and invocant.

Not all alchemists are teachers, and not all alchemists are automatically capable of initiation.

An initiate works to penetrate and discover the secrets of high alchemy. We come to know ourselves as an incidental by-product of feeding of higher entities. We cannot do this by ourselves, or by instinct alone—knowledge is necessary.

Initiatism is the technique of initiation, but almost nothing is ever done directly in the process of initiation—initiatism is a by-product of something else, something within the scope of the alchemical process.

Women in general have certain social and sexual secrets they do not communicate to men. These social and sexual secrets would destroy the illusions about women held by men, and particularly the illusions men hold about themselves, such as the fact that both sexes start as the same thing, and that the organs of man and woman are precisely the same.

In the animal world in general the male is fancier than the female. In human beings the male is only fancier and more beautiful inside in his own mind.

Men are much more vain than women in general, and try to find women who reflect themselves, look like them, and who will enhance their inner plumage and look good draped over their arm.

There are a certain number of sexual secrets that women employ more or less directly during the process of sex. If an ordinary man were to learn that a woman employed them to exploit his weaknesses and male vanity, he would go mad. He believes in the sanctity of women and in his own male allure and powers.

An alchemist has no illusions, and must be able to learn all the sexual secrets—this means that an alchemist will never again see the self as ordinary human beings do.

Alchemists know all the sexual secrets that women must know and share for their survival in a man's world. Some men find the idea refreshing and become alchemists; others go mad or reject those secrets as "old wives' tales" and "female conceits."

Women love from the Feeling Centrum, therefore, their Moving Centrum Sex can be easily made voluntary.

Men, if they love anything at all beyond their own skin, tend to love from their Moving Centrum, therefore, their Moving Centrum Sex is involuntary and their Emotional Centrum tends to be easily made voluntary or nonexistent.

A man must learn to love from the Feeling Centrum so that his Moving Centrum Sex can become voluntary.

Because a woman has sex from her Feeling Centrum, she can become a Moving Centrum actress, while a male can easily be an Emotional Centrum actor.

Man can easily be voluntary in the Emotional Centrum, so he can be polygamous without pain. He can emotionally attach and detach himself to a variety of companions, having no actual interest in his partners either in love or business.

A woman tends to attach herself to a man because she is involuntary in the Feeling Centrum, so she tends to be more easily monogamous, although it has been said that "a woman needs a man like a fish needs a bicycle."

Ordinarily, men and women can both be unnatural; that is to say, men can be monogamous and women can be polygamous, but this is merely a by-product of the present civilization.

Heart disease, aneurisms and stroke are among the primary symptoms caused in males by culturally enforced monogamy, and most males are not really monogamous, which is why there are mistresses, prostitutes and singles bars.

Uterine cancer, breast cancer, alcoholism and severe anxiety neuroses are some of the many symptoms of artificial female polygamy forced upon them by a society which allows easy divorce and encourages males to dominate and betray their female partners.

It is obvious that on the other side of those secrets of women which when known by men may drive them crazy are the secrets of men which, if women really knew them, would equally tend to drive them crazy or make them painfully suspicious, paranoid, sarcastic and endlessly cynical, the very things that would drive anyone to drink.

It is not that a male alchemist voluntarizes the Moving Centrum exactly, he transfers the active sexual part of himself from the Motor and Instinctive Centrums to the Emotional Centrum, within which he is already automatically voluntary, which is to say he then becomes objectively romantic.

Similarly, a female alchemist transfers her sexual love from the Emotional Centrum to the Moving Centrum in which she is voluntary.

This is a very important point. The alchemist does not try to become voluntary in automatic centrums, but learns to operate from a centrum which is already voluntary.

Patience is necessary for this to occur; even after a sufficient amount of time has passed and we feel we have waited long enough, we must learn to continue to wait. We cannot learn patience until we have gone ***beyond endurance***.

One secret of work is that nothing in the Work is fair, but work on the basis of justice. Justice is mathematical; fairness is emotional and sometimes merely an intellectual concept without basis, without foundation in reality.

CHAPTER 31
RITUAL

Ritual is a form of encoded ***initiatism***, the original foundation for encoded messages transmitted through writings, music, dramatic dance, art and other means of communication which endures throughout history. Religious and philosophical transmissions are often destroyed through "ethnic cleansing" and other animalistic actions of human beings in much the same way that all other animals destroy anyone outside their immediate circle.

Real initiation can only descend and ascend from generation to generation—father to son, mother to daughter.

The most profound law of alchemy is "As Below, So Above."

If we were to rise to a higher cosmos and a bottle on a table were present at the time, we could only rise to a higher cosmos in which the bottle and table still existed, but in their archetypal forms. The more clutter, the more we limit the gradation of cosmic concentration to which we can rise, both innerly and outerly.

Another way of saying this is that the more exact the model, the more like the thing itself, the more presence of vibration, and thus the more likely we will reach the higher level of existence in which the archetype also exists and from which our lower scale bottle and table have their arising.

An exact duplicate in very profound detail of a locomotive in small scale, if sufficiently exact in detail, somehow feels more genuine, more ***authentic***; even if only by suggestion; we feel more strongly the vibration of a train when it is correctly represented by the model.

To initiated man, a woman ***is*** the Work. A priestess initiates a man into herself, and yet a man may not enter the temple of Isis, Delphi, Astarte, Laksmi, Shebina, Sophia—very high priestesses equal to Nasrudin in Sufi tradition. A man is not allowed into the Sanctum Regnum.

A woman cannot initiate a man, and yet in the fourth chamber he cannot be refused initiation. A male may not enter the temple where the Ark is kept—the ***Sanctum Sanctorum***, the high esoteric sanctuary.

Above the door of the inner temple is written, "No man may enter here." In ancient days, only women were allowed to enter the Sacred Inner Temple, the Sanctum Sanctorum, yet someone had to go in to clean up, provide the movement of the space, activate the chamber; and certain men, notably Pharaohs and other priests were initiated as women.

We can only become alchemists if we understand that the first step of alchemy is to annihilate in oneself any personal obsessions, passions and romantic notions of ourselves, and only then falling madly in love, but not with a person.

How is this ***agape***, this objective love, possible? And yet, that is the secret not only of the alchemist but also the secret of the healer. To completely—not just partly—annihilate every shred of animal passion and romantic fantasy, and then to fall madly in love.

This is the real basis of all religions, and we can learn this from the Lord's Basic Instruction to humanity:

"Love the Lord thy God."

God tells us what exactly our job is, if we wish to take it. We will know how to find it once we find the Will in ourselves to carry out this task.

CHAPTER 32
THE FIRST ADAM

The first Adam, male and female, completely united into a permanent Self forms a "Gradation of Reason" in complete union, nonseparate, fully flowing in a complete blended alchemical mixture, which is to say, a singular molecular ambient-temperature plasma compound.

The second Adam and Eve...we are not too concerned with them. Their task is to "Go forth and multiply" and this is so automatic, like eating, sleeping and breathing, that it is not hard to accomplish.

The task of the alchemist, on the other hand, is to regain the Garden of Eden, and to recombine the First Adam, the unified self which is neither male nor female.

From the male viewpoint, the recreation of the first Adam is first a problem of penetration and second a problem of alchemy. He must solve the problem of the labyrinth and he must overcome the myth of the minotaur, this symbol of animal passion and romance, the mythological self.

The ordinary centrums are mythological centrums. There are two kinds of ordinary man—mythological and pathological. The Sex Centrum should be the source of all energy, an inexhaustible source of all force—a demand pump. What creates demand?

Necessity.

From the female viewpoint, the first problem is to encourage penetration into the very center of her being which, contrary to male beliefs, is not the vaginal cavity, but the inner spiritual realm within which she lives and breathes, the place of her inner dance—and allowing the alchemical process which means she must be able to overcome her tendency to become an automatic nesting householder and child-bearer.

The way in which a woman could understand how this could be possible is to understand her feelings in her relationship with her children—where she can equally love more than one individual and equally care, equally have in mind, equally go through ups and downs, which is similar to a man who relates to more than one woman.

What makes her able to do this with her children? She gave birth to them—related by more than friendship—by blood. So if not one, then not the other. "If a woman had five children," one said, "it would not be fair to have four others besides me." It would make no sense; that child would get less attention. A single child gets less affection than each one from a group of children. This relates to another fact that if you need something done, go to a shop where someone who is busy will get it done faster than if you go to a shop where everyone is unoccupied and sedentary.

In ancient verse it has been said, "the fires of love are fanned by the fires of love."

How can the First Adam be re-united? The first Adamic Body is, in fact, the "second wind" of the Sex Centrum—ordinary sex is merely powered by the instinct of "survival of the species."

Ordinary sex begins with the automatic process of allowing the abdominal and genital parts to gyrate a bump and grind.

The "second wind" of this automatic instinctive survival force comes from the higher Sex Centrum, powered by a higher will than one's own.

This higher will is the equivalent of dynamo, a generator, an inexhaustible supply of force of energy. In comparison to that, the ordinary centrums are batteries or "wet cells" which can only hold a certain amount of charge, of electrical potential, then they merely discharge and eventually die once they can no longer be recharged by sleep.

In fact, human beings' ordinary consciousness is a kind of sleep which recharges their batteries because they constantly dissipate them, discharging them through various kinds of petty and wasteful activities.

We do not know how to penetrate, and yet even armed with the art of penetration, a male cannot enter the Inner Sanctuary—he must become as a priestess, realize his female nature.

An alchemist who is able to appear in the fourth chamber cannot be refused initiation into the process of personal annihilation.

What initiates a priestess? When she allows herself to be pushed over the brink between life and death—but without passion or romance—to the point of annihilation.

Have you ever come to the point when you genuinely felt that if you continued in a sexual spiral that there would be an extremely good chance that you would die, or have a heart attack, or a stroke? I mean without an orgasm.

Only the dead can be annihilated. We cannot voluntarily allow personal annihilation if there is a shred of personal desire or the urge for ego-survival remaining in us.

The other side of annihilation is the "second wind" of the higher sexual union, which is the First Adamic Body, the Healer Absolute, the Nazorean.

On the "other side" of personal annihilation is also the subjective experience of the Mystical Body of Christ—Advent, Crucifixion and Ascension all at once—three forms of the same experience, experienced as a unified whole, a gestalt "Ding an sich," thing in itself.

Ecstasy is romantic—the impersonal romantic form of the Mystical Body of Christ, the First Adamic Body in the Garden of Eden.

The Holy Ghost is to the mystical body of Christ what attention is to mentation, and what attention is to consciousness, and what consciousness is to presence.

The Holy Ghost moves through the Mystical Body of Christ while the Mystical Body of Christ vibrates, but is static, expanding and contracting equally, both at the same time.

A priestess who has been penetrated fully into her Sanctum Regnum, in which the Supreme Solar Ceremony has been performed, is like a light bulb which has been switched on.

From then on she is permanently part of the Work. However, for many years she can only be working ***for*** the Work, not ***in*** the Work. She assumes her place in the Great Work only when she takes final vows, and accepts the veil of Unification, or Marriage in the Body of Christ, the Holy Grail of Self-Sacrifice, dissolution in the First Adamic Body, the Philosopher's Stone, which itself is the transforming apparatus, not a solid rock, but actually the Power of Transmutation.

Her only hope to be in the Work is to help to form the First Adamic Body and thus become a laboratory for solar alchemy.

Now we must consider solar and lunar entities, processing nectar into honey, processing honey into royal jelly and the distribution and use of royal jelly.

Competitors who cannot beat each other should be partners. The best partner is someone who is equal to our own adeptship, our mastery, a fair match, a worthy adversary.

Each degree of Initiation is yet another level of fusion into the First Adamic Body, or the Body of Krishna/Radha if you prefer, which is accomplished by a series of manipulations physically, emotionally, intellectually, through a variety of mass and energy changes, eruptions of inner energies equivalent to bolts of lightning, dissolution of personal illusions, active nonexistence, ferocious taming of the self, the sly, cunning self which always and in everything seeks to dominate and rule one's inner and outer life.

At various points the alchemist must pass through certain portals which no one may pass.

In ancient times a woman would not be allowed to reach maturity without knowing every subtle sexual and social secret, being taught her mother's and grandmother's secrets.

In modern contemporary language Eve was a clone. Second Adam plus Eve equals First Adam. There is a secret about Adam which was never spoken, yet every woman instinctively knows what it is, and men do not—man must learn annihilation before he begins any real initiation. Annihilation is the first step of initiation. A prerequisite is to be dead to ego, which is almost impossible for a male human being, to die before he dies.

CHAPTER 33
PERSONAL DESIRES

NOT ALL of the answers you discover on your path to mastery will be immediately coherent, and some questions will never be fully answered.

Much of your effort will be devoted to the gathering of basic data, getting a feel or taste for the subject.

We must penetrate the subject in all directions more or less at once. The beginning conditions of the school are being set up—the conditions under which we are forced to die before we die, to give up our personal egoistic willfulness and self-gratifications.

If we do not die to our personal desires we will suffer greatly on the path to mastery.

Either we go through the barriers or we seek temporary rest and relaxation, but going through it again is always worse. Annihilation is not certain.

In order to maintain the "Capstone" mantra continuously, "I wish this to be used for the benefit of all beings everywhere," it is necessary to split the attention during ejaculation.

The "succubus" carries the substance from female to male, the "incubus" carries the substance from male to female.

Female substances are gathered for higher magic—evolutionary processes, coating of higher bodies and the re-unification of the First Adamic Body.

Longevity in the ordinary sense would be an aim of lower magic, although it is sometimes an involuntary byproduct of higher invocation and alchemical work.

Sexual alchemy is not necessary for everyone; not everyone is suited to it. For longevity, it is necessary, but if you cannot tolerate life for its own sake you may as well live out your ordinary destiny, and be done with it.

Some candidates for initiation are suitable for this type of work and some are not. It takes a tremendous amount of discipline and self-denial. One may work for many years only to return to ordinary life, to the ordinary organic desires, and all the previous efforts are wasted.

For work with Alchemical Sex, we must have control over our sexual appetite. Indiscriminate relationships will seriously contaminate our alchemical laboratory, and the effect could last for years.

A single momentary contact with someone outside our alchemical laboratory could ruin our alchemical work permanently, and we could never again work with higher alchemical substances.

Some people have uncontrollable appetites which are cyclic—during dormant periods they may appear to be indifferent to sex, but at other times they are uncontrollably self-indulgent.

Many people think of sex in terms of need.

Some are just conditioned to be indulgent, but others can never discontinue their sexual and emotional self-pampering.

It is easier to make a billion dollars than to make a change in Being. A billion dollars can be made in an ordinary way, but a change in Being requires something extraordinary, something far beyond the ability of the ordinary human being's animalistic urges.

CHAPTER 34
ALTERATION OF THE MACHINE

If you are in a position to work you will be called, but not always and forever, just for one job at a time, like piecework.

Each day you have your name on a blackboard and then if you are needed, you are called.

But you may sit waiting for quite a while, because you have certain specialties and your specialties are not needed at the moment, or the jobs are already filled by others. You may be called for one minute, one hour, one year, or for the rest of your life.

The needs of the Work determine whether or not you may be useful at the moment, based on time, place and people.

The majority of our personal work toward initiation and mastery depends largely upon chemical and electrical reflexes of the human biological machine and its corresponding higher centrums and bodies, if any.

Therefore, we ought to be quite willing to produce the proper sequential episodes in the machine to in turn produce the necessary electro-chemical processes in the machine.

What produces electro-chemical processes in the body is largely our higher emotions.

Ordinary emotions merely reverberate in the machine; real higher emotions do not have organic reverberations, but produce real shocks of higher octaves which can produce real alchemical results within the human biological machine and higher centrums.

Because negative emotions reverberate automatically in the machine, they may be useful; whereas real emotions even though we wish to have them may not be automatically useful to us for our personal alchemical work, but can be made to be useful with the application of special attention and higher energies stemming from invocations and evocational processes.

Thoughts also produce organic reverberations and sensations, but are not as chemically stimulating.

Negative manifestations produce certain electro-chemical reactions in the machine—a machine upon which we cannot act directly.

We cannot take the machine apart, change the chemical valves which function as if they were a device that opens and closes, however and whenever we wish to open and close them, as if we were controlling the flue in a fireplace or the burner on a stovetop.

The controlling factor is largely emotional—a sweeping passion of negative emotion such as anger, righteous indignation, helplessness, hopelessness, despair, organic pleasure, or even ordinary "happiness," a form of self-satisfaction.

Happiness is uniquely subjective because no two people feel the same when they say they are happy. It can be more accurately described in contemporary human life as the absence of pain and a sufficiency of whatever it is that people think they want.

Some people hope to tie all their troubles into a gigantic "Gordian

Knot," to do one single certain thing and thus never needing to do it again.

People are in general hoping to find some sort of cosmic vacuum cleaner which produces the void when it is switched on.

With this special imaginary vacuum cleaner, one need only vacuum once, after which one need never vacuum again because once done, it is done forever. This does not occur with housework, or with anything else in life, so why should we expect it to happen in higher planes of existence?

Fear is a sensation and "wanting to understand it all before we begin" is the foundation of despair. It is possible to evoke fear states characterized by a definite smell of adrenalin and this adrenalized state happens also to produce an electrical odor similar to ozone around the human biological machine's outer wrapping, commonly called "the skin."

It also produces a metallic taste in the mouth and a crisp burning sensation in the nostrils, like being in a swamp.

Transformation sets the stage for evolution. A technical definition for transformation is that it is an alteration of the machine to accommodate evolution. The machine ordinarily will not accommodate evolution.

The key does not fit the lock. The machine must be altered in a certain way electrically and chemically. Therefore, if we are going to work in the Work the machine must be altered in order to produce the lightning rod.

Transformation does not occur in a single flash of permanent enlightenment, but rather it occurs over a long period of time and not always linearly.

Along the way one can have setbacks and failures just as in any long-term project.

The machine is being prepared both voluntarily and intentionally. This long-term preparation of the human biological machine and its associated higher centrums will of course cause a certain amount of subjective personal suffering in the ordinary sense, because we are altering the machine in a radical way and we are inside the machine at the time, like being inside a washing machine or a dryer.

There are a handful of methods for the alteration of the machine, and two of these we will examine. Of the handful of transforming factors, one of which is electrical and the other is chemical, both are provoked by negative emotion.

Negative emotion actually causes sensations in the machine and even in the higher centrums if we permit ourselves to identify with the machine and its states.

However, we must understand what is meant by the word "negative" in the term "negative emotion."

If you wish to alter the machine you must be willing to do what is necessary.

Suppose we wish to change a Volkswagen to a Rolls Royce. This would require massive changes to the engine, the transmission, the suspension and of course extensive frame and body work—by the time we finished, we might as well have bought a Rolls Royce to begin with because we will have to change everything, but as we are, we cannot do so, and must change one or two things at a time, which means that at certain times during this process the machine will not function quite correctly or pleasingly.

Changing the luxury ocean liner "Queen Mary" to a common freighter would be an equally enormous alteration and would result in some discomforts along the way.

In the same way, alterations necessary for the higher functioning of the human biological machine and its associated higher centrums and higher bodies to allow us to take our place in this work are also extensive and can be quite painful at times.

Some of these electro-chemical changes may cause illness, upset, unhappiness, confusion and despair—at those times, these changes may not seem so good.

But just as we do not worry about the significance of these factors which cause us remorse, we need not place significance on those factors related to the electro-chemical alterations of the machine, except insofar as they cause us actual harm, and if we work well, we will not experience actual damage to ourselves or to the machine, just discomfort, which can be tolerated and which is not dangerous.

In order to use remorse for our work we are not concerned with the significance of our remorse—we simply use the sensation of remorse to give power to our will to work.

Tuning into these sensations of remorse and using them to power our work-will requires serious and objective self-study of ourselves as beings and of the workings of our biological machines.

We must learn to correctly and impartially study the machine to discover the sensation of "remorse" in its many disguises. Remorse is the most useful tool as both a reminding factor and to produce the strength of emotion necessary to give extra force to our work-will.

The invocation of presence is called ***remembering***, because we use this force to help us remember that we are a presence, but that our presence, in order to be present, must be intentionally and consciously invoked.

Often we hear the term "self-remembering," which specifically means to remember to invoke presence.

Self-consciousness means that we invoke our own presence; whereas objective consciousness refers to that state or essence-condition in which it is no longer necessary to invoke our own presence because it has by then become a stabilized invoked presence of a Unified Self which does not retreat from the present at any time for any reason.

In fact, this self-invocation is the primary reason for our first efforts at self-observation. We must study the workings of the machine and its primary momentary alterations of state and activity until the invocation of presence and unification of self is fully stabilized.

We can learn to study the human biological machine for its various manifestations and disguises of the sensation of remorse.

Let us say we wish the chemical reactions: "A," then "B," then "C." It may require several months to produce chemical reaction "A" during which a certain process occurs. Then suddenly reverberations wash through the body and the chemical change occurs, and we may learn from this how to produce the changes "B" and "C" as aftershocks of "A."

There are many different kinds of alterations necessary for the machine. There are chemical changes, electrical changes, magnetic changes, mechanical/organic changes, behavioral changes, functional changes, such as mental functional changes, three-brained functional changes, and so forth. The Popcorn Exercise* provokes a functional change. The functions of the headbrain and the tailbrain switch accordingly proper to that of three-brained beings.

The decrease of vascular back pressure and the increase of vascular capacity such as that which can be produced by the use of deep reflex massage by which the vascular system is encouraged to eliminate toxins, is an example of mechanical change.

In this work sometimes there is the production of toxins in various parts of the body which is necessary for the purpose of shocking into reflex certain chemical reactions. These toxins may be organically deadly but chemically necessary for the alchemical process.

This is a big risk, true, but without this risk you will die like a dog, and even if you never seize the opportunity and take the chance of developing yourself in a harmonious way as a unified being, you will die sooner or later anyway.

Toxemia in this work is a definite risk as well as is cell disruption. Everyone in a school, because they work on themselves, is susceptible to tuberculosis, asthma, cancer, heart disease, toxemia, emphysema and pneumonia, all of which are by-products of work-on-self and result from the unusual stress placed on the machine.

But at birth stress is thought to have the opposite effect in such a way that it acts to strengthen the newborn.

On the other hand toxemia and hypothermia produce anxiety and paranoia. And anxiety and paranoia are both symptoms which can be produced from the taking of certain medications. It is common medical knowledge that medications produce chemical changes and physiological changes in the organic body which often result in particular behavioral changes.

For example, Parkinson's disease which results from a certain toxic condition is often treated by a medication called Ldopa, yet the side effects commonly associated with Ldopa are anxiety, paranoia and suspicious behavior similar to what we might see in a patient suffering from that nervous system disease.

Toxic shock is actually a danger of this work. Tuberculosis is a form of toxic shock. And toxemia is actually the underlying cause of many diseases. When toxins in the form of uric acid crystallize in the joints this results in gout. Eventually the organs of elimination become so

---

* See I.D.H.H.B., Inc. Video #076, and Talk of the Month #27 (reprint available)

unaccustomed to not functioning that the toxins which are usually carried out of the body by the uric acid are released into the bloodstream; whereas toxins in the bloodstream are the cause of many diseases. From the blood, toxins can deposit themselves in bone marrow, the skin, the sweat glands, the joints, causing a variety of disorders.

Toxins that are produced as a result of this work are stored in the body, and then they are released. These toxins are deadly. It can kill us first if we do not beat it. But eventually we die one way or another. Evolution is a race, a deadly race against the clock. Once we begin we better hurry—this is why once we begin voluntary evolution it is too dangerous to stop.

In working on ourself and placing ourself under school conditions we have altered the machine thus producing toxins, and then the machine releases those toxins. As invocant of this school, I am producing certain conditions or certain school conditions are being created which produce a certain series of shocks that are intended for our work. But there are setbacks in this process of transformation. Even the weather can affect the process.

Just as in the darkroom, the weather can produce a series of reactions. For example, change of temperature in the darkroom affects the developing solutions in a way that adjustments must be made to account for it. And in the printing of photographs if there is too much ozone in the air the print will not take. Or in the printing process if there is too much humidity in the air the blanket will not pick up the print properly. Furthermore, when painting in oils if there is too much humidity in the air for a period of three days the oils are ruined.

Everything that happens to the body chemically or alchemically ...does this create conditions to invoke an entity or instead does the invoking of an entity create the resulting changes in the chemical or alchemical conditions? Does the invocation of entities cause the chemical alteration or do the chemical alterations cause the invoking of entities?

Invocation itself is the cause of chemical alterations. And electrochemical changes are in preparation for evolutionary transformation—transformation that can accept evolution.

As the Sun of Mercy to Me, charcoal, Sennelier, © 1992 HEI

CHAPTER 35
ELECTRICAL AND CHEMICAL CHANGES

THE MACHINE as it is under the conditions of ordinary life cannot accommodate presence. For example, it is necessary to change the function of the brain by making the headbrain the Moving Centrum thus allowing the tailbrain to be free to become the real Thinking Centrum before one can invoke presence. The invocation of an entity produces radiations that pass through the body affecting change—the radiation, the heat both change the body electrically and chemically.

Suppose I wish to accomplish something with six different people. I will stage a scene, and even if only four people of six are involved, this is sufficient. However, all six people involved will be affected by the event, but the alteration chemically and electrically that I wish to produce will be accomplished.

If we wish to work and if we wish to alter the machine to accommodate evolution, we must be willing to do anything necessary, but the application of common sense is a definite requirement. The disruption with the machine is merely a by-product of the chemical, electrical and functional changes necessary for the alteration of the machine, not a desired effect nor a means of producing those changes.

We are in a life-or-death race, a real struggle to accomplish our work before the death of the organic machine, which is far closer than any human being ever wishes to realize.

The faster and more completely we work, the better—this method is the "fast path" which may from time to time require drastic measures, but not at the risk of safety and good sense.

People in work communities will sometimes use as an excuse for their apparent negative manifestations toward one another that they were treating someone in this way "for their work."

It does not matter whether someone endures the negative manifestations of others as opposed to whether someone points out their observations about another's manifestations, voluntarily or involuntarily because the person's attitude about their inappropriate behavior and the resulting sequence of events and about what they actually did sets the scene for them to feel remorse.

In the course of events and further reverberations, there might be some who experience great internal subjective reactions and others who open their "subjective cinema" by way of exploding negative manifestations toward individuals and the group as a whole, but these are merely reactions of the machine and although they provide fodder for work, are not generally good for anyone and should not really be encouraged.

If we are in a school all our activities and personal suffering can be used for our work, but we should not deliberately make or encourage negativity just to give us something more to work with.

In a school we make corresponding for work. In other words, As Below So Above. We wish to change the machine to accommodate evolution. What difference does it make to just work for machine evolution? Machine evolution just for the sake of machine evolution is absurd and unnecessarily painful for everyone.

In the same way it is ridiculous to identify with the nature of events that happen to us by calling them unbearable, insane, ridiculous, disappointing, absurd, painful, petty, joyous, exalted, and so on. We can put labels on everything that we have done, if we wish; nevertheless, no matter how we categorize our experiences they still produce chemical change in the machine.

Even if we know what is coming the chemical change still occurs because the automatic nervous system will respond when given forewarning of upcoming events. We can even know what is coming and react to it. This relentless assault of events which evoke almost unbearable personal suffering may seem unfair, but if we are working toward alchemical mastery and higher initiation into higher spheres of existence, we are working against time—the organic machine is a time-bomb that will soon go off—and we must meet and endure all those unpleasant conditions which come with the territory.

At a certain point, after the crucible starts getting hot, we cannot break apart. That is the danger; it might burn us out organically before it burns out. Usually when it locks down we have several hours before we can get out of it. If we have not locked down to this degree, then we have not got it. It is not a huff and puff effort but very galvanic.

Galvanic means in the body but not spasmodic.

To demonstrate this to ourself, spread the fingers apart on one hand and feel the tension from the stretch. Continue feeling the mounting tension and try to slowly curl your fingers down to close the hand. Now continue to spread the fingers and try to uncurl them to open the hand.

Using isometric force, imagine arm-wrestling with an imaginary opponent. Feel the struggle which ensues and let the opponent win a little at a time. Now imagine fighting back; feel the force of pushing your arm up.

This is exactly what we want to do with Alchemical Sex. If we are not putting powerful isometric effort into it, we are not doing enough—it could be said that our heart is not in it.

At the same time, all this must be effortless.

The secret to passion with adoration is the secret of endless effortless isometric power.

There is a point at which the body starts to heat up, a point when we wonder why we ever got into it, and yet we must go all the way through—the process itself is inexorable, although there are points of exhaustion, despair, discomfort and there is always the temptation to take the orgasm and run.

Noninitiates are unable to understand alchemy.

We start with the metal called "lead," but it is not ordinary lead. Every metal and salt in alchemy has a different meaning other than the obvious.

In Alchemical Sex we start with gold and end up with alchemical gold by passing ordinary gold through all the various alchemical processes. One of the processes is invoking the presence of love in order to harness but not become identified with the "heat" of passion and to use this "heat" to fire up the alchemical furnace and to produce the ***plasma effect***.

It is utterly impossible to harness ordinary organic sexual energy. The presence of objective love can harness the higher sexual energy and turn it into an invocational alchemical process.

The natural organic tendency is to allow ourselves to slip into passion and orgasmic withdrawal, but what we really want to do is harness the heat of passion.

The activity reaches a certain intensity, a magnetic intensity, as would a magnetic bottle full of plasma in a cyclotron or linear accelerator, then we focus the resulting collected force and harness it to a specific application, such as coating higher bodies, invocation or the building of the First Adamic Body.

We use the force of will, and are not identified with the organic state and have no interest in orgasm; and therefore we could also stop the force of passion if we chose to.

Substances help us to invoke; but only with natural magnetism evoked from higher substances can we make angelic clusters and work within them.

While the man can be said to be the weaver, the woman forms the loom, and in the final stage of the process of invocation, the male partner in Alchemical Sex will tend to vanish into what we call the Angelic Body, which is to say the loomed fabric.

The male participant is the catalyst and as he is personally annihilated in the alchemical process he indwells within all those essential selves who when taken as a single entity, compose the Angelic Body which is that exact entity being invoked.

We are in many hidden ways permanently knitted together and fellow invocants even more so.

Only with natural magnetism can we knit into an Angelic Body, although from other forces we can obtain substances for this process.

We begin with ordinary gold, or the passion of sexual contact. Then by tempering, quenching and rebuilding with the alchemical processes we finally tame the ordinary gold, the ordinary passionate sex of the machine, to become an invocational form of alchemical gold. Along the way we feed the alchemical fire of the alchemical furnace with both male and female semen.

Love harnesses passion, so the higher the level we allow the passion to achieve, only harnessing it at the last moment, the greater the invocation will tend to be, provided we do not give ourselves to organic passion and the violent spasm of orgasm.

If we have no Will, we are not able to harness passion at its highest point. We must have Will in order to invoke the presence of love. Love is the harness of passion.

We must have a natural magnetism between us in order for there to be sufficient quantity of force to harness. It is not rare to have some degree of magnetism with a woman with whom you have sexual contact, but that magnetism is usually chemical. This must be electrical—not chemical, but electrical fusion.

Another big difference between sex and invocation—in sex we hate our dependency on one another, just as we hate anything we are forced to do. With sex, we must have sex—we are driven to have sex with our own species and we hate what we must do.

Therefore, in sex is invoked the presence of hatred, if not of each other. In invocation is invoked the presence of love because in invocation we choose to invoke and so need not hate each other for our dependency on one another.

For an Angelic Body we need earth, air, fire and water. This has nothing to do with astrological signs. This is a requirement for alchemy.

Alchemy is a recipe for assembling a unit for the invocation of higher entities, coating higher bodies and reforming the First Adamic Body, and the recipe works exactly as would a recipe for baking a cake or making a gourmet meal.

Think of fusion on a molecular level. When the first Adamic Body goes to the second Adamic Body we have mitosis or fission—the body is split into two. In doing so, on a molecular level, the molecules are actually split apart. If we reverse this process we get fusion, the molecules recombine on a molecular level.

Now extend that concept through the whole body, a ***Klein Bottle*** with only one surface, no inside and no outside and when you make the two one, you get two or more masses occupying a single space in complete fusion in which all bodies occupy the same space at the same time, a feat impossible in any ordinary universal sense.

The mechanicality of organic life is so profound and its effect is so powerful that we must be absolutely certain there is nothing lacking in our earth education and no sense of having "given up" something important for this work, no sense of personal sacrifice or loss.

In short, we must be absolutely certain there is nothing here for us, nothing remaining to be acquired, accomplished or experienced, no sense that we have left something out of our Earthian voyage.

Absurdity, greed for metallic gold and general disbelief and sarcasm are various safety factors for all serious alchemical and invocational data.

Now you have enough data to recognize more safety factors, for example, silliness, ridiculousness, outrageousness, wackiness, peculiarness, paradox, comic exaggeration and conscious foolishness.

CHAPTER 36
THE SECRETS OF THE ALCHEMIST

ANYONE SERIOUSLY studying these subjects would learn in the very first laboratory experiment that contamination changes the result. Even an amateur photographer knows better than to dip the emulsion into the developer or pour the compound into the developer or to expose undeveloped film to bright light.

If we are beginning to learn ordinary chemistry in which the chemical experiments occurred outside our bodies we could easily understand the need for Hermetism, the isolation of mutually contaminating chemicals from one another.

But should the contamination occur within our own machines and the prevention of contamination interferes even slightly with the pleasure-seeking activities of the machine, somehow the idea of chemical contamination in relation to work on self seems just too absurd. And we quickly find psychological arguments to deny what we are able to accept medically, biologically and chemically in the abstract.

It simply becomes necessary to understand that what is true in the ordinary chemical sense must be true in esoteric chemistry. Esoteric chemistry obeys the same laws as ordinary chemistry. Cosmic laws do not change just because of activity. We still must use the same cosmic laws even if we do not like them.

One of the great advances in chemistry was discovery of contamination and the means to at least partially prevent contamination. The results of contamination are not necessarily always bad. Contamination simply prevents an experiment from being duplicated exactly.

The idea of contamination is not limited strictly to chemistry, biology, physics, mathematics and other sciences; all obey the same laws. The argument is generally given that esoteric chemistry obeys very different laws and that the general chemical, biological, physical, mathematical laws can be ignored.

One example clearly demonstrates the ignorance and stupidity of this idea. The same idiots who think chemistry has no place in work on self and the Work in general, will also have no idea that cooking of ordinary foods is entirely a matter of chemistry—both inorganic and organic—taking into account mixtures of salts, metals, hydrogens, carbons, amino acids and so forth, and that each meal in combination and in relation to the fluids of organs, blood and cells produces serious alterations in the balance between acid and alkaline which in turn alters the chemical functioning of the body and its several brains.

We have already seen even if we did not yet know exactly how the period of breath can alter mood and the functioning of centrums. We also know from personal experience that changes of diet, even simple changes of water from different geographical localities can radically alter our chemical and psychological functions.

Our work does not proceed independently of these functions so it can be easily seen that chemistry plays a large part in our work.

If we also understand the importance of data cell colonies in the Work and the effects upon them of even the smallest chemical changes then we can see that chemistry really is the foundation of our work, not just some philosophical idea.

A chemist who refuses to recognize the laws of chemistry is destined sooner or later to endure life as a clerk in a dry-goods store.

One well-kept alchemical secret is that the skin is an organ of perception and can be used as such. In most individuals it has descended into the realm of involuntary unconscious. Men tend to keep their arms, forearms and back alive, whereas women tend to keep their chest, buttocks and hands alive.

Sensation on the skin may be converted to sexual sensation. The second secret is the conversion of all skin sensation to sexual sensation.

The third secret used by an alchemist is the adoration of the Magi. The mask is always before us. Actively and professionally the alchemist works to adore the mask, that patchwork quilt which is the Face of God.

A woman naturally knows how to milk a man. Men do not know how to milk a woman. Organic man has no idea how to milk a woman of her substances, nor does he care about such things. In ordinary sex he has his way, and takes the easiest course.

One great secret in knowing how to cure any addiction is knowing that withdrawal is painful.

Although at first an addiction might be pleasant, eventually the pleasant effects wear off and continuation in the addiction is merely to avoid the unpleasant effects of withdrawal.

Animal sex is sex for procreation; it is the lowest form of sex—biological sex. Sporting sex is for those to whom biological sex, romantic sex or commercial sex is not enough. All these forms of sex are at the same level with the same obsessive-compulsive spasmodic orgasmic result.

A person may first pass through taboos, then sex for miracles, searching for a slightly more exalted form of sex, but it is all out of boredom because when you get right down to it, sex is as boring as any other activity.

Those who attain sexual skills beyond organic sex find that it requires a certain impersonal freedom from all conventional sexual categories, activities and results.

People tend to remain socially and sexually categorical because they are told to and are afraid to break those barriers. Those who do not obey the categorical imperatives tend to be vilified by the establishment, whatever that may be at the time, and it varies rather widely what is permitted and what is punished. Continued Alchemical Sex can cause detoxification from personal addictions, and therefore some personal and egoistic pain.

A man can use female manifestations to pull her toward him. He mimes a woman's manifestations in order to accommodate to her style and then recreates her drama—and then, in her own inimitable way, the woman activates her drama.

Just because it is voluntary does not mean it is phony. Because it is voluntary we are not identified.

If we wait for the body to do something authentic, it will never succeed. All of this must be learned. Do not expect to know or understand this concept immediately and without personal data personally experienced.

In feelings of cooperation one automatically arouses those substances exactly necessary for alchemical processing, but we must put our own personal work aside for the duration of our participation in this Great Work.

We can compare the human biological machine to a large and complex commercial chemical factory with its huge cylindrical storage tanks, many buildings, walkways, girders, pipes of different sizes connecting complicated machinery and general air of activity and production.

We can use the minimum efforts and energies necessary to make an alchemical laboratory by merely clearing a smaller area in the larger general chemical factory and set up our laboratory on a small scale.

Our little alchemical laboratory is just big enough for our alchemical needs, not enough to cause upset or damage to the factory as a whole.

The much smaller alchemical laboratory produces less quantity, but sufficient quality of substances to serve the operation and to produce the results we wish to achieve.

There is no one voyage or lifetime that is alchemically speaking "better" than any other. Use your personal voyage through organic life as just a beginning part of life, encompassing many existences in many forms, some of which are organic and some not.

If we do not see ourselves involved in an endless life, then we are only involved with one small part of our whole possible struggle to evolve into a higher consciousness.

Constantly we ask ourselves: "How am I doing? How do I feel?" When we hear ourselves talking like this we are caught up in our personal life and cannot extract from it what we need for work.

Ordinary human beings are doomed anyway, since eventually we will die. We seem to be satisfied because we do not know how to obtain something more and are not aware of the possibility; our dreams and imaginary attainments keep us asleep to real possibilities.

CHAPTER 37
THE BODHI TREE

TO TRULY GAIN entrance into the world of initiatism we must commit a form of esoteric suicide—a nonphenomenal form of ***hara-kiri***—we must develop the courage to take a vow to never again succumb to the pleasures, pains, automatic sufferings and desires of ordinary organic life, no matter what—even if starving.

We must teach ourselves to sit patiently without expectation under the Bodhi tree and to remain there, ignoring all offers of personal powers, enlightenment and other transitory rewards and at the same time, we must learn to not respond with twitching and swatting to all the little unpleasant buzzing and biting insects of life's continual annoyances, impulses and distractions.

Even if things go very wrong, we cannot go back on our vow to never again live an ordinary life. We obtain what we need only when we work for the Work, not for ourselves.

Buddha made a mistake by accepting Buddhahood. He was offered power; he refused. Devils, demons and gods tried to entice him away from the Bodhi tree. He refused power over time, power over space, offers of food, drink, companionship. Each time he refused the simpler more immediate remedy. Only when he became Buddha was he willing to walk away from the Bodhi tree. If he had only waited.

He thought that it would be sufficient to take the offer of nothingness, but even the mistake of accepting Buddhahood can be used for work, as illustrated by the following story:

Two Zen monks visited a geisha house. They both returned after several hours and the Roshi asked, "What happened?"

The first monk said, "I went, I made love, and I came back."

"Well," asked the master, "What was the result?"

"The thing was in the moment and it no longer is," the monk replied.

"Very good," and turning to the second monk he asked him what had happened.

"Master, I was able to maintain my Zen every moment; not once did I give in to joy or ecstasy."

"You rotten son-of-a-bitch!" the master roared, "What of the poor girl's feelings? She is not a Zen monk, you know!"

To jump off the cliff of personal expectation and personal desire is to commit esoteric suicide. We have to have real knowledge to commit esoteric suicide in such a way that it does not affect anyone else, and also in such a way that we are absolutely sure we will never be forced to break our Big Oath, and that we will hurt no one in ordinary life including ourselves as a result of our self-inflicted Ego Death.

We must have discipline which cannot be learned or acquired. Either we have it or we do not. The discipline required is the discipline to not break a Work vow.

When we commit esoteric suicide, if we ever break that vow, only suicide remains and our life will be miserable from then on. We can make an analogy with a monkey who lives among humans then tries to return to the jungle. The monkey will not be able to function or survive very well when he returns; it would have been better to have stayed with the humans.

Somehow we have to find the discipline in ourselves and then do it. Somewhere along the line we have to call a halt to the personal garbage. If we take the Big Vow we cannot indulge in personal garbage ***ever again***. To do so is like an alcoholic going back to drinking, and only a binge can be the result—there is only one opportunity to "dry out" in the esoteric sense. ***We are not given a second chance if we "fall off the wagon" even once.***

If we can be seduced, then we did not really commit esoteric suicide. Real candidates for the Work have an unshakable aim. If we commit esoteric suicide the work must notice us. When we become a serious candidate our name is entered in the roll books of the Work. From then on it is all a matter of effort and the will to work.

In ordinary life we can have anything of an ordinary nature that we think we want for a price, but in the end it will always be empty.

In the Work we cannot have anything we want, only what we actually need, which usually far exceeds what we want. We will not have what we need for the Work until we give up what we want for the ego. That is why it is called "esoteric suicide."

We literally give up the whole of our future life, quickly, before it is too late. We do not get many opportunities to commit esoteric suicide. But we must never commit esoteric suicide unless we are sure we can remain dead to ordinary desires.

We will get all the help we need on a superficial level, but no help on the "dark night of the soul." For that time of self-examination we are on our own. That is why we work together; mutual support keeps us strong in our Work Will.

Endowed with Glory, charcoal, Sennelier, © 1992 HEI

CHAPTER 38
SACRED SEX

The word ***Shakti*** comes from the root-word ***Shak***, ableness. The complete name translates to force of ableness. Devotees of this force frequently inhabit the crematoria of India and Tibet, performing ritual intercourse, during which they become identified with Shiva and Shakti, the cosmic couple.

For this purpose they employ incantations recited with the aid of a ***mala***, or rosary. Coinciding with this, they assume various postures and cultivate specific erotic passions and adorations, which are then directed first toward the divine couple, and later, when they have achieved the complete restoration and evolution of their Adamic Bodies, they direct from within their newly produced Adamic-Body-chamber, in which they now have immortal life.

The three primary forces issuing from the goddess ***Shakti*** are:

1. Passive, heavy darkness
2. Blazing motion, passion and aggressions
3. Harmony and tranquility

The dark aspect also assumes the aspect of ***Kali***, the destroyer of Time—"I eat myself to maintain myself"—while ***Shiva*** becomes the maintainer—"I keep myself within myself by absorbing myself back into myself."

Both in India and in Tibet slave-girls of God similar to the ***Gopis*** of ***Krishna*** were brought into the temples. These were the temple prostitutes, similar to the Whores of Babylon, dedicated to serve their male partner, but only for the purpose of Sacred Sex.

Their duties were to the temple, to sweep, see to the lighting and placement of new candles, to anoint the shrine, place flowers and to dance and sing for special occasions. The dancing and singing were extremely provocative sexually, and sexual energy was used to provide the force necessary to draw the god down upon them. In Greece and Rome, similar mediumship was employed.

In ancient India and Tibet, the temple girls played an important part in the temple's activities, for they offered a ready counterpart for a male visitor's magical sexual activities without the need for him to acquire concubines which might disturb his household routine, domestic harmony and economic stability.

The ritual in which the girls were adopted into the temples was the same as for Catholic nuns today which was a marriage ceremony to the god, in which she became the wife of the divinity.

Prostitutes at these temples were not there to serve pleasure-oriented men. There were town-prostitutes who were available strictly for pleasure. In the same way, Shaktis and Dakinis in Tibet would offer their services to initiates only.

CHAPTER 39
COMMON FACTORS FOR ALCHEMICAL SEX: POSTURES AND EXERCISES

1. Vajroli Mudra.
2. Yoni Mudra.
3. Viparitakarani.
4. Shakti Kalini Mudra.
Removes fear of death and gives power of the Yoni Mudra.
5. Vayarvi Dhyana Mudra.
Skywalking-destroyer of old age.
6. Guptasana.
7. Virasana.
8. Vajrasana.
9. Varisara.
For use in drawing semen through the bloodstream.

The rhythm for altering deep and shallow strokes should be either in the 3-5-7-9 periodic structure, or in the 1-4-2-8-5-7 structure.

There are about thirty postures for intercourse—only a few of which are suitable for westerners due to restricted pelvic and leg muscle action, unlike that of people used to sitting on hard floors.

Here are the common factors for all Alchemical Sex—

1. A discussion of the cosmic principles involved for visualization.

2. An affirmation between the couple that they both are in agreement regarding the spiritual use of the energies of sex.

3. Preliminary arousal—stroking, kissing and caresses must not be neglected, and should be protracted in the extreme.

4. Actual postures for intercourse, such as Cat and Mouse in One Hole, Bamboos Near the Altar, Reversed Flying Ducks, Wailing Monkey in Embrace with a Tree, etc. Choreographed in sequence for aesthetics—and agreed upon in advance.

5. Movements: deep/shallow, slow/quick, slanting thrust/straight thrust...In all there are nine basic styles of movement and six basic styles of penetration.

Some examples of styles of penetration are:

General breaking through enemy ranks, also called Hunter breaking through forest with a sword or flail, also called Farmer flailing rice stalks.

A sparrow picking grain
A ship in a storm
Prying an oyster open to get the pearl
A pestle grinding in a mortar
A bird trying to escape its cage
A serpent weaving at the entrance to its lair
A cobra striking a mongoose
A pearl dropping through heavy oil

6. Instructions for the man as to how to inhibit his orgasm.

7. Instructions for the man as to how to draw forth from his partner's vagina the Yin fluid.

8. How to combine the Yin fluid with the Yang semen to make converted Yang, or converted semen.

9. Auxiliary practices, such as oral sex and genital, oral drawing of fluids.

10. Oral drawing of fluids from the other two primary points of secretion.

11. Medicines and diet for a couple.

12. Cures for impotence or frigidity.

13. The yogic technique for combining semen and female effluvia and forcing the resulting substances to ascend to the brains of both partners using different techniques for male and female for this operation.

14. The use of partners for gathering of effluvia and semen.

15. The post-sexual visualizations.

16. The enlargement of the forebrain and regeneration of cells.

17. The direction of converted semen into the higher body.

18. The application of converted semen, along with breathing techniques and a special diet to be used during the period of this action, for longevity or immortality of the physical body.

19. Preparation for the entrance of an immortal into the Cave of Ancients, also known as the home of the Arhats or Adepts.

20. The conscious conception of a child.

21. Prenatal care for a child conceived during Alchemical Sex.

22. The postnatal care of a magical child.

Use of tantra for collection of substances, transformation of substances into useful coating substances, precipitation and electrolytic deposits in cells and along muscle system.

Nervous system's use in generating voltages necessary for electrolysis.

Use of erotic manipulation in the nervous system for generation of voltage, amperage and presence of salts in solution.

Ingestion of proper types of salts for use in coating higher bodies with the electrolytic process of tantra.

Psychological preparation for use of tantra for work purposes rather than biological survival of the species.

Catalyst is viro/bacterial—transmission by "alchemical infusion."

Electrical catalyst for precipitation called "Shaktipat" by yogis.

Contamination/chemical balance/pH factors of substances.

Transformation of lower substances into higher.

Acculumation of alchemical gold for higher body coating.

Generation of electrolytic current for coating.

Generation of electrolytic current for transformation of substances.

Oracular contact with higher entities.

Dissolution of ordinary functions of the brains, temporarily exposing essence-perception-and-consciousness.

Experiences in higher seances unlimited by reciprocal feeding and lower emotions.

Dissolution of human limits, belief systems, taboos, behavior patterns, interactions, romantic scenarios.

Discipline over automatic organic reactions of Moving/Instinctive Centrum, reproductive urges, romantic notions of the Moving Centrum, etc.

Cooperative effort of the partner to transcend personal experiences, goals, etc.

Familiarity with higher entities in-the-subjective and in-the-objective.

CHAPTER 40
TANTRA WORKSHOP EXERCISES —ANGELIC CLUSTERS

Balance is an important aspect of life and of Alchemical Sex. We must learn to force the organism to arrange itself in a balanced state, to distribute forces over a number of bases. A base is a single body or body part. It is important to sink into the gravity centrum of a selected body or body part and then to place an equal amount of weight on it.

There must be some airspace between adjacent bases; for example, the buttocks includes a minimum amount of airspace. This exercise is done by one person and then extended to two or more participants to make a cluster, in a workshop setting.

The number of bases may also be varied from 1 to 48 with each different number of bodies. For example, one body on one base, two bodies on six bases, five bodies on seven bases, twelve on four bases, twenty-four on one base, etc.

This cluster formation should be able to be held indefinitely, with no erratic breathing, until the signal is given to move to the next grouping.

Upon the signal to hold the cluster posture, immediately assume and freeze into the posture, holding it until a break is called.

Some clusters may be held longer than others, and in a training situation, clusters may be held for observation by others. Visualize and create classical tableaus, each of which communicates a definite concept to a viewer.

Now without talking, stroll with your partner as if in a garden six thousand years ago. Upon signal, fall without discussion into an erotic posture with your partner.

Do this several times. Everyone parcipitating in a group exercise should stand or sit quietly and, upon signal, assume the suggested erotic postures without verbal interaction between individuals, creating a "temple frieze" effect, that is of carved marble statuary on a temple edifice.

Repeat this again in two lines facing each other, and then, with partners standing side by side in one or another of the lines; when the signal to begin is given, drop into the suggested posture together.

Now repeat the body base exercise with your partner, creating erotic tableaux of one base, two bases, up to ten bases. Now do this exercise in groups of three, then four, then five.

Sitting opposite your partner in a cross-legged position, maintain solid eye-contact for a few minutes. Then move into an intertwined leg posture with your partner, still maintaining eye contact.

Proceed to perform subtle wave-like motions with the whole body. These gently rocking motions or undulations are done in time with a slow deep drum beat.

Then move into the stop-start movement called "staccato." Here you may find a greater sense of detachment and consequently an increasing ability to observe. Staccato movements are regulated with signals from the instructor; be careful not to anticipate the movements.

This exercise is carried one step further by assuming your favorite sexual posture and moving the pelvis in staccato manner. Sixteen beats in and sixteen beats out. Some of your erotic programs may be triggered by this group exercise.

With your partner, lie on the floor, intertwining bodies as close together as possible. The aim is to let your body sleep, but not let your mind sleep.

To keep the mind alert, perform the counting exercise—of counting up to 100 by ones—then come down by twos, then go back up by threes, then go back down by fours, then go back up by fives, then down by sixes, then up by sevens, up through eights, nines and tens.

Your mind should be active, but the body completely relaxed. This is called the "Scissor Exercise."

Stretch up as tall as possible, reaching for the ceiling, and then stretch taller and then taller still. ***Super effort is only possible when strong effort is being made already.***

With a group of fellow workers, build a pyramid. Mark a route of carrying stones and then begin lifting imaginary stones, creating muscular isometric tension in the body proportional to the weight to be lifted. Repeat this lifting, carrying, unloading and returning to exactness.

Maintain an internal counting between 0 and 100, up by ones, down by twos, up by threes, down by fours, etc. Keep counting up and down and continue this while working and during rest breaks. If you lose your internal count, begin again.

The Asanas—after doing the "Ham-Sah" breathing, it is important to take a cleansing breath. Next, lie flat on your back. If necessary support the small of your back with palms down. Draw your knees up to the chest. Take your time with these positions. Do not move abruptly. Lift your legs into the air in the "candle position." Spread your legs into a scissor and then rotate them. Slowly come down out of this position and resume the lying down position. Do a cleansing breath and sit up slowly.

Sit on the floor, spine erect and legs stretched out in front of you. Now draw the left leg up bending it at the knee, so the sole of the foot rests against the fleshy inner portion of the right thigh, toes just above the knee.

Closing your eyes, reach with the right hand to grasp the toes of the right foot. Follow with the left arm and hold the toes with both hands, relaxing and stretching the body in an acquiescent curve. Letting go of the toes, open your eyes.

Straighten your limbs again, resuming your original posture and repeat the toe-grasping ritual using the left set of toes. When you have stretched out that side, open your eyes, straighten out and take a cleansing breath.

Now get down on your knees and lower your head until your forehead touches the floor. Place your arms along your legs on the floor, palms up.

Bring your arms slowly forward, sliding them along the floor until arms are stretched forward as far as possible. Now your palms are facing the floor.

Bring your head up slowly and begin arching the back, sliding your hands along the thighs.

Spread your feet apart and bring your buttocks onto the floor. Slide your hands further and shift your weight onto your arms and legs. Arch your back until your head touches the floor.

Remain in arched position. Raise your pelvis as high as you can three or four times.

Then bring yourself back up into a sitting position slowly. Take a deep cleansing breath—exhale and then return to normal breathing.

CHAPTER 41
THIRD BRAIN BEING

RATHER THAN ALLOWING the organic machine to initiate our climax as would ordinarily occur, we wish to initiate it ourselves, as a voluntary action. Ordinarily ejaculation is not voluntary.

Ejaculation is ordinarily part of an organic-involuntary cycle in the Moving-Instinctive Centrum.

To make ejaculation and the manifestations of orgasm voluntary, we do not wait until the organic machine begins its involuntary cycle leading to climax. Before this occurs, we ourselves initiate the manifestations of climax and voluntarily allow only a small ejaculation as an exact means to provide a specific substance which is used for the opening of additional inner chambers and psychic domains.

For most human beings the whole question of orgasm and ejaculation is involuntary and is not a subject for discussion except in a bragging contest. Usually they will wildly spend their force with no possibility beyond their involuntary palpitating-self-oblivion.

If they happen to produce more than one ejaculation it is as a result of this same palpitating-self-oblivion. They are driven to it by their involuntary moving-instinctive impulses. They are not in possession of themselves. Any animal can do the same.

In this way, we are no different from any other animal, although we like to think so. The main difference between humans and animals is that human beings have the possible means to become voluntary, for which is required an extra third brain. Humans in the organic only use one, and at most—as a result of accident—two brains. Organic human beings never use the third brain, even accidentally.

Ordinary orgasm can be said to be the involuntary manifestations of Moving-Centrum sex, while voluntary ejaculation is initiated only by the impartial "I."

We wish to separate ejaculation from the involuntary part of ejaculation which we call "***orgasm***."

The reason we wish to do this is because we wish to remove orgasm entirely from this involuntary manifestation. To voluntarize our manifestations to some degree.

Transference during ejaculation is an exchange of a very small amount of higher "refined" alchemical substance, and this substance, when transformed, is then directed into the female partner through her chalice. It is held in her chalice and returned to the source of life in this way and then passed back to her male partner.

When the semen is ordinarily transferred during involuntary manifestations of orgasm, it is mostly sperm which is carried by the semen. When semen is transferred in the voluntary, it carries a small amount of sperm, not meaning that the sperm is not potent, but that the number of sperm are sufficiently lower to make a completely different substance, in addition to which, the substance has been transformed through special activities including the activities of prolonged sex. By making the ejaculation occur outside the domain of the involuntary, ejaculation is removed from the involuntary domain and a special chamber opens.

Ordinarily this chamber is rock hard and impenetrable, even if the man's member may be three feet long and like a donkey, still he cannot penetrate to the alchemical alembic under ordinary circumstances. She must open the special chamber and she cannot open the special chamber by thinking it open, or hoping it open, or wishing it open, or any other means except through gradual change in her glandular activity which is brought about by the extraction of ejaculation from the involuntary domain of the male.

So ordinary man is only able to enter the chamber which we call the "red lotus chamber." This chamber extends just to the cervix. The "blue lotus chamber" extends further, not a great deal, but somewhat further, past the cervix. This is the first genuine opening which is brought about by the switching of the timing of ejaculation and through the action of producing fifty or sixty ejaculations. Thus he is able to place the ejaculation in this chamber which is much farther past the cervix than she is able to make accessible under ordinary circumstances.

Then through a special contact which is called ***Madonna Breast***s, another chamber is opened for the yellow chamber which is the second available special chamber. But the third chamber, the gold chamber, we know about. The red chamber is accessible always. The blue chamber is accessible through Madonna Breasts. Red is through passion.

Then the golden lotus chamber, the final chamber available and accessible, is available through the male giving his life force.

If he gives entirely his whole inner self, if his whole life force goes to her, even if that occurs, he is willing to do this. He is willing to do this in the same way that someone who is under the domination of a vampire is willing to give blood—the same feeling, but not hypnotic. That is to say, voluntarily able to sacrifice himself with no feelings of pain, no regret, completely impartial, but not impartially through hypnosis or narcosis.

These chambers become accessible to him and they become accessible to the semen which otherwise is stopped. Now in this case, I am not interested in uterine implantation.

We have gone past the cervix and in each of these chambers, a special secretion is released by her upon reception of transformed semen.

When we say transformed semen, we mean semen which is not contaminated by the involuntary. That is to say, by involuntary manifestations of orgasm.

These special secretions make possible a certain absorption of semen through that chamber passing upward along the centrums for transformation and to be passed back down.

Several substances are generated which are not ordinarily found in the vagina, but which can be present under certain special conditions.

She then becomes what is called an "Initiate Priestess," which means that she is able to supply very special substances otherwise unobtainable and which are then transformed several times as this transference occurs back and forth between the Alchemical Partners.

CHAPTER 42
THE MOOD OF THE PARTNERS

PROLONGED SEXUAL CONTACT is not a guarantee of success. It requires a special female mood, and the giving of one's life force.

The organic and psychic chambers are capable of transformation of substances. They are in themselves capable of generations of special substances, and more importantly, they are capable of absorption of semen in different ways.

The absorption of a certain amount of semen over a long period of time provides the glandular trigger for the opening of the next chamber if the mood is also activated which requires an all-centrums-cooperation within oneself and the invocants in the circle.

In each case, the organic trigger is the number and amount of seminal ejaculations which provide the organism with the glandular demand for the opening of the next chamber in the same way that a fetus makes glandular demands for the opening of the vaginal passage—the birth canal.

The male is drained of life force which the female partner can return to him through breath, but which he can also collect as a bee collects pollen.

The partner will change from supplier to receiver. Each in turn receiving and supplying life force and substances.

As the chambers open, the female partner must be impartial to the opening of the chambers. If she becomes enamored of this process or becomes identified with the opening of her chambers, she can easily fall into the involuntary and either close the chambers or sour the contents.

A beginning technique is to focus the concentrated attention on oral contact, with much kissing, the hands on or around the head primarily in the hair and the back of the neck.

It is necessary for the male to evoke in himself those manifestations which would ordinarily be appropriate only to romantic love. Now the female partner must evoke in herself voluntarily the Moving Centrum manifestations of passionate love.

Thus the male becomes female, the female becomes male. The manifestations will be through the mouth and the hands. This removes the power of the Moving Centrum which is a lower psychic energy in which we ordinarily place our sexual attention.

The female partner always knows exactly where to place the attention. She cradles the head of her male partner; she knows exactly how to do this. Every woman is skilled in this art.

A male alchemist will learn to follow the female partner's movements, not to initiate his own or to control her movements or posture, and to mimic her manifestations and to take from her the exact clue to her openings.

The female partner will communicate through her manifestation, how to open her pathways and chambers from moment to moment. If the male partner follows these manifestations exactly, with precise reflective mimicry, then he will be attentive to her body and psychic language when she speaks through her sexual senses.

So in this dance, she is the leading partner. The male alchemical partner is always in the passive, and the female partner is the active and guiding force.

CHAPTER 43
THE VAGINA ALCHEMICA

The inside wall of the vagina is called the "Red Chamber." The venom producer supplies the venom, which is extracted by the magician or priest, from the red chamber. The venom is indrawn into the penis by the process of vacuum absorption, and is precipitated into the scrotum where distillation takes place. The distilled venom results in the production of "protohari."

Transformed semen is the substance offered within each of the chambers of the elixir producer, located just past the sphincter which opens into the "Blue Chamber."

There are specific keys used by the priest to dilate each of the sphincters of the alchemical chambers, from the red to the blue, from the blue to the yellow, from the yellow to the gold, and finally, from the gold chamber to the fifth chamber which is an alchemical alembic where distillation and collection of substances takes place. This is the chamber where the feeding of the solar entity takes place. The keys used are specific mentations and Moving Centrum manifestations. Mood is engendered in the process by the combination of both, but especially triggered by the mentation.

To open the gates of the blue chamber, the mentation used is, "I wish this to be used for the benefit of all Beings everywhere." The Moving Centrum manifestations are nonpassionate, with the use of breath. To dilate the sphincter into the yellow chamber from the blue, the mentation used is, "This effort is ***in*** the Work ***for*** the Work." The Moving Centrum manifestation is the Madonna Breasts.

For the next opening into the gold, the mentation is of giving every last drop of one's life force to the Beloved, like a moth that flies into the flame. The Moving Centrum manifestation is a specific oral manipulation. To open into the fifth chamber, the mentation is invocation of the solar entity. The Moving Centrum manifestation is the catalyst. Substances are then placed in this final chamber or temple, which serves as food for the solar entity.

The substance transformed in the fifth chamber is Alchemical Gold. As the solar entity feeds on this, a "backwash" occurs through a form of "reverse EMF" or Electro-Magnetic Force and some of the gold is absorbed through the walls of the vagina of the priestess, and some is absorbed by vacuum and osmosis into the penis of the priest. Byproducts that are not used form a sediment on the bottom of the chamber. They are precipitated out through a filtering system. The priest can then share some of the alchemical substance with the venom producer.

We can use this exercise for self-observation. When we move from one chamber to another through openings of various sizes, we can view that as passing through a portal.

We must ask ourselves why we moved from one chamber to another; what motivated us to do this? Actually take a small notebook with you and record these observations. There may be more than one reason for any activity, so record all your reasons. At first this will slow you down and affect your movements, but soon your regular pattern will re-establish itself as the note-taking becomes habitual. This is a very powerful exercise if you are able to do it without lying to yourself or others.

CHAPTER 44
FLOORS OF THE CHAMBER

IN AN ORDINARY SPACE, people are all separate individuals, into their own games, with their own personal agendas, personalities, beliefs and activities both internal and external.

People have intellectual ideas, roof-brain chatter going on. There are opinions, agreements and disagreements, likes and dislikes. People have personal trips. There is no connection with each other.

We make a psycho-physical explanation for everything that happens here. There is an outside world connected to any ordinary space. You came in through the door and can walk back out through the door. The sounds you hear can come from places "outside." You bring your dream into this room, you make associations with things that happened in the dream.

Astral World: you recognize the chamber. It is not ordinary. You did not walk in through the door, you woke up here. You still remember the ordinary state and are looking down at it.

A few mild sensations may happen—tingling, clarity. People come out of themselves somewhat, may form ***cliques***.

You are aware of the group and recognize them. They are familiar to you, and it seems that you have known one another for a long time. The group gets together; all are playing the same game. There is fellowship. The light brightens. There is a sense of heightened perceptions, telepathy. You have a bond between each other.

There is no outside in a "Klein-Bottle" space, the archetypal space of Higher Dimensions. You cannot get out without descending. The energy is high. Facial changes are observed, the body may grow, you may feel uplifted. Your senses are acute. You have a feeling of clarity. People look different, the space is noticeably different. Visual and auditory phenomena. A queasy sensation in the stomach, or nausea. Time is slowed down.

Causal World: there is a slight energy drop—a pregnant, expectant feeling—the calm before the storm. Stillness. The light gets subdued, filters out, gets diffused. You see and sense flatness.

On the causal plane you are able to recognize archetypes. You see the players, not the characters. Faces and identifies interchange; it is more fluid. Being together.

Here there is an interval, a safety valve—the dream is a way of keeping you from going to the archetype. You do not go there when you do not want to. There are guardians at the gates. A shock is needed to get through the interval; a Key.

The Archetype: all hell breaks loose. Things melt into each other. Stars within your form. Intense sensations. Feet keep being pulled down, going and going, there is no end. One of the games of the archetype is creating other worlds. There is no time sense here.

There is no communication, because there is no one with whom to communicate. You are alone, All-One. Sounds all come from you. If you look into the eyes of someone else who is there, you share a special secret.

Those in the work partnership already exist and always have existed in the archetype space. Either you are in that archetype, or you are not. If you are in that archetype, it is your homeroom.

In order to leave the archetype without descending, it is necessary to have gone through a transformation. The fragmented being reunites. The work partnership must be together in the room and must tolerate each other for one moment. One moment might as well be eternity.

If you are in the archetype and are able to leave without descending, you will see a corridor when you open the door. Even if the teaching space appears to be in the country in a field, for example, in the archetype, there will be a corridor which leads to other archetypes. Such as:

To surrender to the chamber and its natural inhabitants and events.

To be in this chamber, not on the way to some other chamber.

To do nothing until the chamber provides the data for appropriate activities.

Respect the chamber and do nothing to violate it by habitual momentum.

Trust that the chamber is the same Face of God (FoG) as always, just in another form.

To be in this chamber and leave your baggage from previous chambers outside.

To be aware of yourself, the objects, the function and appearance of the chamber, the light, the mood, the people, the sounds. Observe objectively and impartially.

To tolerate your work partner and allow a blending to occur, even if the result is eternal and irreversible.

Do nothing for one moment.

Do not rest on your past data, habits or attainments.

Do nothing from your own previous experience. Do not inflict events from other chambers.

Be present and take the risk of being present.

Look actively with high attention for opportunities to make evolutionary efforts.

Make an effort not to make an ordinary organic effort.

Be aware of people and objects as shapes of light and dark in the FoG.

Take data literally, unless otherwise indicated.

Place attention on the chamber in concentrated diffusion.

Listen to the sounds of the chamber.

The chamber ***is*** the teaching!

The chamber is an archetype, if we can fixate the vision of the chamber as an angelic being or as the Face of God (FoG).

Everything you need to know about the chamber is in the chamber—the chamber provides all data necessary in the chamber.

Assume the angelic post most corresponding to your source of attention.

Things that prevent us from having the force to be in a chamber are negative emotions, ordinary sex and fantasies—get the main points of any available data ***verbatim***.

As powerfully as you are able to arouse attention in a chamber, you are awake.

When you fall asleep in a chamber, you disappear from the chamber.

Sit still. Do not lie back on the floor. Do not lean against walls, etc. Do not fidget.

No note-taking.

Do not get into negative emotions. Do not blow away Power Centrum force.

No eating in the Work Chamber.

Keep each other awake.

Do not drift off.

Invocation is not a passive event. Be attention-active and machine passive.

If a question comes up, work on it to refine it, penetrate it as deeply as possible. Keep your attention on the question if it is important. If not, then pass to another subject of attention.

Be still. Do not entertain. If you have to do something, observe with full attention.

Shekinah is an illusion between Sandalphon and Metatron, so that neither has to be female. Sandalphon and Metatron are twin brothers. They never see each other; they always see Shekinah. And what do these two dark and awesome angels do?

A genuine three-centrum-being finds a two-centrum human being—one individual isolated and acting and feeling alone—very strange. This is the ordinary Adamic Body, not the First Adam. It can be formed at least temporarily for practice.

Shekinah is the illusion, and yet she is the only reality.

The Shekinah is at once the mirror, the reflection, and that which is reflected in the mirror. Nothing she sees is like her; she is the mirror of the mirror. The mirror is the only reality, and it has no dimension whatever.

CHAPTER 45
BIG BANGS & BLACK HOLES

SOMEONE WHO IS IN THE WORK does not necessarily get work. There are many work ideas very unpleasant and seemingly very unfair—such as the idea that there are some who will never be in the Work no matter how much effort they exert.

In the story of the "King's New Klothes," as given in ***Angels Healing Journey****, the Shekinah is the embodiment of evil and represents the clothes covering the naked King, the Face of God, which is composed of angels knitted together in a cluster.

When we see the Face of God, we see what God sees; we see through the Face of God. The Shekinah is the veil which prevents us from seeing the Face of God. The last veil, the last thing we see before we see the Face of God is Satan; we see Satan. If we do not penetrate further before the Face of God, we see Satan and often are driven away

*1997, Gateways/I.D.H.H.B., Nevada City, CA

in our quest assuming that we have travelled in the wrong direction.

Man is the third smallest part of God; below him are the animal and mineral kingdom. However, there are no more than ten parts in all.

There must be both ends of a vibration in order to make an invocation work and, in the same way, there had to be a House of King David and a House of the Priest Aaron—the line of kings and another line of priests, in short, separation of church and state.

Jesus was believed by some to be the Jewish Messiah who would destroy the Romans and restore the Holy Temple of Jerusalem.

He lived his life almost exactly as described in the Messianic Prophecies of the Jews, written and collected since the capture of Jerusalem and the surrounding territories by the Romans—Simon Magus and Joseph of Arimathea were actually the top contenders, but Jesus, whose Jewish name was "Isa," number 14 on the list of possible Messiahs, was the "tie-breaker" between the two warring factions of Jewish priests who were to choose the Messiah from the list of candidates.

Jesus had access to all the secret writings of the Messianic Prophecies, since his uncle was the Chief Priest at the Temple of Jerusalem and his cousins, John the Baptist, who announced that he was the Messiah, and Lazarus, whom he apparently raised from the dead, were well-placed to help him. Most of his apostles were also members of his family.

Jesus was supposed to be half from the line of kings and half from the line of priests, the product of both lineages.

If we were in an objective space there would be no differences between us; it is only subjectively that there are differences. Maintain your individuality; do not try to be someone else. What you can be is a cosmic maintainer. Do not react to this, simply do it.

Objectively speaking there is a necessity for both ends of a stick, and in a work chamber there must be a dichotomy—black and white, red and blue, good and bad, dark and light, warm and cool, intense and gray.

This need for dichotomy expresses itself in various ways.

When we ascend into a higher chamber in which we are able to view some objective archetypal drama in its unfolding, we are playing a character, but these characters are not us.

The attitudes they hold are not our attitudes. We can think of these forms as hollow; we can fit inside and be privileged to watch. Sometimes when we act out or reveal our presence by interjection of our egos, we are ejected from the space.

To stay in a place forever, that is the real price of immortality.

The Absolute sometimes tumbles into what we would call a "writhing space"—it folds back on itself and begins eating its own tail.

We could if we knew how, align ourselves to the space of the Absolute and bring the writhing to a halt.

What happens to us subjectively is that space drops away until we are fully exposed to nothingness. During this eternal moment, our entire form is open to the Void, to the infinite expansion of space into the nothingness of the Void.

It is dark outside and filled with stars inside, and our face is in every direction at once—we are fully and completely open and vulnerable, and we can feel it.

At this point we should be at our most alert ever in our whole lives—no tension must build anywhere, no muscles must twitch; even the slightest tension can destroy the stop. If we do it really well we can hear the eternal chanting and singing of angels filling the space within.

When viewing this space, one must not move in an ordinary way, as one would in an ordinary chamber in lower orders of space and time. There is nothing of the phenomenal in this space.

There are a lot of sensations in the higher space, but they are not the sensations of the body—vision may mislead the senses, but not higher sensations of the electrical field which is oneself.

The third factor is that we tend to hold a very, very basic assumption that we are always on planet Earth and that we always know where we are and who we are and that we are able to understand what is going on. We hold on to the idea of being in a particular time and a particular place and being a particular individual.

The concept of suddenly being elsewhere and elsewhen and being someone entirely different without warning and without distinct indications of this fact can be very disturbing.

Your safety factor is to think that you are a person. This is where the "Law of Irony" comes in—it requires discipline under the Law of Irony in order to penetrate the veils over the vision. A vision is not just visual, it is also tactile and emotional.

When you are able to extend your sensations throughout the universe, a peculiar connection takes place in which one single organism exists in that space.

It is utterly alone and if it is having sex, it is having sex with itself, because there is no one else but itself.

We can develop that concept in order to directly see the Absolute in the mirror of the self. Some time, along the line, you can use the mantra "I am a figment of my own imagination" or "The mirror is the reflection of the reflection."

When we see reality the way it really is, we will be absolutely convinced we are hallucinating, but actually, we are hallucinating now.

Only a work partnership can and should use Alchemical Sex for the purpose of invoking entities for data and transformation. The primary requisite is to be free of the tendency to involve oneself in casual encounters with others. The partnership must be hermetically sealed for the duration of their work together, however long that may be, often extending many trillions of lifetimes, across time and space and through many convolutions and evolutions of many universes.

Stars are formed by Hydrogen gases collapsing into a gravity well, a Black Hole. Eventually all stars explode into dust and are recycled into stars again. Virtually any and every physical thing you run into is composed of some substance which was once part of a star, because it requires the heat and pressure of a star to convert Hydrogen into anything higher, even Carbon; so technically your body is composed of stardust and everything you touch is also stardust, some of which comes from stars so distant and so long-dead that they are older than this universe.

Each universe is composed of matter which has fallen into a Black Hole until it reaches Critical Mass and explodes in a "Big Bang" into its own universe with its own expanding galaxies and star systems with their invariable planetary systems encircling them, in a closed general system within which are open systems acting as if independently under the Laws of Improbability and Uncertainty.

CHAPTER 46
WORK ETHIC

"HERMETICALLY SEALED" means exactly that—no intimate connections with anyone outside the circle except socially, with the obvious exception of family and friends; no sexual connections outside the Hermetic relationship whatever, and an unbreakable fastidiousness to keep oneself ritually clean from all contaminations whether mental, emotional, psychic or organic.

Hermetic self-discipline means "As Below, So Above." This is the sublime link between lower and higher cosmoses and must not be broken if the partnership is to achieve any real results.

Partners must naturally possess a fierce loyalty to each other and a strong dedication to the Work, to be a free agent, a black sheep who has burned all bridges behind him. An alchemical relationship is isolated from the outer world yet is part of it at least nominally, ***for the duration;*** it is cloistered away in relation to its work and the exact methods of work.

Intimacy is taken for granted but not abused; intimacy on all possible levels. Verbal, food, water, interests, all for the conservation of force. Alchemical Partners must know that they can trust one another by experience, not just by vows. A partner in Alchemical Sex must be tested thoroughly to determine their ability to remain nonviolent under the worst possible conditions, and so on.

Someone who has been very pampered or who is very self-pampering, who uses everyone and everything to contribute to their own self-masturbation is dangerous to the relationship. Considerations are never personal; the interest of each partner within the Hermetic Seal is always tempered by practical sense, with no personal agendas.

This means no "shagging after every car that passes," like a dog, or being attracted-by-every-distraction. To be dependable and steady in an alchemical relationship means to endure the work ethic far beyond the point of boredom and to be dependable in terms of personal predictability. We must not manifest what we cannot afford to pay for.

To be in an alchemical relationship requires full participation, to make a shared-unity, a vehicle in which to learn, to know, to discover "Philadelphia"—the City of Brotherly Love, or "Agape" together. In an alchemical relationship there must be allowances for work which are boring and also for efforts which may be cathartic. We must be able to take the salt and the sugar impartially without judgment.

In an alchemical relationship all centrums are involved in some degree of organic and psychic compensation. Mood is part of this, which could be called "Plastic Psychosis."

With a high degree of impersonal attention, we can learn to study impartially the manifestations of someone whom we happen to know is in a particular state of altered or everyday consciousness.

We can study and imitate at least the posture of the state—the subtle nuances, tones, timing, transition and vocal pitch.

If we can correctly adopt their posture and tone, we can understand at least somewhat the scope and basic concepts they hold as a self-image and maybe even their world view.

This "sacred acting" is a form of voluntary adaptation, which the ancient Greeks called "happenings" and which were part of their theater performances. Greek playwrights were not the same as today's playwrights; they considered what they did to be part of an attempt to eavesdrop on the lives of the Gods by adopting the postures and roles of various characters playing against each other.

One exercise used by both comics and actors is to repeat what someone is saying as simultaneously as possible which puts you on the same wavelength.

At some point this can become genuine telepathy, tuning in to what someone else is thinking, following the same thoughts together.

It is important to understand that thoughts do not arise independently—the mind tunes into thoughts by tuning out other thoughts. Approximately 28,000 thoughts pass through the mind every second, but the mind sees only a small percentage of these, and ignores all others. In dreaming and deep sleep, the thoughts ordinarily tuned out may come to the forefront. Some of these thoughts can be predictive, some passive and some reminiscent.

When we perform the same movements, the same exercises and the same breathing, emotional prayers and mentations, we may develop a collective identity and consciousness.

This collective identity provides an Etheric Body for a larger entity.

One example of collective consciousness can be found in concerts or large religious or political gatherings.

Various presences require different numbers of bodies for their descent into the phenomenal world—clearly, the entities which descend on rock concerts are very different from those which tend to congregate in churches, temples, small religious rites or alchemical operations.

"Drawing Down" or "invoking" requires gathering of a group with a common goal, quietude of presence, impartial emotional states and definite higher emotional, psychological and even physical alignments.

This collective consciousness and the provision of a cluster for "momentary possession" by higher entities was the original purpose of temples, rituals, ceremonial theater, ancient rites and today's church services.

In the middle ages dervishes entered Western Europe as ***jongleur***—jugglers, street entertainers—who performed various forms of public theater for the purpose of gathering crowds, manipulating their moods and using them to provide the basis for invocations, which sometimes precipitated vague thoughts of personal evolution in some of the more open and courageous curious onlookers.

If invocations are not allowed in certain civilizations, which can occur for various reasons—some of which are political, some religious fanaticism, scientific superstition, or simple apathy which often occurs in the ordinary course of time in every civilization no matter how enlightened it may become at one period or another in its history—cultural and religious crises can develop on large scales, having profound effects upon organic life through the resulting ethnic cleansing and religious warfare which are the inevitable result of suppression.

An invoked presence may seem benevolent or malevolent, but we should only consider its relationship to the Work, not to our own values and standards.

Malevolent presences are also necessary to life and evolution, and we may someday come to understand that they are only malevolent to our ordinary personal and cultural views, taken in relation to our own aims, wishes, desires, fears, beliefs and attitudes.

With practice we can learn to distinguish between "benevolent to the Work" and "malevolent to the Work," which is our only concern at present, but we will not be able to distinguish accurately if we persist in viewing experienced experiences through the veils of personal preference—"like" and "dislike."

The province of work partners is to build higher, more elaborate "Landing Fields" for specific presences at specific times, when certain chemical, biological, psychological and emotional changes are produced in exact accordance with precise invocational methods, under Divine Grace and Guidance. The same is true for Alchemical Partnerships.

CHAPTER 47
ALCHEMICAL RELATIONSHIPS

The process of "imprinting," or deliberately implanting definite and specific psycho-emotional images and effects upon a space or an object, is the reverse of psychometry, which is to say, we are psychically writing rather than reading an object, and this effort generally requires the cooperative efforts of a coherent and knowledgeable group of high initiates. This can be accomplished through alchemical means combined with psychic techniques which we have discussed in detail in ***Visions in the Stone****.

Artifacts which have been psychometrically imprinted in this way and which date from pre-Babylonian to Egyptian eras in the Fertile

*1989, Gateways/I.D.H.H.B., Nevada City, CA

Crescent can generally be activated by an initiate familiar with the technique of reading objects which have been exposed to psychometric influences.

These artifacts are often found in ancient sites and can be quite easily decoded and viewed by any trained psychic.

Tarot cards, which date back to Ancient Babylonian and Protodynastic Egyptian times, if properly drawn and colored in their exact correspondences, can yield information from other artifacts ordinarily inaccessible, which is to say, the cards can act like "relay stations" for ordinarily inaccessible artifacts, artifacts which are "locked up" in certain ways, "encrypted" in ancient spells, or which are simply not present and available for study at the moment.

Precise and exact copies of artifacts can also have the same exact effects that the originals would have. The majority of "Unlocking Keys" to alchemical data contained in ancient artifacts and which are available from invoked entities are from the higher Emotional Centrums.

The organism is part of the environment. Organs and the organic self are actually ancient recycled artifacts, and virtually every physical object is made of stellar particles, some of which can be as old as 700 trillion trillion years, coming from entirely different universes through Black Holes.

The Organic Body contains a major part of the data we wish to acquire and which we need for our alchemical work, if we can learn to treat it as an ancient artifact.

When several conversations are available in one space, we can decode it as a single conversation, which can be useful to our alchemical work and to our evolutionary efforts.

Organic life is a single organism in its basic function, although it may appear to be a concatenation of many different kinds of life. The most common form of life or half-life is the virus, and protoplasm is common throughout the universe, connected by a collective consciousness into which we can tap if we practice the method of contacting this part of our consciousness—we can learn this technique, which was extensively covered in ***The Hidden Work**** and also in ***Secrets of Angelic Invocation***.

This form of tuning into the collective consciousness should and can

*1991, Gateways/I.D.H.H.B., Nevada City, CA

be part of the life of every human being on the planet, but due to evolutionary imbalances and several evolutionary accidents which prevent the development of higher centrums in human beings, hardly anyone today is interested in the enclave which can tune into the Universal Vortex.

The lock or seal on the door of an alchemical relationship is human, ordinary reactions and values. If we have ordinary reactions and values we cannot enter an alchemical relationship, and if by some chance we did get in momentarily, we would not want to remain.

In an alchemical relationship substances are shared allowing the partner to obtain enough of the substance necessary to build higher being bodies.

In an alchemical relationship partners must have a balanced sense of humor with compassion for the other. In fact, without humor there can be no discipline.

When we crystallize our higher being body, we must do it at the correct moment. There is a point we reach when we have attained the maximum and must have the courage to take the leap and crystallize then.

We are building toward an opportunity to crystallize an immortal form and the courage to take that opportunity. We are building toward a certain moment for which the timing is critical. The fool in the Tarot is the ignition point; we step off the cliff to crystallize.

Everything must be paid for. Hospitality has a price, but it is the host who must pay. Those who give service must pay, those who are served cannot pay. We must pay to serve.

In the Work or not, one must be able to accept responsibility. If one does not have a ***tonic*** (roof brain) running constantly, one may be able to hear ***harmonics*** and ***overtones***. A work partnership is work, not play, not sexual indulgence.

The story of Dracula—but the real story—is the story of the Work. Dracula was a man forced to suck the blood from young women, a job he found personally extremely unpleasant, in order to survive. Dracula was a vampire.

In the Work it is also necessary to suck people's higher blood, which they would not use in any case, to use for work. In a work partnership, this "blood sucking" is done knowingly and willingly. The alchemist takes from the woman, but then he must pay her for its use by being her drone.

A candidate for the Work is someone who is in the Work, but has not yet accepted the responsibility—his work has not yet been developed, although to accept the responsibility is not to guarantee admission to the Work.

A work circle gathers when the call goes out, by decree. With force of magnetism, parts of a higher dimensional body are re-collected from the work cell colonies of the individuals gathered.

There is no reincarnation, no transmigration of souls, but there is eternal continuation, which to the ordinary consciousness is not necessarily desirable.

How long does an elephant exist as an elephant, a tortoise live as a tortoise, a rock exist as a rock, an amoeba live out its life, a virus survive as a virus?

Subjectively they all exist the same in time, and time is merely a local effect of gravity, and gravity is in turn a local effect of space, which is an effect of expansion of energy as it converts to mass. In this universe, nothing can survive longer than "seven days," which is a way of saying, "the whole cycle of creation."

CHAPTER 48
TRANSFORMATIONAL TRIGGERS AND ENERGY PARAMETERS

Transformational Triggers

Conditioning
Adjusting Energy Levels
Grammar for a New World—I am—I-verb/am-noun
Somatic Scale
Chart of Emotional Connections with Muscles
Chart of Access
Alert to Inert—Degree of Awarenesss
Active to Passive

Energy Parameters

Physical Effects of Invocation:

- sudden sweating
- night sweating
- change in breathing pattern
- release of gas
- change in blood pressure
- nausea, vomiting
- diarrhea
- urination
- itching
- hot flashes
- emotional reactions
- odors
- bruising
- soreness
- twitches/tics/spasms
- vibrating
- shivering
- lightness
- spatial disorientation
- confusion
- disorientation
- grogginess
- unusual hunger or loss of appetite
- sexual arousal/unusual continued stimulation
- heightened sensory perception/optic brightness
- irritation/ annoyance/ short tempered/ impatience
- loss of inhibitions/sense of freedom
- lightness
- phlegm
- weakness
- dizziness
- frequent unexpected out-of-body experiences
- floating sensations
- feeling of detachment
- rapid random mood changes
- numbness

CHAPTER 49
THE GODDESS

PRIESTS IN THE ANCIENT WORLD were originally intended to service the priestesses sexually for the good of the community, and also to clean the temple grounds and to keep the temple in good repair and appearance. They were the ones who were taught to invoke the agricultural goddesses...one goddess in particular...into the priestess.

A woman is considered ritually unclean in virtually every ancient agricultural religion.

The Malamat was a filthy man; he was ritually unclean, untouchable. He had to sleep with each harem wife the first night to break the hymen. He knew the ritual practices; he was highly trained, highly skilled and he taught her how to wield sexual powers, how to use her vagina as a weapon.

He taught her the customary secrets of the woman's trade, tricks of the wives' trade. And also "old wives" were counted upon to teach the younger women sexual secrets, but the function of the Priest was also to invoke the goddess directly into the consecrated body of the Bride.

The whole idea of the marriage ceremony was originally to invoke the goddess into the bride. It only later became contractual when it was necessary for every woman to have a man to take care of them and to decide the rights of inheritance, which in ancient times always passed through the women of the tribe.

Catholic Nuns today are "married to Jesus." This idea is very different from the original ancient intention, and very different from the original Jewish traditions from which Jesus had his arisings.

In many tribes the male would perhaps take as part of his obligation to his wife, the obligation of also having sex with and supporting her sisters, nieces, cousins, and so forth, or any women who were on her side of the family who were unattached.

The concept of a "dowry" came from this idea of a man accepting obligation to care for a woman and supporting her family as well.

And if there wasn't a dowry, some of the women of a family might be sold into slavery to make a dowry to allow the husband to support the women he was willing to take responsibility for.

Remember also, up until only a few years ago, 13 was a common age for a girl to be married in some southern states. And in some cultures, even recently, the age went down to three and among several cultures which survive today, including the Mormons, several wives are not at all uncommon.

This was certainly true of the early agricultural societies as well. Very young girls could be used to produce children because the death rate was extremely high and the life expectancy was extremely low.

Twenty-three was the average life expectancy because it was a warrior's society, and because the diseases were completely absolutely unchecked.

In Western Europe, particularly in Spain, France and England there has been a movement since the destruction of the ancient religions to bring them back. One of these that formed in Western Europe was the Witchcraft Cult—the cult of the Wicca. Cult in this sense doesn't mean anything negative; it means the same as the word sect or group. Cult actually means a unique group or lineage, so you could say the lineage of the Wicca.

This represents religion before the imposition of Christianity, but no matter what they say in today's form, Wicca is a protest against Christianity in addition to the original religion—the reaction to Christianity as well as the original religion. And the original agricultural religions—by the time the church thoroughly stamped them out had become household religions. Here's what happened:

During the fourteenth, fifteenth, sixteenth and seventeenth centuries—what is called paganism, but what was actually an ancient religion, an agricultural religion in which the goddess of the moon who controlled the tides and controlled the seasons—the moon goddess was the primary focus. She was the centrum—actually the fertility goddess—and her helpers were also fertility goddesses of various kinds. They were the centrum originally of these household religions.

In other words, the hunting gods were dropped from the Pantheon. And even the major agricultural gods were dropped. The goddesses were retained and brought into the household. Now they were protectresses of the household.

Imagine yourselves to be in the same plight as the woman of the late dark ages, with a simple choice of marriage or prostitution... A very thin veneer of Christianity lies over the ancient religions which are still very much buzzing and very much around, but in the form of superstition—household charms, fortune telling, lesser magic to insure one's own crops or to ward off evil, to keep disease from the house, pestilence, and so forth, and as a woman—you could not leave the household because if you left the house you would be killed or sold into slavery or put to work in what's called a "work house" for unattached women.

In fact, a woman whose husband died was subject to the work house if she didn't have some money saved and children or family to care for her.

She could not remarry because the laws of the church didn't allow her to remarry unless her husband was dead, then she could remarry ...only after a suitable period of time during which she was subject to the work house. A man could not support her, even if he wanted her—and generally they didn't.

Or she could become a prostitute. There was no such thing as a bag lady in those days. There was no such thing as a woman owning her own business or property. The property was all in the man's name; if she didn't have a man in her family, she could not own the property.

If she were the sole surviving heir, the property went to someone else or went to the state or to the church. She was evicted from the property and sent to the work house. Even if she had been a baroness, if there was no male heir, she was kicked off the property and the property was seized.

She had no life of her own. She could not leave the house. What her husband said was law. If she didn't like it she could go to the work house. He had the right to kill her, to beat her, to sell her and to sell her children or to kill them, as he chose. He had the power of life and death over his whole family. No one else had that power, and no one except the church could stop him.

She did not choose where she went. When she was of marriageable age her family arranged the marriage in most countries. She had no choice over who her mate would be. She lived with a man, she gave birth to his children, she cared for his children, she kept his home, she obeyed him and she was sweet to him on pain of death. She had no power whatever.

Is there any wonder then that a movement began in the twelfth century, giving women of the fourteenth century power in the household, although it was invisible. They were absolute total slaves to the men...and incidentally, if the baron wanted her for a night, he had the right of the aristocrat. He could just take her for the night, or if on her wedding night he decided he preferred her, the groom had to send the new bride on her wedding night to the estate of the aristocrat, and he would return her in whatever condition he wanted to return her, if he ever did. This was the condition under which she lived.

If she lived in a pigsty, she couldn't just leave the pigsty because she would then become subject to the work house. She could not work for a living. She could not earn a living under any circumstances any which way except in prostitution. And if she were caught in prostitution, she could be killed, depending upon the circumstances. The life expectancy of a prostitute at that time was about what it is today—three years—the average.

She had no way out. She couldn't go anywhere. If she were caught travelling by herself without her husband, she was treated as a runaway slave and subject to execution.

She and her husband were owned by the aristocrats who owned the property. They were tenant farmers. In effect, they were slaves. They could not leave their land. It wasn't their land even though they technically owned it; they didn't own it. The feudal baron owned it...or the child owned it. One-tenth of everything they grew went to the church.

Depending upon where they lived up to, in some cases, ninety percent was taken by the church and then by the local baron, and then by the state government—the King—leaving them ten percent of whatever they grew. Worse than that, the people who took the taxes took them in grain and in livestock, and so forth, and took them at different times of the year or at different times relative to each other.

So ninety percent of this and fifty percent of that and ten percent of that, and so forth, which sometimes meant that they ended up with not enough really to eat, not enough to live on, but they were not allowed to earn anything or make any money outside their own demand, their own farm.

They took everything; they left almost nothing for the peasantry. They took the best breeding stock and killed it for food. The stupidity of the Western European Aristocracy is absolutely unequaled in terms of what they did to destroy themselves.

You'd think that that would be done better today with our intelligent civilizations. For instance, why would we take the best human breeding stock and send it to war and leave the completely unfit available for breeding during wartime, during the highest pressure for breeding? And yet, we do exactly that.

The Roman Legions were encouraged to have homosexual relationships. There is nothing like protecting your lover to make you fight hard.

The collapse of the Roman Empire signalled the loss of the matriarchal society and began the enslavement of women. Although women were brutalized all throughout history, the first thing you think of about one city state raiding another one is the rape and pillage—pillage comes second, because rape and murder of women and children is part of the "ethnic cleansing" so common to all animals of every species, including the bipedal apes called "man."

And that's the reason for the suicides of Masada—the primary reason is the women ***knew*** they would be raped and the children would be killed anyway, and the men knew they would be killed. So to avoid all that they simply committed suicide, because they knew how they would be brutalized in the hands of the Romans.

The history of human beings is really pretty grisly, but I want you to understand the growth of the new witchcraft. There was an ancient witchcraft in which the goddess did not play a very large part.

In the new witchcraft in the fourteenth, fifteenth, sixteenth and seventeenth centuries, the goddess played the central part because the women were brutalized, absolutely enslaved. And they have no way of escape except through mental and emotional release provided by the Wicca, what was the Cult of the Goddess.

They began an underground religion which was actually called the "house" religion or the "kitchen" religion. In fact, the implements that were used in witchcraft were implements of the kitchen. The broom is a kitchen implement in a household. It was the symbol of the woman's power.

By the sixteenth century women were using aconite, belladonna and other herbal narcotics in ointment form to transport themselves to the ***Sabbat***—the witches' meetings.

In other words, they were getting stoned just like many unhappy "Soccer moms" of today who are trapped in the suburbs.

When the Catholic Church became aware of this underground movement, its force, it was an enormous movement and very, very well organized. The grand covens were organized by coven masters who were the heads of covens who were in themselves cellular groups that had other covens, and so there was one major coven of thirteen members, in which each of the thirteen members was the coven master of thirteen covens.

It was organized primarily by Catholic Priests. When it was discovered, the Catholic Church went after it with a vengeance, and then took on all the characteristics that it has today. The reaction of the Christian Church to the Pagan religions caused the suppression of magical literature from the fifteenth century on and really from the twelfth century in many cases.

For instance, the twelfth century in Majorca in the Spanish domain generally from Spain to North Africa, and then throughout France and Germany, Hungary, Austria, Bulgaria, Romania and Yugoslavia, from about the late thirteenth century, and then from the beginning of the fourteenth century in England and the Scandinavian countries, there was a powerful suppression from Rome against magical literature and against any research which was not directly related to the Christian religion which was why some of the very serious early astronomers in Western Europe were threatened with being burned at the stake.

Leonardo daVinci did not dare to keep open records of what he did and what he thought. Anything which existed outside the realm of biblical orthodoxy was kept in cypher, in code. Alchemy was encoded.in Christian terms in Western Europe, just as it was hidden in Islamic mysticism and poetry under Islamic iconoclasmic suppression and today is encrypted in psychic terms.

There Is Nothing Which Can Draw Me Into Sleep, charcoal, Sennelier, © 1992 HEI

CHAPTER 50
TREASURE HUNTING AND ALCHEMICAL GOLD

What you should have learned:

1. That the process of finding gold on the river, whether it be by using a dry dredge, suction dredge, high bank sluice box, metal detector, or just an old fashioned pan, is a perfect analogy for finding alchemical gold, or Work on Self gold.

2. That if you break out of your normal operating limits, you can withstand all types of sensation which you never thought you could.

3. That after you see the first few flakes of gold appearing, you begin to realize you could be facing a lifetime of extremely hard work, and to not be fooled by the initial enthusiasm.

4. That, whenever possible, you do not start panning out the finds for the day in front of any tourists who may be standing on the riverbed watching. That at all times you exercise discretion, as a normal operating habit, and do not discuss things in front of others.

5. That there is such a thing as teamwork, but as far as you are concerned it is some vague notion, and that the last thing you want to experience is a pseudo sense of security.

6. That everyone out there has a different idea of how things should be done and that is one of the reasons we got into this mess in the first place. Also that behind the idea of how things should be done, there is a hint, or a smell of an all universal operating principle, which operates in everything that is done.

7. That learning to look for gold is an art on its own, and once mastered can be applied to the search for any type of gold, in any type of terrain, anywhere on the planet. In fact until you have mastered the art of looking for gold, you probably will not find very much.

8. That as you were scraping away the layers of moss, dirt, clay, etc., you were going back in history, more like antiquity, and that the river of life has flowed along the same lines as a gold-bearing river. That every flood, which brings a high water mark, also deposits fresh layers of gold.

9. That the idea of old moss as the hidden source, the unassuming, well-disguised places, is an old esoteric secret. The hidden monastery that you pass every day, that people in general in a hurry always pass by could be exactly what you are looking for. The purloined letter is hidden right in front of everyone.

10. That everything you do out there, is or could be, a mirror for the Work. That it is all applied knowledge and that applied knowledge is the first step to understanding. And if that does not get applied—then what does?

11. And possibly that the most important lesson of all, that you worked the dry-vacs wrong, and then learned to use them correctly later on, and learned to use them better.

12. That if you learn to operate any machine correctly the first time, then you have a problem. If you do not make any mistakes, how do you know that you are doing anything wrong?

What you should want to do:

1. Definitely learn how to find places rich in gold, then learn how to work them. You have to find a way to mine your gold once you have found it.

2. Talk to the river people, learn how to find good information and then what to do with it. Learn what common sense is, and how to apply it.

3. Try and understand in a practical way, how to apply the techniques of treasure hunting to Work on Self.

Safety Procedure on the River:

1. Do not work alone, always in pairs.

2. Do not leave anyone on the river alone under any circumstances ***with no exceptions***.

3. Do not stay alone at the river overnight with no exceptions.

4. Do not carry heavy loads such as equipment, etc. on your own; always travel in pairs.

General Procedure:

1. Do not drink the water unless you are sure that it is safe and that you know its source.

2. If you are not feeling well, tell someone so arrangements can be made to move you if necessary, and while it is still possible.

3. Make sure your campsite is in a good position, so if it rains you will not get washed away or flooded out.

4. Bash, ***burn***, (This does not mean to start a forest fire and wipe out half of California in the process. Exercise extreme caution with fires at all times.) and bury all rubbish and food scraps—especially food scraps.

5. Make sure that when you go to a camp you have all the necessary equipment, that it is in good working order, and that you have plenty of gas and oil supplies. ***Check your food supplies.***

6. Exercise extreme care with firearms; treat every firearm as if loaded, at all times.

7. Do not leave groups of people on the river without some means of transportation, i.e.: in case of accident or a sudden need to go to town.

CHAPTER 51
THE LOVER AND THE BELOVED

IN SOME MONASTERIES, particularly one of the monasteries at Mount Athos, there is a repetitive prayer which the monks use. This prayer is first brought into ***Kriya*** form, then it reaches a feverish pitch at which point a clamp is placed over it to harness the force, pacifying it and creating a contained explosion like a nuclear explosion within the bomb itself which never reaches the cataclysmic mushrooming outpouring of an explosive release.

There is a secret in the Bible which says, hide your light under a bushel. A bushel of wheat was equivalent to a famous coin, the ***Shekel***.

The shekel was the typical price of one lamb which one could bring as an offering at the Temple in accordance with the instructions given by the Lord in the Old Testament.

The Shekel was the only type of money permitted near the Temple. One could not bring ***coin of the realm*** into the Temple, because Roman coins carried the face of Roman emperors and representations of human forms were not permitted in the Temple, hence the money-changers—not money lenders, but money changers—outside the Temple, so that offerings could be converted from Roman coins to Jewish coins and brought to the Temple as offerings.

The shekel had on it the inscription, ***"The Lord thy God is One."***

If you understand what it means to hide your light under a bushel, you can easily see that the religious fervor manifested in many contemporary churches does not encourage containment of the Force, the inner light of religious inspiration.

In the Last Supper bread was dipped into the wine, then into salt, and then the bread was eaten, which is the equivalent of the sacrificial lamb.

The explosive power of the ***Kriyas*** in Tantra are similar to these elements of the Sacramental Meal. Religious fervor reaches a feverish pitch and the resulting spiritual explosion is hidden under a bushel-basket, which is to say, contained in the Chalice, the cup which catches the blood at the Holy Sacrifice, the Man on the Cross, as described in the volume, ***Man On the Cross****. This is the so-called ***"Lost Secret of Tantra."***

The force of the Sex Centrum begins to vibrate and move from this force. How is the force of the Sex Centrum brought into pacification so it can be contained by the Sacred Chalice, the Cup of the Alembic, and brought into use for alchemical work?

First we must know that is possible. If we use sex energy in an ordinary manner, continuing until orgasm is reached, then we must be satisfied with the uncontained explosion. The contained explosion is the Secret of Tantra, and the secret tends to keep itself, because most animals prefer the uncontained explosion of sexual release and have no wish to contain it.

There is a difference between an atomic fission explosion and atomic fusion. Fission is lunar, fusion is solar.

---

* Volume in preparation by Gateways/I.D.H.H.B., Inc., 2003

When our attention wanders, we should put it back, otherwise it will go away or wander in the endless fields of the Astral Plane. If we can keep our attention on containing the explosion and remain calm and passive throughout the sexual contact it is easy to contain the explosion and we will be able to harness The Force all day long.

This is not something we can discover just by thinking about it, reading a book or seeing a movie. It is not a passive thought brought about by the process of automatic association, but a proactive process which develops from a series of realizations which in turn are brought about by a combination of active experimentation, discipline and cognitive functions of the higher centrums.

The Method of Alchemical Sex can only be discovered through the Adoration of the Beloved, which can only be understood through direct experience and experimentation in higher realms and, in the objective sense, organizing within oneself a "corresponding" in the higher centrums of what can be called "The Adoration of the Face of the Beloved."

Loving gratitude transforms lust into love. Passion which has been harnessed can transform lust and sexual slavery into the objective form of romantic love—Grateful Adoration of the Face of the Holy Beloved, under Divine Grace and Guidance. This is precisely how the chalice is placed over the explosion, and requires some skill and perseverance to gain a true understanding of the exact process.

Imagine a horse already completely acquiescent to the saddle when the saddle is first put on. The horse just walks around. That horse is never any good for anything and has no spirit, just a stable-plug bound for the glue factory. Now take a horse with unbroken spirit and work with that horse to become one with the spirit of the horse. You need no saddle, no bridle for such a horse. You have developed a relationship between equals, and in that horse you have a friend for life, full of spirit, yet willing to take a knowing and skillful rider at need.

You can learn anything as long as you need to know, and if you need it you are given the data whether you want it or not. I told you how to contain the explosion, and I did not tell you how to contain the explosion. You know, and yet you do not know. That data is not attainable by merely thinking about it or asking more questions; it came from antiquity, yet you see it in front of you, and can only be penetrated by asking in the right way, which means by actually carrying out experiments and being willing to keep trying, regardless of the failures along the way.

When is it best to start exerting your will over the horse's will when breaking it in? You give the horse its head. Let it run; then at the height or peak of its excitement, you exert your mastership. Then and only then do you harness the horse. That is the time to "place the Chalice" upside down over the explosion.

"The Harnessing of Passion" was rediscovered by Saint Francis of Assisi, who learned it from Sufi initiates in the Middle East.

Saint Benedictus rediscovered ***"The Secret of the Inverted Chalice."*** The Inverted Chalice was widely depicted in art during the ninth to fourteenth century and was the basis for the Legend of the Holy Grail, which was added to the Arthurian cycle long after it first appeared. We can compare this concept to the Ancient Egyptian symbology of the Overturned Chalice in the Four of Cups of the Holy Tarot, the secret communication and initiation method used by Egyptian Priests for many centuries, which survives today as a simple card game and precognitive device used by psychics and fortunetellers.

Until the chalice is overturned, it is only evoking ordinary passion, and an upright Chalice does not contain the explosive nature of The Force.

In the passion of The Christ, Jesus the Nazorean, or the Healer, reenacted the ritual of the Invocation of the Presence of the Christ, the Man On the Cross.

He did everything possible to get himself nailed to the Cross, which was at that time a very common Roman punishment for rebellion among captive peoples; through his suffering and the containment of Passion on the Cross, The Christ descended. The presence of Christ came down, enveloped the Passion of Jesus the Nazorean, and thus he contained the explosion, transformed it into something else, and then ascended above the Cross, transcending organic life itself.

The only way off the Cross is through the Cross—to contain the Passion of suffering and the torment of the soul which is separated from the One, to turn the Chalice upside down, and clamp down with the Chalice on the Passion with the Force of Adoration of the Face of the Beloved, which is a very good description of the Process of Alchemical Sex.

Prayer powered by the Sexual Force is the most powerful prayer we can possibly perform, but it is useless when the sexual energy is that of animal sex, orgasmic lust.

Only humans are capable of transforming sexual energies into prayer. No other animal can do this, and no other animal is capable of prayer in any form. Most humans are not able to, nor interested in, nor willing to turn sexual energy into anything other than satisfaction of lust, much less into the Force of Prayer. The harnessing of the Sex Centrum at the height of its passion and the denial of self-satisfaction and lustful gratification for use as an intense form of Prayer is not typical of human beings and is a taste which must be developed; it does not come automatically with the life of the human biological machine and is alien to its ordinary functioning.

Imagine waiting for the height of passion and then enveloping the height of passion with adoration, literally sailing into a different octave, an entirely different wavelength of the Spectrum of Existence.

Suddenly the Motor and Instinctive Centrums are totally subdued, denied their ordinary satisfactions and transcend the organic into a much more powerful sphere of existence.

Adoration transforms a lover into the beloved, the nonphenomenal corresponding beloved. The phenomenal corresponding lover requires the total harnessing, no leaks, of passion by adoration.

With this Holy Presence powered by the sexual energies which are contained in the Chalice and denied lustful fulfillment, we can experience what it is to be One with the Holy Spirit, the mirror itself and not the reflected or the reflection.

Rather than more ephemeral it becomes the more real, more tangible, more present. Presence is in this sense actually a tangible objective substance. Once the Method has been mastered we can do this all day long without the need for physical sexual stimulation, by finding the emotional basis for love.

Nude With Armbands, E.J. Gold, charcoal, Rives BFK, © 1987 HE

CHAPTER 52
SECRETS OF THE DAKINI

We will find fragments of these ideas in many traditions. Eventually annihilation of the personal self and the urge for personal satisfactions is the result of such work in these realms.

By reversing ordinary sexual roles, the male following the female partner wherever she goes physically, emotionally and mentally, the beginning of conversion of Passion into Prayer can be achieved, but this is difficult for a man.

The male must put aside his excitement and the urge to thrust. Just as a woman learns in childbirth, the male must resist his urge to bear down, his desire to penetrate, and simply follow her wherever she goes and be passive in an active and attentive way, enveloping himself in a veil of Adoration, not of lust.

He must understand the woman's view so well that his gender-identity is not threatened by surrendering to her initiative.

He must evoke from within himself the Presence of his own Feminine Force, and from this inner force, "learn from the inside out."

He must apprentice himself to the female presence within himself, who will teach him the ways of a woman. Then she thrusts. The pump is reversed; the flow goes the other direction.

He accommodates to her every movement and mood. A woman knows instinctively how to follow a man's every motion. Usually he initiates, she follows; now in order to master alchemical methods, we must reverse this ordinary organic process.

The male must learn to allow her to lead him where she will—"Wither Thou Goest, There Also Shall I Go."

As with the sitar and tabla, it is possible to reverse the lead and the response.

He learns to answer her, and she in turn learns to build passion, to thrust, to bear down, to push, to evoke passionate response without lustful satisfactions.

He learns to pay attention with Adoration; when passion reaches its crescendo, he simply answers her passion and they transcend together into a higher realm, not allowing passion to fulfill itself in orgasmic release, but in an ecstasy of another kind.

Without training it is extremely easy for a man to flip into lustful orgasmic release, which is the Dark Side of the Force, and is merely the flip side of Anger and Frustration.

At the crescendo of nonorganic passion, through the invocation of the presence of objective love—through invocation of adoration, we perform a deliberate act to invoke the adoration of the presence, clamping down on the organic passion which suddenly begins to burn with an intense white heat, bringing it into a slower, more productive heat. This is True Alchemy.

The heat begins to build and build, as controlled explosion after controlled explosion occurs within the Chalice. The Chalice begins to heat, transforms into the Crucible, and then becomes a heat resistant Chalice which burns white hot.

At this point, an otherworldly glow begins to infuse everything—

reaches maximum; then the heat slowly begins to dissipate, die back down to embers. It does not melt, it fuses and dies back down to a very small warm point, ready to use again.

What occurs as a result of this activation is what is called ***"Transformation."*** In other words, Transformation is a natural by-product of contained alchemical heat contained to a point of fusion. Transformational side effects take place naturally but as by-products of Alchemical Sex, not as the primary objective.

William Blake shows a picture of objective prayer; it looks like a father-mother in the yab-yum posture; it depicts a female angel with her legs wrapped around God/Jehovah.

This is actually reversed. In this technique she would stand, thrust, and he would contain her with his legs wrapped around her. It is God portrayed as a female angel, the Shekinah, standing and thrusting, and he is wrapped around her containing her passion with adoration.

Man in nature is a pump, but by the application of attention, intention and energy, he can reverse this automatic organic flow.

Most Tibetan ***thangkas*** show the male standing, with ***dakinis*** on him, she with adoration. The black ***thangkas*** of the ***Kagyu*** and of the ***Nyingmapa***, show the reverse and were used in the inner temples where a specially trained priest and priestess remained. The Tibetan terms of ***dakinis, devas, asuras*** correspond, depending on what order, with the same entities we talk about as angels, archangels, principalities, powers, and so forth.

Angels are not a cultural phenomena; angels are very real. However, the most common descriptions of angels are merely cultural and religious phenomena.

An invoked presence is nonphenomenal by definition; it does not have a phenomenal formation. What matters in an invocation is who is there, not what you see. Never mind what happens—it is who is there that is more important. The presence is more important than the manifestation; the manifestation is unnecessary for pure presence.

It is said that the Tribe of Israel is intended to reunite the Shekinah with the Absolute. This does not mean once and forever, because the Shekinah has been reunited with the Absolute many times before. But through periodic fragmentation and inattention, the Shekinah and the

Absolute break apart. They can be reunited not only through Objective Prayer, but through the arousal through any form, not just sexual, of passion and containment with adoration.

The Absolute is burning with love for the Beloved. The eye in the pyramid represents the eye that is in adoration of the Beloved. Adoration is the capstone on the pyramid. The invisible capstone, an invoked presence, nonphenomenal—that is why we do not see the capstone placed on the pyramid which covers the pyramid and becomes turned in on itself until a heat develops.

First we must consciously overturn the Chalice which immediately transforms it to the crucible, and the furnace begins to burn with intense but slow heat.

When completed, the fire begins to glow hotter and hotter to an intense white heat. This takes time, sexually speaking, and may well require continuous work anywhere from a few hours up to as much as eighteen hours to achieve this finely attuned heat.

In other forms of Objective Prayer, the intensity can be brought about in a different way. There can be a ritual in which a certain type of passion can be aroused, capped by a precise form of adoration, corresponding to that higher form of objective, impartial passion.

To try to cap one form of passion with another form of adoration not in correspondence crushes and destroys it. Human beings ordinarily try to destroy adoration with passion.

Because males and females do not objectively know these ideas, it is almost impossible for an alchemist to find a partner who knows enough to reverse or transcend ordinary animal sex.

If you understand what it means for a man to invoke the presence of a female entity into himself, and learn all her secrets from her including the big female sexual secret which takes the form, "Let him have his way with you; show him a good time; show him you are having a good time," and when he is finished, do not press the issue, and do your best to let the reverberations die down by themselves.

Another way of saying this is that when a man is finished, all the force is washed out of him. Once a woman is "turned on," she is never finished—maybe days later, the reverberations will die down somewhat, but they never completely disappear.

A male Alchemist must learn to follow the reverberations, help her to follow the vibration.

A woman is, rightly so, terrified to fully arouse herself; she uses certain manifestations to turn it into a straight transaction, to convince him to have a good time and that she is having a good time.

She uses manifestations that are flattering to him. Most men, if they discovered that they are selected by the women, and that she is the director, in fact, of the encounter, would be horrified. She plays him like a fisherman plays a trout, cunningly, allowing him to believe that he is free, then sinking the hook and reeling him in.

Most men are very easily flattered. If they knew that calculated, exactitude manifestations form the major part of a woman's lovemaking they would look for the nearest shotgun because of what they would think of themselves. They are very flattered and convinced by the dramatic, convinced of their superior lovemaking because of her passion.

The secret of the woman is that she does not turn herself on; it is simply a straight transaction. This is the pity of human sex. Women do not know male secrets.

Unless she is secure enough to know that her man will follow her reverberations, it is all an act, calculated theater; she may enjoy it or not.

Her manifestations are designed to maintain the relationship and thus her security and the security of her home and children, to fulfill the DNA-directed nesting urges and territorial imperatives she feels, and of which she is, if she is organically inclined, a total prisoner.

On the other hand, when you see a man lost in the clouds of passion, he is really gone. What you see is true; it is no act, and this loss of self is his real goal, annihilation into personal oblivion.

The way of the shaman is to become a man with a woman inside him who is his teacher; to teach him the way of the woman.

A woman does not need to learn the secrets of a man; she is infinitely accommodating and not threatened by gender reversal by taking the manifestations of a man.

She can get into pants and not feel threatened, but when a man puts on a skirt he feels threatened—he is in drag and if he lives in a repressive society, he can be made to feel shame, but oddly enough, that very same society will easily accept women in men's clothes.

A woman, even with no alchemical training, can adapt quite easily to the passionate, while a male without alchemical discipline has great difficulty adapting to any form of adoration.

In fact he must have his body or nervous system finely attuned, which takes serious training and skill, and he must learn to respond as a woman's body, emotions and mind will respond.

He cannot do this just by reading and thinking about it. This skill requires patience to develop, and it also requires the presence of a female entity within him, to adjust his nervous system accordingly, to teach him by inhabiting, occupying him, something close to mediumship or possession.

CHAPTER 53
THE SECRET KEEPS ITSELF

A PSYCHIC or Spiritualistic Medium goes fishing and grabs for everything; true Shamanism is knowing exactly what you are after, and throwing away everything else. A Shaman or Alchemist does not get caught up in the phenomenal self-gratifications which may engulf a Medium.

The secret of the real monasteries is exactly the same. Remember the passion of Jesus, the adoration of the Christ. Jesus was a man who learned to invoke the nonphenomenal entity called the Christ. For a long time Jesus was just a healer, a medium, a psychic.

By accident in the second year of what is called his ministry, he discovered how to invoke the Christ on himself. He put himself in the position of necessity and learned the secret of the Christ—to invoke the Christ on himself.

Before he was just an ordinary man, after he was transformed into something far beyond a man, something very different from a man because he was able to call down on himself the presence of the Christ which over time had a transforming effect.

Over a period of time the presence of the Christ became so powerful that it resulted in the annihilation of Jesus, and the arising of a new form of the Christ. Jesus learned from the Christ, to be like the Christ, so he became Jesus Christ, Jesus who had become the Christ.

The operant laws are the same; yet each case is always slightly different, different specific conditions. Conditions for the invocation of the Christ require time, place and people—set, setting and participants.

The equation holds for conditions in the equivalent, but we change variables in the equivalent.

You hear and you do not hear. In order to take advantage of these sexual secrets and alchemical results, you must have will, unity, powerful attention and necessity. If you do not, you cannot use this data.

Why would prayer be associated with sex? Such an association is the dirtiest, most repugnant thing to Westerners—prayer being the least likely thing to be associated with sex in the West, but not to Eastern religions and philosophies.

Prayer is associated with the most holy, sacred activity in a church. So in this way, the Secret Keeps Itself.

If you wanted to keep a secret, where would you put it? On the mantlepiece labeled ***"Top Secret, Open Me, Read Me!"***

If you wanted to perpetuate something, not have it tampered with, you would hide it in something that would be taboo in every culture.

In all the descriptions of sexual containment, the man seems to have a more difficult task. He must go against the fear of a gender-threatening situation.

If a man tries to imitate a woman, he plunges into a false overblown caricature of femininity and overexaggeration of what he thinks is feminine, creating a cartoon of a woman.

If a woman tries to imitate a man, she goes for masculinity, and then she looks like what is called a "bull-dyke." Both resemble a bad actor who overplays a role. A "bull-dyke" is overacting the male part, having aggressive manifestations and cruelty, but this is not a man, just as an "overblown nelly" is not a woman. Masculine and feminine manifestations do not tell the real story—it is inside, not outside, that male and female exist, although physically, both male and female organic forms have exactly the same internal organs.

In order for a man to learn a woman's secrets—how a woman wraps a man in adoration—a male must have a teacher, and the teacher cannot be from the outside.

For this it is necessary to join the Seaman's Union. It is well-known that nobody can join the Seaman's Union just by walking in the door, because you cannot join the Union unless you have been to sea for six months, and you cannot go to sea unless you have joined the seaman's union—the ultimate "Catch 22."

Similarly, we cannot call down a female entity unless we know at least some of the female's secrets, and a male cannot learn the secrets of feminine force unless he can evoke from within himself that female entity which is his "better half." One must find a way to break that dilemma.

Two serpents eating each other's tails, ***ourobourous***, the Taoist formulation of yin and yang is a double spiral-helix, one with a spine of white, the other with a spine of black.

Every woman hopes to find a man who is able to develop this side of himself and enter into her private world. A pretty boy will understand less, as a pretty woman will understand less.

The prettier or "cuter" the man or woman, the less chance they have to understand these principles, because they are not driven to understand.

We always look for the wrong thing. A woman is trained to adore; the male is trained for passion. He looks for sport, another roadside attraction, another conquest, another victim; she looks for the pretty boy, the softer, more romantic and gentler sort who might be able to treat her as she wishes to be treated.

The couple is doomed to failure when they select each other in the phenomenal by organic rules and desires. What you see is what you get. In the nonphenomenal, what you do ***not*** see is what you get, and if you are a serious alchemist, this is what you are looking for.

CHAPTER 54
SELECTING A PARTNER

IF YOU KNOW what you really want in a partner, you can make a non-mechanical, nonorganically driven selection.

What kind of partner you select depends upon whether your personal, phenomenal self or your work, nonphenomenal self is more powerful.

It is hard to give up your personal drives, your desire for organic satisfactions.

To go without satisfaction a long time, to learn how to live in the nonphenomenal, you must be patient. You might not be strong enough to survive the journey to a different stream. The most often asked question is, "Are we there yet?"

You do not recognize what you are looking for; you do not recognize when you see it. "I cannot wait any longer, I am tired of waiting..." This sounds like children in a car, going to grandma's house. "It is taking too long..."

We have come to a point where man's ability to accept the technology we have has gone beyond the intolerable. The same idea follows with sensation; man goes along with it, then over a certain point he wishes it to be gone—to be rid of sensation, to eliminate sensation because he feels as if he does not have control. Sensation is nevertheless there, no matter what the reason.

Ordinary help is impossible and special help cannot be given, except under special circumstances. At the same time you must live according to the idea as if that option were available to you.

If you ever catch yourself in the middle of a yawn try to close your mouth while you are yawning—that is what it is like to clamp down over passion—it is the same or similar sensation. Basically you are containing an explosion, which is not easy. The trouble is adoration has no payoff for a man, nor does a woman derive any payoff from passion. She does not derive from it what a man derives from it. She can only derive manifestations of passion; she will feel something, although not passion.

A man once out in space...he is gone, and one cannot get him to take a sharp turn in any direction. A woman at the height of passion can stop and look at her watch, tell the time, and in fact, often thinks of it.

I am talking openly about things which are extremely secret. However, it does not matter; people rarely actualize what they hear or even learn. For example, there was a man who became a millionaire from selling real estate. He wrote a book and was interviewed telling a nationwide audience his method. He also set up classes to teach others how to become a millionaire. When interviewed he reported that from the study he made of those who attended his classes, he discovered that people who meet with the slightest setback, or with whom a problem arose, or who had the slightest consideration about his system are those who leave his classes or quit their efforts to become a millionaire.

The frustration syndrome is one barrier. Someone who tries to follow what he teaches without changing anything to meet the conditions he encounters does not see the principles. There is another barrier—the barrier of failure which actually is an important part of learning.

The millionaire reported that it did not bother him to fail. For two years nothing happened except hard work. It never seemed as if he could see the end of the tunnel.

His follow-up study on his students revealed that most people collapse long before they see the light at the end of the tunnel. Some people go through the whole process and start becoming a millionaire and through some quirk do not feel deserving of it and therefore cause themselves to fail. There was one person who succeeded in becoming a millionaire and did not enjoy having the money; so he dropped everything, dissolved all his assets and became something else. Actually only a few people who studied this method followed through and succeeded in their aim.

Conception is not a consideration in alchemy; there may be conception, there may not be. The consideration is a completely irrelevant question. If it is not irrelevant you need to examine your attitudes and how they will affect the magical operation.

Alchemical Sex is not sex. It may look to you like sex, feel like sex, smell like sex, but it is not sex. Passion is harnessed by Adoration which does not mean control but rather to contain an explosion.

People essentially say, "If I do not meet any of the conditions of alchemy, can I still do alchemical work?" They already know the answer—of course not.

I cannot do your work for you, nor can I give you the inner discipline you need for such work; all I can give you are the basic conditions for work, hints, fragments and clues.

If we ask a mystic, one who has seen God Face to Face as it were, he or she will tell us that there is no such thing as social religion; it is irrelevant—there is only God.

Someone who is truly religious cannot comprehend the need for ritualized social religion, which is to say, a church which imposes ritual upon others and insists on only one way to see God.

We are on a journey to see God. What are we going to do when we arrive? It is like going on a journey to our place of business, but when we arrive there, we must get to work.

It is not enough just to say, "I have arrived." It is not appropriate to announce your arrival, roll up your sleeves, arrange your desk, make a few telephone calls, powder your nose and then do your nails.

By the time you get ready, it is all over. You must arrive ready to work, do your work, then leave. When the whistle blows signalling the end of the work day, do not stay after work hours. Follow the union rules. Take your breaks and take them when you are supposed to so you do not disturb everyone else's schedule.

Someone once asked me what my objective work is. I will tell you now. I am a tailor; that is what I do for a living. That is my objective work. I am a tailor in the sense of making suits—sheers, denses, opaques. A lot of sheers, in fact, my fabrics are so sheer, you can see right through, completely, 100 percent sheer. They give perfect support, perfect contour and perfect fit.

My grandfather was a tailor, and my great grandfather was a tailor, a very bad one at that. In Russia one did not need to be a good tailor. In Russia there were only two sizes of costumes—too large and too small. One size fits all was invented by necessity and came into being in the Roman Empire. The toga is "one size fits all," and the only difference is the little safety pins.

One can stumble into these secrets but not have the keys, the catalysts, and one cannot find them without special help. Ninety-eight percent one can stumble into; the other two percent one must rely on transmission from the ancients, depending on some data passed on from antiquity.

For two percent we rely on transmissions from the ancients; we need help of a special kind. This also depends on the risk. The more serious we become the greater the risk. The less I think you can take, the less demands I make on you. The more polite I am the less I respect you. The more I berate someone, the more I respect them.

We like to think we have achieved a lot; it is nice to think we have achieved something already. Actually you have not taken the first step. If you had, it would be obvious, visible at a glance. The same way as the nonphenomenal world is visible at a glance. So far, we are just gathering the data and re-establishing basic ideas with which we are working. Then you will be asked to take a step, and the step you will be asked to take is the one thing you think is the most irrelevant, least applicable to your work, most ridiculous and the most annoying thing.

CHAPTER 55
DATA CELLS

YOU MAY WONDER how it is that I have so much data available to me on so many different subjects. It is possible through accumulation of organic and inorganic cells which are data-corresponding to accumulate data with them and through them.

The apprentice system is learning by doing, in what is called "on the job training." You cannot possibly learn enough in one thousand years to do the Work, so you must get help from someone already in the Work.

You are not a walking encyclopedia, so you must have within your easy reach the cumulative experience of tens of thousands or even millions or trillions of years of many different realities viewed through the eyes and processed through the brains of many different types of individuals who have achieved many things on many different levels.

We want to be able to retrieve and absorb the data instantly, and this we can do by accessing data colonies within our organic cells—this can also provide data for us which can lead us to yet other data colonies not ordinarily accessible, and through Alchemical means, we can find and obtain other higher levels of data colonies which are not organic and which are virtually inexhaustible fountains of knowledge.

If you can capture a scout, the scout can sometimes tell you where the general is. We can also reach and work with data cells and data colonies that are not actually there—that are long dead, perhaps trillions of years ago, which come to us from other star systems, other galaxies and even other universes, through Black Holes and Space Strings.

If you cannot access data cells and data colonies, you do not hear and do not see, and have no real knowledge other than that of direct experience gathered by yourself in local time and space, which is a small amount of very limited data which will do you little good and which may not be relevant to your work.

You are capable of receiving the full impact of trillions of years of experience in a single instant. For instance, suppose you knew totally instinctively everything that Paracelsus had ever learned, and could apperceive this in one brilliant flash.

You are entirely too casual. You are not careful enough in how you keep yourself. You cannot prepare dirty ground to receive clean seeds. The whole idea of Purification is a practical idea, upon which all spiritual work rests.

In the same way that you would, for instance, sterilize soil before you start certain delicate bulbs, certain rose bushes—you sterilize the soil first. It is a very elaborate process, not things you just dump in the ground and expect to grow. You do with beans, corn, even tomatoes, unless you want very special and very fine tomatoes. Some kinds of Italian tomatoes have to have the soil sterilized.

In order to receive data cells, you yourself, your soil, your organic form, your organic body must be clean, be sterile, free of poisons, pH-balanced. Ph-balance is almost the equilibrium in your work. None of your human civilization values are going to hold.

None of your social games are going to be of any value to you or of any use to you, and they will be disastrous. If you hold onto them, even for a little while, you will find that at some point, first you are confronted with the idea, with the definite dilemma of having to give these up. One or the other has to be sacrificed.

Either you can have a life as you know it—have your organic destiny—or you can have the Work. You can either have personal aims or the work aims. And the work aims will never serve the personal aims, and the work aims never bring about what you personally want to have happen for yourself.

So if you think you can satisfy or achieve the satisfactions of a personal aim through the Work, you are in for a horrible disappointment. And if you think you have gotten rid of these civilization scars, the scars of romance, the scars of normal and imaginary life, you are probably mistaken. Even the very best have fallen, on the basis that they thought they had eliminated the scars of romantic, imaginary life in themselves. What is worse is your search for instantaneous intimacy, whatever that means.

You come into the world alone and leave the world alone. If you think that you are not alone, it is an illusion. You are alone. You can be among friends, but you are still alone. If you are unable to be alone you are doomed to be alone. If you do not mind being alone then you do not have to be alone.

When we work on ourselves, the cells of our body begin to undergo a transformation. This transformation can be interrupted at any time, up to a certain point, but it is a very long time before they cannot be interrupted or reversed. We can be thankful for that because it is possible to make mistakes along the way and we do not want to crystallize ourself in an organic way as we are now.

The cells of the body begin to crystallize by the accumulation of higher substances. The organism is a chemical factory, as well as being a machine in general. There are definite chemistries involved. It is actually a very elaborate chemical factory. The balances of the chemical factory are even more exact than the balances of the machine.

The chemical factory takes in certain foods. The foods are threefold—food, air and impressions. Actually these three kinds of food are ***contained*** in food, air, impressions; they are not those things themselves. The substances that are contained in food are brought into this system; they break down and produce certain chemicals, in air, and then in impressions. They are broken down into certain chemical compositions.

Among those chemistries are certain chemical elements in very trace amounts, which when exposed to electrical charges in the body, begin to create entirely new substances for the body which are not native to the body, but which are native to the body's chemical factory, at a certain point. You could say that they are refined substances. The chemical factory produces only so much of these higher substances per day. These higher substances are those exact things upon which Lunar Parasite feeds, which we call the moon.

Because Lunar Parasite takes that which is not used by the chemical factory or by the machine itself, at the end of the day one is ordinarily left with nothing of higher substances. All the higher substances have been used either by the factory or by the machine or by Lunar Parasite, leaving nothing whatever. Yet these are the substances which we use for work.

These are the substances which are the basis of our work in the Alchemical Factory, the alchemical laboratory. We want to change it from a chemical factory to an Alchemical Factory which means we begin with those substances which ordinarily the chemical factory ends with, which means further refinement of those substances and then their use. But how are we going to further refine something that we are not left with, that is taken from us everyday?

First of all, we must learn to disallow Lunar Parasite's theft of these substances. Second, we must learn to produce additional higher substances which we ordinarily would not produce, and which are produced by a special kind of suffering which is the nonmanifested negative emotion.

By nonmanifesting negative emotions, we begin to accumulate

more higher substances than we would otherwise accumulate. There are more details, but basically the idea is the chemical. But there aren't nearly enough of the higher substances even for our general use, let alone our Work use.

We must prevent the loss of higher substances and we must generate additional higher substances. As we do this, the cells in our body begin to crystallize in a particular way. If we worked at this for some time, the entire body would crystallize cell by cell in a particular way. Should these crystallized cells survive into the future and be absorbed by someone who is receptive organically, they become part of the organic formation and begin to take root and colonize themselves. These crystallized cells begin to reproduce the personality of the body of the individual in the Work who has separated from the Organic Body.

The Organic Body which remains, decomposes, finds its way to other bodies eventually, and is absorbed by a body. Even one cell is sufficient to begin to take root and begin to form this colonization—to colonize and reproduce itself among human cells, among the flesh cells.

Data cells are absorbed into ourselves in a variety of ways—by ingestion, aerosol breathing and by any means by which a cell can find its way into the body.

Sometimes by sweat absorption—in fact, sweat absorption is a very common vector for the exchange of organic substances.

The only cells which concern us in this work are those which are crystallized. Unfortunately, they can also be crystallized as a "Lunar Parasite" and what we hope for are data cells and colonies which are grounded in the Work, not in Lunar entities.

Inevitably, some cells find their way here and there. They can even be cells which have been charcoaled through cremation, but the formation in many cases, survives. The ashes contain enough that it can be transmitted through the ash. In fact, the ashes of Saints are very often used on the bodies of devotees.

These crystallized cells are an indirect result of the accumulation of substances. The substances, as they accumulate, begin to crystallize the cells nucleically. The cells then do not break down in the sense they do ordinarily. One of the effects this has is that the body would exist far beyond its ordinary deterioration.

The degeneration of the organs means very little to the contamination of the body. The organs have less to do with the running of the body than the cells in general.

Would it be possible for this Organic Body if I were able to crystallize higher substances?

No. Accumulation of higher substances would have the effect of crystallizing the cells little by little. Let us say that the body was cremated and some of the ash found its way into the drinking water of someone. And his body is prepared, his general organic presence is prepared, clean, receptive to it, then the cell can take root.

If it can take root, then it can begin to reproduce itself using other cells and begin to form a definite colonization which, at a certain point, begins to become powerful enough to exert a definite psychological force and even to take on a full personality, which would be a reproduction of the original personality to some degree.

You would be able to draw upon the experience directly as if it were yourself, so that the memories of that individual are your own memories. The knowledge of that individual would be your own knowledge. Suddenly you wake up one morning able to play the violin, for some inexplicable reason.

To some degree, some types of crystallized data cells have already entered your organic form. If you did not have crystallized data cells in some already quite advanced colonies, you would not be here, could not be here, right now. You could not sit here unless you had these.

Certain data cell colonies can take root, others cannot. There are some data cell colonies which cannot take root in the presence of certain forms of negative emotion.

Certain negative manifestations which produce acidic qualities, which throw the pH balance off sufficiently, cannot take root. In the presence of certain romantic moods, data cell colonies are unable to take root. Certain types of cynicisms make it impossible. Certain types of ultra beliefs make it impossible.

There are very exact conditions for the rooting, sprouting, germination of data cell colonies. But also, there are some, which under the most adverse conditions, can take root, although they are only good for Magnetic Centrum. They create a cellular Magnetic Centrum. Magnetic Centrum is cellular; it has nothing to do with iron filings. Someone in there says, get to the school—drives you to the school.

Data cells and colonies are directly linked to your knowledge, understanding, experience, and so forth. Which means that right now they would not be that useful. You have to somehow combine stability and a steady state mood with love-sickness for the Work. And a Moving-Instinctive Centrum stability.

Genetic transmission means that you inherited it from your grandfather, or greatgrandfather, greatgrandmother, grandmother. It came through your family lineage. What I am trying to get you to understand is, it can come through a hamburger, sweat, a handshake. One cell, if it takes root, can form a colony. It cannot come through DNA because data cell colonies are carried nucleically. They are not carried in the amino acid chain exactly.

You carry it in the nucleic fluids, which even though they become dessicated, have the minute particles which immediately on resuscitation reform themselves electrically to the brain. They have nodes, synapses, synaptic junctions, and so forth. But in a very minute formation, in the cellular water. It is like embryonic fluid, amniotic fluid.

The ashes of a Saint can be formulated and ground up with other substances which make its ingestion and assimilation possible and the sly man can take this and know more Yoga than a yogi who studies for twenty years—just by ingesting the ashes of a great yogi—if it takes.

Hopefully, we have the introduction, first of all of sufficient policing colonies which kill off the organic cells as they come in or as they try to form a colony. The organic colonies will lose, but this is bacterial warfare which is well within the cellular structure of the body. If it should happen, then it happens. The organic cell colony becomes too strong. It is one of the dangers.

In preparing ground, fertile ground for introduction of seeds for germination, there is always the danger of introduction of weeds, some of which may choke out the intentional plants, maybe completely—maybe choke out the whole garden. We have to burn out the whole garden and start over again. It sometimes happens that a garden can be overtaken so strongly that we have to turn it over, burn it out, and introduce killing solution into the soil and allow the soil to remain fallow for a year or two before we can reintroduce plants, and before the soil is cleared enough of the poisons for anything to grow there to be safe to us.

CHAPTER 56
WORK INSTINCT

Some people say that if you throw seeds on the ground, some will grow and some probably will not. But usually the ground is not fertile enough or is too fertile. The pH needs to be balanced.

So what you are doing is not the Work, unless furrowing, plowing and so forth are the Work. These can happen ***before*** the Work or concurrently ***with*** the Work.

If you did not already have data cells you would not be in the school. But you do not know how to use them. There are a very small group of "Seekers After Truth." Everyone has to have a little Lubovedsky—love of knowledge—a little Prince Mukransky—a patron—but also someone who has been everywhere. Everyone has to have a Soloviev.

If you translate these words you would see that each represents a definite type of data cell colony in the old man's general organic presence.

For something to be achieved it has to be a deactivated defused desire. Sometimes things can be accomplished that are exact and definite, but these are very ordinary things. For example, it became right to go sailing today. Not before has it been right.

You have to wait for an exact opportunity and be awake enough to recognize it—and take it—which means that if you are going to take advantage of an opportunity or a moment of freedom, you cannot be too busy and involved in anything else. Because the opportunity is very subtle, it is easy to miss. Even the slightest distraction can throw us off. It can be any distraction at all.

For example, in the bazaar, the passing of a pretty girl can distract our attention for a moment which could be ***the*** moment. Perhaps we are distracted by our hopes for an idea such as monetary reform. We can even be distracted by these ideas ourselves if we are too much in the formatory. Even the Movements—the most objective thing we can do with our Moving Centrum in the beginning work—can be a distraction, but they would be no distraction unless we knew how to see an opportunity.

Opportunities never come in the expected form—never. If they conformed to our ideas they would not be genuine opportunities, but simply more of the same.

What is more of the same?

Have you ever been to a university? You have paper? Did you ever hear of a degree called B.S.? Everyone knows what B.S. means. Well, M.S. is "more of the same." Have you ever heard of a Ph.D? Ph.D means piled higher and deeper.

Do you wish for more of the same? What do you wish more than anything for yourself?

To prepare for the Work is not so hard. Any idiot with just a little discipline can do that. But to find the Work, we need to be like a bear catching fish—very quick, very exact and very patient. A bear knows how to wait. He never goes to sleep until he accomplishes his aim. If he goes to sleep for even one second, the fish may escape his attention.

We must be very watchful with attention for the Work if it passes our way. This we can practice by being watchful on ourselves, but we must not be too caught up with ourselves to catch the fish.

What does the Work look like? How will we recognize it when it goes by?

How does the bear recognize fish? He is hungry and he knows food. For this he needs no school. If we could catch the Work with instinct like Mr. Bear catches his fish, then we would not need a school. Much of the Work in preparation is to be able to recognize the Work and be able to catch it, and of course, to speak its special language and perform its special tasks. For this, ordinary man has no instinct whatever, and from ordinary man we came. If anything, our instincts are the worst possible, almost always the reverse of what they ought to be. But instinct cannot be readily taught.

I did not say it would be easy. Instinct is always taught by indirect means. To catch the Work must be done by pure instinct. It must come from the skin; formatory is too slow. We must be like a mother to the Work. A mother always instinctively recognizes her children no matter how they may have changed in appearance.

A certain amount of preparation is required in the beginning for anything to happen, but then at a certain point it is just a question of finish work.

Once the major parts of your house are up, the finish work can be done more or less at leisure. Then one can begin to live in the house even though the details are not complete.

I do not store data; data passes through me like a shower. I transform data and use it like food—food, air, impressions and data. For example, I use food and discard waste. Most people do not discard; they save it in the brain or nervous system. I use data like food, so rather than storing knowledge, I am left with understanding.

Data is like lower or negative emotion, understanding is like higher emotion. Understanding is an inchoate formation of how and why, not attached to anything. Data contains who, what, where, when. I am never that interested in the why of anything. The how interests me occasionally.

When we take in food, what happens? We pass it through our body and dump out the waste products. Before the waste products of data are discarded I have a rainbow shower. The rainbow shower is a shimmering shower of change, the result of which is understanding. Everything that is a genuine part of me is affected by the data in some way. The changes are very minute. Data in itself is useless; it only clutters the brain. Every day I take a good healthy data dump.

What about special meditations, for example, the cathartic meditation?

Catharsis is a cathartic—you get the same result; you take an enema before the food has a chance to act.

What about fasting from impressions?

If we do not eat between fasts, then fasting is absurd. If we are using impressions and data properly we do not need to fast, we have no constipation of ideas.

It is very important to take a good healthy data dump sometime during the day. The process to understand how this is done is understanding itself. Understanding of that happens as we start to do it.

For example, in the 40s we had the technology to send a rocket to the moon, but no one said it could be done. There was one transformational trigger that was missing. It was not anticipated by any Science Fiction writer. That was that the moon landing would be telecast live in color. Until somebody says it can be done, it cannot be done.

Data stored for a long time is a waste product. Data does get involuntarily stored. Contemporary human's main pathological illness is involuntary organic storage of data. Our educational system conditions us to save data. Contemporary humans do not know how to learn. I look at a book and when I look I remember about it. I sense, feel, smell and touch ideas. I do not process the book as words.

I can taste better than I know. Most of my process of thinking is taste. I feel food, air, impressions, ideas more than I process through words. It is an inchoate body inside me slightly smaller than my real one. This body contains everything necessary for my operation on a daily basis, even exotic pondering. Everything I use each day has to be relearned new. I have a vague taste of what it must be. I am operating on minimal memory, just enough to retain the taste.

The illness of involuntary organic storage of data is a direct cause for the disease of tomorrow. For understanding today you do not need tomorrow today. I do not even know if I was alive or dead yesterday, but I can taste it. If I do not need to know something why retain it?

Organic humans prefer to think they possess what they do not and do not possess what they do. Self-love and vanity prevent them from ever becoming fully aware of the terror of the situation. They live in a limited reality which is different from a fantasy. They prevent perception of reality by fantasy.

A person infected by a poisonous lineage may try to continue in the Work. They can only go so far and then they become anguished by their inability to continue.

At some point one is not subject to poison lineage. This point is reached after transference, after the third transference. The poison lineage only affects the organic.

Figure Study #77, E.J. Gold, charcoal, Arches, © 1987 HEI

CHAPTER 57
HABITS

It is possible, through concentrated attention and effort, to eradicate the effect of one's total past existence throughout time and space—that is to say, the results of our essence-habits and, through the combined effort of attention and will, to continue to direct oneself along totally new lines of behavior, by replacing the habits that are already there with entirely new ones.

At the death of the body the re-establishment of the habits that were there before are re-instituted if one has not replaced them with new habits, and one becomes the same as one was before birth—one's essence will not have really changed unless the old habits were fully and profoundly replaced with new habits.

One's essence—using the term "essence" to describe the Body of Habits, which survives beyond thought, beyond the mind, beyond the body, beyond the identity, beyond knowledge—can be altered permanently beyond the time-space discontinuum through this combined effort of attention and will.

The effect of a new Body of Habits can be felt and sensed during the Alchemical Sex experience. Through constant practice, a new Body of Habits can be brought into a permanent and stable condition, which means that one will not tend to "revert to type," which is the fate of those who only change behavior in a superficial way, and not in the Deep Self.

To "awaken the essence" means to create consciously an entirely new Body of Habits, through the process of replacement and constant reinforcement through the use of attention, powered by will.

One does not do this by ***merely deciding*** to change a habit and having it change within the instant. The "decision" to change a habit is not enough, because within moments, a different "I" will emerge and the decision will be lost and forgotten.

Even full recognition of the habit does not bring it out of automaticity. One cannot reprogram that which is beyond the mind and beyond thought through the mind and through thought. In short, one cannot metaprogram on a lower biological level. One must go directly to the high level program of the essence itself, and the application of constant will and attention are necessary, far beyond the mere "wish" to change and a momentary decision to do so, as one would make a New Year's Resolution.

Occasionally in ordinary life we will reach this level of metaprogramming simply because we are living on a repetitive basis, but ordinarily one does not actually change habits and cannot change them without replacing them with something else, something of equal force and equal weight.

At some point, if it becomes a matter of life and death, of urgent necessity, one can find the will to make these changes, and the continued will to work at them until the changes become permanent. This "will-to-work" expresses itself only over a period of years, never over a single weekend workshop.

A result of Alchemical Sex might be that we go into a condition of high certainty on some personal issues, but we must ascend to the level of work in which work becomes almost an obsession in order to work on our basic Essence habits.

Habits are the only thing about us that will survive the death of the organic self, which is to say, the body and the mind.

Our organic identity will be lost at death—our sense of connectedness and personal organic memory will be lost, but our habits and tendencies will not.

We are nothing more than a surviving accumulation of habits—that is the real us—just a bundle of habits.

This is what makes us unique, in a sense. And, in another sense, in quite a more real way, it makes us not at all unique; it makes us the same in so many ways. Our real uniqueness cannot be expressed while our accumulated organic habits are dominant over our Essence habits.

We finally become unique as human beings when we can consciously replace organic self-pampering gratification habits with Essence Work habits to the point where they really, actually exist.

If we consciously replace an old established organic habit with a new one which reflects our Will to Work, the first time we create that new habit does not mean that it is a habit.

It cannot be called a "habit" until it is habitual, which means, when it has replaced the old habit fully and completely, and we no longer need to consciously create it, even though it was in the first place intentionally created.

We cannot begin to create a habit deliberately until we can see that there is a problem with our old organic habits. Only then can we even begin to learn how to make and keep a decision and to actually carry it out, not just once, but with integrity, to its fullest possible completion.

Integrity simply means that we will feel the same way about it tomorrow as we did today.

Some of the habitual things we do on a daily basis are self-contradictory. We have many different attitudes. All those attitudes rob us of our real power, our energy, taking these forces from us and using them to keep themselves alive and to feed their desire to survive.

Usually there is so much garbage in the way of doing work that Alchemical Sex has a secondary purpose, which is to say, it becomes valuable in clearing away some of our personal garbage.

There are so many habitual attitudes and actions within us which have become so automatic that we cannot see them, although others can easily point them out to us, that they make it impossible to view them through their pervading presence and ordinariness.

This prevents us from understanding our ordinary habitual manifestations and from even seeing them clearly, and in this way, prevents us from arriving at the Deep Self, so by providing the necessity to change those organic habits which through familiarity have become invisible to us, Alchemical Sex becomes valuable for our Self-Knowledge as well as in other higher ways.

Many humans are incapable of creating emotions, rather than letting emotions just happen, but this form of "sacred acting" combined with intentional changes in posture and other automaticities provide us with the means to exercise our will and make it work for our work.

The ability to alter even the smallest organic habit depends on so much work beforehand, and represents such a powerful ego-threat that, once again, The Secret Keeps Itself.

Those who have too much ego in the way, and for whom the body and emotions are everything, are simply not prepared for the Work, and regardless of how much effort is put out toward them, they have no inner will, no strength, no power over the ego, and so they never really are ready for the struggle that precedes entry into the Work, because they are too attached to their personal problems and agendas to do any serious work at all.

Someone who is so important that how they feel, what they think, what their attitudes are, are more important than the Work itself will in point of fact never develop the will to work under ***any*** condition that could be set up in a school.

All the "body work" and mental-emotional massage techniques in the world will not help someone who is totally committed to the Way of the Body and the Power of Personality.

Alchemical Sex is valuable in the sense that it deals with the body by by-passing the body to a great degree, and it is valuable as an indicator of higher cosmic chambers that are accessible to those with the will and attention to ascend to them, yet it is not valuable if it becomes a substitute for real therapeutic action.

If the body is producing our emotions and all our thought-forms, and our emotions are so potently overpowering and overwhelming, then we are not ready for this high-powered form of work on self, and might be better served to find something a little less challenging to the ego.

We have the innate ability to make a decision to allow our psyche, body, emotions—our whole personality structure—continue to be a problem for us, or we can make a decision to have the work on ourself be a solution.

We can make the choice between having our psyche be a problem, or facing the Problem of Reality, and then the Work becomes our real problem which we must solve through the application of attention, effort and will.

If our body, mind and emotions are more powerful than we are, and we need some leverage against their demands, we can use Alchemical Sex as a device to gain this leverage and to find within ourselves a fulcrum against which we can apply the force of will and attention.

If we do not choose this path of applied effort, will and attention, then we doom ourselves to remain as weak in Essence as we were before. If, on the other hand, we apply the tools of Alchemical Sex for a higher purpose than our own gratification and pleasures, and put our work in a completely different category, then this becomes a usable and workable tool for Self-Knowledge and Mastery—not of others, but of ourselves.

If we are able to keep ourselves on this path of continual alteration of organic habits into Essence Habits, we will find that we are constantly reinforcing the conscious creation of new work habits and that it is these new work habits which actually begin to change our lives. Nothing else will change our lives but the substitution of new Essence Habits in place of old organic ones.

Strength and Beauty, E.J. Gold, charcoal, Sennelier, © 1992 HEI

CHAPTER 58
BODY OF HABITS

TO MERELY WISH for change is to whistle in the wind.

We can, over a period of time, with a great deal of continual reinforcement and purity of intention, through a long and arduous path of effort, actually create a new identity which is permanent and which survives the death of the organic self.

In other words, we can create an immortal mind and new Essence Identity by merely using the opportunity of living an organic life as a human being to alter our habits and to use those new habits as modular components of the higher self.

Without this effort, we remain a hodge-podge assemblage of tendencies accumulated from the sum-total of our collected organic experiences—a blend of many forms of identity, mind, emotions and memory.

Ordinarily we are just an accumulation of unconscious habits—a completely unconscious random accumulation. This creates the ego, which is itself a localized random accumulation of organic habits and DNA directives, together with learned cultural imperatives and personal desires.

We must die to this organic self before we can be reborn. We must, as has been said before, die before we die. We must accomplish this ego-death long before we lose the ability to consciously create new habits because we must not only create new habits, we must apply them and work to replace the old organic habits with these new habits which we have chosen or created for the purpose of altering our Body of Habits.

When we first become willing to consciously create new non-organic habits and to forgo our desires for self-gratification, we have passed the First Test of the Work.

We can begin with small habits first, then work up to bigger and bigger, stronger and stronger, habits. It is not until we are able to consciously create a big habit and to replace a very powerful organic habit with that new habit, that we are actually able to cease being a collection of randomly accumulated habits.

Changing your life in this way requires a great deal of attention, integrity, courage, interest, self-honesty and—most of all—will.

We must be truly committed to this course in order to last through it. It takes most people who attempt this alteration in Being an absolute minimum of twenty years. This is definitely not the short path, which is to say, it cannot be accomplished just by deciding to do it, nor by taking one or two weekend workshops, and certainly cannot be accomplished merely by reading a book or watching a video or listening to a tape while driving to work.

We have a body and a mind, and they can be said to reflect our habits. But our habits can be said to equally reflect our body and mind. Our actions, our attitudes, feelings, sensations, thoughts and relationships all reflect whatever dominant habits are currently operating within us. But those dominant habits also reflect our attitudes, actions, thoughts, emotions—they mutually affect each other.

I will give an example of this. We live today in a world in which science operates, and the scientific laws are what are the operant factors. Now, conceive of a universe in which the laws of magic are operant factors rather than science, such as that described in the science-fantasy story "Wall Around the World."* Science does not work, the laws of magic do. Do the laws of magic work because everyone agrees that they do, or does everyone agree that they work because they work?

The point is that our accumulated habits are accumulated long before we assume this body, but the moment we assume this body, the habits create a body-matrix, enter into the three nervous systems, and begin to program the nervous system, brain, mind—which is separate from the brain—and all our attitudes, behavior patterns and personal psyche.

They form our ego-mind and control our bodies, and then the environment reinforces those habits which it requires as dominant.

This means that not all of our habits are visible; one of the functions of a school and one of the artistries of a teacher on this path is to make visible to us those traits or habits which are not visible to us, but which direct and influence us all the time.

If you could see your habits as clearly as others can see them, you would know exactly what to do to change yourself and thus your life. But because they are habits, they are outside your vision, out of reach of your attention—which is the very definition of a habit—something which is not under your conscious control, and yet, if you were able to see them, you would know which habits to substitute and which habits are exactly the right habits to substitute; the right new ones to put in place of the old ones. We can get help from others in this way, because they can see in us what has become, through familiarity and unconscious repetition, invisible to ourselves.

We try to preserve unconsciously accumulated habits and still try to do work on ourselves of some kind or another, in fact even try to enhance the unconsciously accumulated habits as if those are very, very valuable, very real, and very workable, and we pretend to try to change ourselves without actually working to break down the ego without breaking down our unconsciously accumulated habits. This, of course, leaves us helpless and in exactly the same condition as the day we started. Real change is achieved through repetition, not direct change.

Substitution is the action required; this occurs only under repetition and stress, because only by fully exposing the Essential Self can we actually reach and reprogram an Essence Habit.

---

* by Theodore R. Cogswell, in: ***E.J. Gold's Retro Visions;*** Gateways Books and Tapes, 2003

Take the example of working on a car. Sometimes parts of an engine have to be taken off in order to get to parts that are deeper inside the engine, and we cannot get to parts that are very far inside it until we remove some of the things that are outside or in front of it. However, negative or dangerous stress is not usable in this way, and therefore we do not create negative stress factors to help someone change their habits.

Some individuals, in order to protect their psyches and to prevent themselves from actually undergoing change, will go into negative stress—this is a completely automatic "knee-jerk" reaction to ego-threat.

Such an individual is really too important for this work, and their need for gratification is too strong.

We must, in order to be ready for this arduous path, lose all interest in ourselves in the personal sense, in what becomes of us, in what is becoming of us right now, how we feel, how we feel about things, our current opinion about things we demand, the conditions that we require in order to exist, and our personal agendas and need for personal gratification and self-pampering—in short, all these obstacles must be completely out of the way before we can even begin work on ourselves.

At the same time we must be extremely interested in the possibility of conscious life and service to the Work, but not interested in a certain state that we expect for ourselves as a result of our efforts, because this "higher self-gratification" may never come, and is in itself just as much a trap as any other form of self-gratification, no matter how exalted it may seem.

So we must have transcended altruism, grasping for absence of personal discomfort, and certainly we must have progressed beyond the idea of personal eternal bliss, and into an appreciation for conscious life without necessarily requiring or demanding gratifications of any sort.

The ***Book of Sacrifices**** is an eighteen-point program for creating conscious habits. However, I did not go into any detail in this book. I only point out that it is possible and give some hints as to how to accomplish a full and complete change of life.

But not everyone goes through those sacrifices exactly as they are outlined in the book, and the required actions are not always the same for each time, place and person.

For some individuals it is extremely comfortable to give up the material life and enter into the spiritual life; for others it is much more

---

**The Joy of Sacrifice*, 1987, I.D.H.H.B./Hohm Press

comfortable to be a spiritual groupie; and for still others it is even more comfortable to be "on the circuit" and to attend weekend workshops and seminars with all the spiritual celebrities.

Where are we right now in the school in relation to all this? How much longer is it before we get to the place where we're going to be doing the sacrifices?

We do not realize that we are doing these things, that we are being taught something, and are working on something individually. Luckily, it is not required that we are aware of the process in order to be in the process.

There are Alchemical Sexual techniques for using the energies along the axis of the body in order to move our consciousness out of body-space and body-ego.

If we move ***along*** the axis of the body's electrical field, we will accomplish one thing, and if we move out ***across*** the axis of the body, we will accomplish something else—the first effort will take us into ETA—ExtraTerrestrial Activity—and the other will keep us in TA—Terrestrial Activity.

But before we even learn the simplest tricks and effects of Alchemical Sex, we should understand that Alchemical Sex is usable for anything—even for enhancing our accumulated organic habits—and that it requires great discipline to use it for the formation of a new Body of Habits.

There is a function of ego-defense against ego-threat, a form of self-importance in which an individual will only agree to carry out an instruction when the basis becomes fully understood by the body-mind.

This automatic ego-defense must eventually be transcended, because there are some instructions that we may not understand while they are given and perhaps only understand later, through the accomplishment of the thing itself.

There are those who continue to believe that they can decide to work based on which teacher they like the best—which usually means which teacher will allow them to remain as they are.

Someone who has abandoned all possibility, all hope, and who no longer has any possibilities or interest in organic life may at that point of hopelessness and despair be able to actually accumulate the will to perform the arduous tasks necessary to do the work within themselves in order to prepare themselves for the Great Work. So a great deal of our work together is preliminary and preparatory, to bring ourselves to the point of decision and will.

Do you understand why this barrier of personal ego-threat is so important to transcend before we can even begin to think about seriously working on ourselves or working to prepare ourselves for the Work?

It is imperative to let go of all the ego things, all the desires for self-gratification, all the self-pampering and lying and veils of deceit before beginning work.

There are a great many preliminary steps that we are already doing in terms of consciously creating new work habits, but we cannot actually do anything real until we no longer hold as important what will eventually become of us.

The idea of self-importance is what creates spiritual "groupies," those who go moving from group to group constantly seeking and searching for their own enhancement, always looking for the "best" school, the "best" situation, the "best" relationship, the prettiest people, the nicest environment, the most respected and admired teacher, and so on.

All these ego-demands are barriers to the Work. If we understand that those are barriers, we understand a great deal about the human psyche, and of what it is composed. The fears, defenses and avoidances of the ego are exposed and only then, when we can see how we avoid confronting these issues within ourselves are we able to address real work and to begin to work seriously on ourselves.

The Samsaric Ideal is to succeed at something in which there is a ***personal*** future as one is now—but when we are in the Work, we must be absolutely indifferent to our personal future. When we want a personal future we cannot have it; as soon as we do not want it anymore, we can have all we want. There is a point at which we can decide it—the way people generally are—we cannot just decide to get rid of our habits.

This process of transcendence of personal ego gratifications and will and power over our organic imperatives requires continual reaffirmation, and in this area we will be constantly tested.

CHAPTER 59
ORGANIC SUFFERING

It is impossible to understand the entire process of transformation—why it works, how it works, what it does. Yet we have been convinced by organic life and the concept of total personal knowledge and understanding that we must first understand everything about our path before we make our final commitment to it.

The final step is endless, but so is the very first step, and we must realize only one thing before we take that first step. Nothing more can be known at this time, but we can know one thing for sure—that we will not get any rest from this point on, and never again enjoy the personal comfort of hypnotic ignorance and sleep.

We will have to learn to live without the comfort and rest of a life lived in dreams.

Allowing ourselves to remain steeped in an unconscious existence through unconsciously accumulated habits, we have always enjoyed the comfort of personal organic suffering, because wrapped in the sedations of world-illusion and the ecstasy of personal pain, it is in fact possible to feel nothing.

We must experience the loss of our organic suffering to some degree before we enter fully onto the path—only then we will know whether we will be able to endure the absence of our world-illusions—whether or not we have the courage to remain on the path forever. The price of immortality is immortality.

If we can imagine paying this price endlessly—paying the price of organic comfort, ecstasy of pain and the illusions of sleep—we might think twice before we take the first step, but if we knew what we were going to have to endure in any discipline we might never begin, so the choice must be made by the will, and the price must be small compared to the pain of remaining as we are now.

The alternative to work on self is organic bliss, and a certain kind of peaceful hypnotic sleep, reinforced by continual ecstasy of pain and suffering.

Do not think of conscious life as being the ultimate possession of something which is valuable, which would enhance in any way our existence, or which is exalted, something to reach for. It is not gratifying, fulfilling or heroic. Think of it as a curse, which is quite acceptable once we have gone beyond a certain point in our understanding of ourself, but until this point, totally excruciating.

It certainly is excruciating to someone who is committed to having a specific identity, set of relationships, and who has certain definite goals in mind, things to get, things to do, things which must be accomplished, places to go, people to meet, obstacles to overcome, and success and achievement. And for an individual who certainly likes the relaxed, calm, steady state, a condition of no rest, no comfort, no peace of mind and total uncertainty would be rather excruciating.

Social and cultural demands may or may not take one away from this path of work. Sexual needs, even imaginary ones, certainly will, if we are not very strong. And if we are really weak, then even small cultural things will take us away.

Men will tend to be taken away more through sexual and business things—through ambition. Women will be taken away more through not being able to find the right man for themselves, and may go off searching for this man.

One of the things we are going to be using Alchemical Sex spaces for is to find out what our relationship is with this planet and this universe, and with other humans, and with the body, the mind, and so on. Because, we in relation to all of these factors, is what creates all the possibility for us to actually do any work. Also, realize that we have, although it is not dominant, all of the male and female sexual programs. We have cellular programs within us. All these are operational; not all of them are dominant. That is why it is cultural reinforcement, because we have biologically both male and female programs. Now we certainly, as beings, have male and female programs; we do not have as essence, any particular sexuality.

If we are extremely weak, and we abstain from sex, thinking this will save us from temptation, and then suddenly we come across someone who is very sexually attractive, very powerful, but totally disinterested in the Work; we could easily sell our souls to be with them and to follow them wherever they go, even if it forces us to abandon our work path.

If we are very, very highly influenced by the whole agenda of "relationships," it is suggested that we get involved with someone who is powerfully in the Work and is already very dedicated to it, so we will not be drawn away by this organic desire.

To properly select new habits which we will use for the formation of our new Body of Habits, we must select these new habits with some degree of higher knowledge, or we must accept the suggestions of those with knowledge of these principles.

We must know exactly what it is we want. We must know what kind of soup it is we want, then we can select the ingredients and select the pot to cook it in. In other words, then we can select and create the chamber, fill the chamber with those things which represent the chamber we are trying to program in. And of course we really need to understand those chambers very well.

Once crystallized, to decrystallize takes a very long time. That is why the human lifetime is so very important because we have in it the option. The fact is we cannot be anything this time around, but we can program ourself to be anything next time around. In other words, this is a place of selection, not a place of manifestation—this is not what it seems, the planetary voyage is not at all what it seems to be. It is not as solid as we perceive it. The symbols of this chamber are not as we perceive them. This is a chamber of selection.

To choose a set of habits with knowledge requires a little bit of willingness to become, first of all, a scholar to some degree and then to be able to throw that scholarship away and become a worker. The habits start in the Moving Centrum, but of course all centrums have to be invoked in order to be effective over a lifetime, to accomplish something on a much deeper level, to program ourselves to take a certain angelic form, with a certain ability to do. Imagine every day doing this four to eight hours a day depending on how many years we have left to ourselves or how many months in terms of our intensity of work. In order to accomplish this particular thing, we could conceivably do it.

CHAPTER 60
CHANCE FOR CHANGE

In some cases there are those who have done nothing and are turned away simply because they have formed the habit of laziness to the degree that they cannot accept the discipline of the art, in other words, not the discipline of the teacher, of the master, of someone else nor of the coach, but their own discipline of the art of transformation itself. This is what we mean when we say "to accept discipline."

The American Way is to totally avoid anything having to do with discipline. There are some people who literally go to pieces, collapse emotionally, go into hysterics because of being critiqued on their art work or creative writing.

They expect to remain untrained in the arts, undisciplined in their craft, and yet to merely put their art on exhibit or to have their unedited and unproofread writings published and to have it admired by everyone, and in America, this concept is fully reinforced by ignorance.

In the end, such artists and writers learn nothing, because they are content with the adulation of biped hominids.

Part of learning is to put what you can manifest into what you know in front of someone who knows more than you and who can tell you where you went wrong.

In mastery of the self, it is no different from mastering anything else. It is hard work; a lot of it is repetitive, boring; if we don't have the innate ability to "hang in" when it gets boring, we will never last the course.

If we need constant continual titillation, we will discover that we will be overwhelmed by sheer boredom.

Every day we put in a program deeper and deeper; every day we run the grooves deeper and deeper, into a new life, but this requires discipline. The secret is "hanging in."

We wish to get good advice before we start developing habits that are unchangeable and bad—bad in the sense of what we wish to accomplish—not bad objectively. Those habits can become so crystallized that they cannot be changed at this time.

We would prefer to be in a group of professional musicians or professional dancers than among a group of amateurs who are all looking to us for advice. In the course of a professional career we would want to obtain the finest results possible. Most of what we learn is learned in about twenty minutes, then we go practice it and then come back and face the music.

There are some things that we will have done that will have been wrong, we just did not understand. We should accept the corrections and then go do them, apply the corrections then come back and get checked out again. So each of these things is done over a period of time, a level of refinement is attained, more and more professional quality is obtained.

It is really important that we realize that professionals require from us that we are able to accept correction and are able and willing to learn—not stop learning—asking questions—not stop doubting—use doubt to develop a self-check, "Am I doing this the right way? Am I doing what I intended to do? Hey, where have I gone off? Is this the direction I was going?"

As soon as we understand the options and make a selection from those options we find that the basic programming structure, the ritual that we adopt is very simple and is given to us in strata—first on the gross level, then with major corrections and then with smaller and smaller corrections until the refinements are down to the point where you almost have it—all we need to do is go out and practice it, so we go out and practice it without trying to become at this point a professional; we just practice it.

We have a chance for change, a taste of what it means to enact this change, to make it occur and know that the means for such change is available to us.

When we accept change or go through the next change, we have no particular idea what we will manifest as, what mask we will wear. The mask includes the mind; the mind is part of the mask. The mind does not belong to us, it is not ours, it is how we process information and it will have an entirely different set of feelings, attitudes, beliefs and understandings. The only thing that will be the same is us. However, if we are our mask, then we die; we no longer exist if we identify with the mask.

If we identify with that which does not change, we do not experience death as change. The simplicity of being is what we own—a few basic things which we own, the rest is borrowed for the chamber or the play in the chamber, and when we are no longer in the chamber then we do not know what tools we will be given—so best to learn to use any tools we are given to become very adept at adapting to different tools, structures or realms. Do not just explore the realms, become adept at using tools no matter what form they appear in.

Scan all aspects of the planetary presence—particularly the contained shape—called "the biosphere"—projected by the planetary presence. Begin to collect yourself from wherever you left parts of yourself and bring those parts of the totality of your attention into the present chamber. Begin to collect yourself and scan the contained shape which results from this psychic action. You will then be doing what is called "sitting"—the true meaning of the word "Seance."

There are two forms of intellectual reason—rational and emotional.

Nonphenomenal vision is intuitive and self-evident, visible to the naked eye; the more naked the eye, the more visible the vision.

It is impossible to convince someone of something which is nonphenomenal by rational argument alone. The attention must be called to it by a direct summons.

Habitual beliefs change only as a result of experience, and even then the experience must be so convincing that current beliefs are momentarily annihilated. Only then will one give up the old belief, and then only grudgingly.

Necessity for work comes only through experience; by first trying the presence exercise and seeing that one cannot be conscious just by deciding to be.

CHAPTER 61
AL-HAQQ—"THE TRUTH"

I HAVE PRESENCE; I have momentarily invoked the presence; I have total presence; I have total unique presence; I have total unique subjective presence—the same as attention of presence—I have total unique objective presence; objective consciousness; the unveiled vision of the Face of God, which we have nicknamed the FoG; the Naked King, viewed without his consort; the King's New Clothes, also called the Vision of Phenomena.

We must hit a "big ***Doh***" every moment with the invocation of presence. There is a strong tendency for the octave to devolve after hitting the ***Doh***—we think we are still doing it but really we are just experiencing the reverberations from the first ***Doh*** until it degenerates entirely. Each time we think we are hitting a new ***Doh***, we could actually be hitting a lower and lower note, until we arouse the force to hit a real new ***Doh*** once again.

After self-invocation has been mastered somewhat, the next stage is an intermediate step; the intentional placement of attention on presence, taking care to separate the illusion of consciousness from this activity.

With this method of work there is no immediate payoff. We may work for years without any apparent change. With Kundalini Yoga, etc., daily payoffs can be obtained.

Presence must have an equal force to the present; then the third force, the AM can form itself by the mutual reciprocal blending of the two primary forces. In some Arabic languages the sentence is constructed I HERE, with no AM, which promotes ignorance of the third force.

Everything we see in the world is third force, although we cannot see the third force itself. All manifested forms result from the third force. ***Al-Haqq***, the Truth, is the patchwork quilt viewed as a whole thing in which no one form is more significant than any other, and all forms exist as a fraction of a whole.

All forms are merely light and shadow playing across the Face of God. Where is God? The last place we would look...right before our eyes! In Arabic, there are other words for truth, but only ***Al-Haqq*** means ***The*** Truth.

Everything in life is against the Work; everything we encounter, every organism, etc. Nature is against the Work. Human beings even as we are, serve Nature and Nature serves God; therefore, humans indirectly serve God. The Work is for the direct benefit of the Unveiled Kingdom.

Nature's plan for human beings is that they ultimately provide waste products, including someday our own Organic Body, as fertilizer for the benefit of the planet. As we are now, we serve nature's purposes admirably, by transforming food substances including ourself into one form of nitrogen or another.

Nature's original plan was for humans to serve a much higher function than we now fulfill. Human beings have degenerated; we cannot fulfill our intended function. A more highly evolved human serves Our Endless Creator in another way impossible for others, but we must struggle against Nature in order to evolve and to take our place in this higher organization of work.

Nature is like a big bully. If you beat up a bully, he becomes your friend. Once you have beaten Nature, Nature will fear you and be your friend. You will be able to work for a new world in a higher, more efficient way.

Nature is God's secretary. She is there to keep people out of the boss's office who do not belong. Sometimes someone may pass the secretary and have nothing useful for the boss; or manage to steal and cheat his way into the boss's office, then in the end be cast out.

Our primary test of new people in the work-community is whether they are able to discover that they are not really conscious and can see the importance of working to become more than just imaginary-conscious.

There must be a balance between presence and phenomena to produce the Harmonious Human Being, the raw material which can produce a worker for a new world. In music, if two notes are struck with the proper interval between them, overtones and harmonics will result, but if one of the notes is slightly off, there is no result.

When the invocation of presence exercise was given to the early groups, it was given as I AM HERE NOW, to draw presence into the present with complete abandonment, going the whole hog and the postage. This is abandonment in the Sufi sense, not in the American sense of grounds for divorce, but what was not given was the invocational means to draw the angelic self into the present.

Identification is when the identity is submerged in the phenomenal vision and for which Invocation of Presence is the only cure.

Pondering is very different. Pondering is intentional directing of attention of all centers on an imaginary thing, that is, on an idea which has not occurred and may never occur, or upon something that occurred in the past or is occurring in the present in which one is not directly participating except as the ponderer.

The idea of pondering carries with it the baptism of thinking, feeling and sensing. Baptism in the old sense of total immersion with presence. Who is present cannot be identified. The cure for identification is presence. To whom or what is identification referring to? It refers to I whether real or false.

What does this tell us about identification, whether it is real or false? Presence is the cure. Identification is a technical state of existence; actually a condition in which "I" has become immersed in the phenomenal vision.

The attention of "I" is glamourized in the old sense of glamour. The word means fascinated in the old, hypnotic sense. In the original sense it meant magnetic fascination. Even though we know the attraction is unreal, we are hopelessly drawn to it.

Magnetic fascination is something with which almost every woman wishes to be endowed, if not in her Being, then in her vivacious personality; if not her personality, then with her face and body; if not her whole body, then perhaps her breasts, or her hair, or face; if not her whole face, then perhaps just one feature of her face, such as her eyes, or her nose.

Years from now you will look back and be amazed that you did not see the truth. How many people have experienced this with the presence exercise—realizing what is there, that they could not see before? People come to me constantly after reading notes from talks I gave years ago, and they cannot believe I said the same things then, but that they had not seen it.

It often takes a lot for knowledge to penetrate our thick skulls and thick skins. It takes a lot of pain for us to learn anything new. No one offers us the pain; we simply insist on it. There are much better ways to learn than the way we do. Unfortunately, there is no way to coax you out of the habit of inflicting pain on ourselves to learn, until we are ready to move ourself out of this horrible habit.

In order to invoke, we must first evoke. The simplest thing about an invocation is that it depends on a mood or series of moods. It depends upon definite knowledge and exact data and I make a distinction between the two. What kind of data? At least, the exact data of what to do if something goes wrong. And believe me, things can go wrong—sometimes horribly wrong. There are things that can happen that may make you wish you had never started.

CHAPTER 62
CASUAL SEX

MANY PEOPLE prefer to have casual sexual encounters. Why?...Because the excitement of the first encounter, in which one is caught off-guard, is automatically powerful even if at the same time superficial. Most people would prefer to maintain casualness, even to the extent that with marriage partners, for instance, they will ignore each other for several months and then engage in a sexual encounter to achieve the same result—first encounter excitement.

An initiated individual will endure a long period of unsuccessful encounters in the knowledge that eventually even though the encounters may be unsatisfactory for a period of a year or more, provided the encounters are maintained, they will surpass one-thousand-fold the first encounter syndrome. One-thousand-fold is a phrase I carefully considered when I said that.

The force of such encounters can by no means be achieved in the first encounter. Just through laziness, fear, insecurity, vanity, and maybe a few other things such as hungers, most people are not willing to go through the period of mastery. Everything has a similar period during which non-success and even utter failure is experienced—dance, theater, art, music, writing, chemistry, housekeeping, driving—things get worse before they get better.

In gambling the first encounter syndrome is called beginner's luck. Then from that point on, gambling becomes steadily, considerably worse for a long time. If one can afford the inevitable losing streak for the first year or two, mastery is possible or more possible.

Most people cannot endure the loss to their vanity. This is the reason the first year of marriage is considered the most dangerous. The first year at a job is considered the most dangerous as well as the first year at a university. Most people leave the university the first year, the second semester to be exact, because they can never repeat or duplicate the instantaneous success of the first week or the first month.

This relates very strongly to the Second Wind Phenomenon, which states that when we are unprepared for and least expecting something, we may very easily achieve it, the first time. The second time and after that everything is on guard. The whole mechano-organic colony is on the alert for any possibility of the first sign of success. And so it is also with invocation. The first invocation is free. After that, everything is downhill, downhill, downhill.

I have had numerous talks with people who have been responsible for other circles of invocation, which many call schools. They have noticed that the same people tend to circulate from school to school. They even know which ones, where they have been, and where they are going. They are transients; they make the circuit. We see them here. They come, they go, they stay awhile and they leave, and we even know where they came from and where they are going next. They are called spiritual bobbysoxers or cult hoppers. They are after First Encounters of the Spiritual Kind. They are always on the hop. They move on and start again as a virgin in the next town.

The lure of prostitution is simply first encounter syndrome. It is never as good for a long time as the first time. There is a magic to it—the magic is, one is not prepared for it. Rather than spend the effort to penetrate, they go on the top. It is just vanity. There are even some people, if you can imagine this, ask any psychologist, particularly a marriage counselor, who deliberately provoke arguments, fights, battles of some kind in order to separate periodically, briefly and then to bounce back for the benefit of the first encounter syndrome. They argue, fight, split up four or five days, and get back together all for the first night syndrome.

We inevitably begin a losing streak as we begin penetration. Penetration begins in the dark, and, the beginning of penetration we go into darkness. This is the significance of the cave, what the cave is—the beginning of penetration. Once we enter the cave, we can be sure we are beginning penetration. It is murky, dark, dull, dull, dull, boring, boring, boring, flat, tasteless, nonepisodic.

If we were looking for a word to describe the first trimester of penetration, boring would spring to mind. It goes on and on, day after day. All efforts seem meaningless, useless, besides which, it is very boring. There is simply no excitement to it, really. If you ever wish to have a really boring time, just try penetrating something or other in a really serious way.

An analogy—you have surely noticed this in the higher echelons of education such as junior high or high school; there are three kinds of students in an ordinary school: the Tortoise, which is to say, the slow learner, insecure, unsteady, uncertain, not too bright, but willing to work very hard to understand and the hare who is speedy, secure, certain, arrogant even, who finds everything a breeze and a snap, who brags, I never even had to crack the textbook the whole semester. Hares may be identified by the small map pin stuck in the lapel—a symbol of membership in Mensa and there are different colors signifying different gradations of I.Q.

The third character we shall call the Athalete. The Athalete is a product of the Nucular Age. He thinks in broader terms than other students—terms like scholarship, half-time, broadjump, beer, commercials. He expects to be in school just long enough to make the major leagues and anything else in sight. He is excited by only three things, the third of which is a waving pompom.

We already know the story of the Tortoise and the Hare. The Hare has a serious case of First Night Syndrome and manages in leaps and bounds to stay entirely at skin level, although not without dramatic flair. Meanwhile, the Tortoise plods on day after day. Suddenly the Hare looks up to find that the Tortoise has passed mysteriously into realms impossible for him to attain. He wakes up to find himself still at the starting line and is he ever bored, bored, bored. And so he looks for another university where he can start all over again as a virgin, and maybe this time, win the race. But, what of the tortoise? The tortoise never knew that there was a race. To the tortoise, competition is a foreign word meaning nothing. The tortoise is even too stupid to stop after all possible attainments have been attained and so becomes eligible to unguessed-at-splendors, because he did not know they were impossible, unattainable, unachievable and non-existent, as do all hares and athaletes everywhere. The End.

Did you ever see this syndrome in school? Did you understand something about the Tortoise and the Hare Syndrome? There is the fast-starter who zips along thinking everything is okay and the slow one who plods along slowly, uncertainly—not periodically—but quite often surpasses slowly, imperceptibly the Rapid Rabbit. The rapid rabbit is forced to ride again, and again, and again. What difference does it make if the rides are free, if they go in a circle? Besides which, they are not free, they only seem to be free.

There are some people who simply like to go back to the beginning and start again because they like that first rush. If we cannot stick with it, we cannot penetrate. If we cannot stick with one, we cannot stick with another. If we cannot plod on long enough and hard enough, and stick with it on an ordinary basis and endure—suffer voluntarily on a daily basis the inevitable consequences of boring, boring, boring—then we cannot penetrate anything.

There are certain people that no matter what you ask them to do, they will; even if they cannot, they will try. Other people are not even asked because they do nothing anyway. We cannot have a community where everyone does everything. There are always those who do some things, and always a few who do nothing. There are always a very few people who do nearly everything in a community. They are the ones, the small minority who have the lousiest time, the worst conditions, complain the least and are always bailing someone else out.

They are the first ones to lend you money even if they do not have a cent to their names. They are the first ones to rush off to do an errand even though they are busy and have a million things to do. They are the ones who scrape a windshield no one else is willing to do. They are the ones who notice the light bulb needs changing. They are the ones first to rush over to help on childcare. They are the first ones to offer to do dishes. They are the ones who pick things up that people have been stepping over for days. They are the first ones up in the morning, and the last ones to bed at night. They do the invisible things. They are always working, yet will always take something else to do in addition to what they are already doing. They always have time to stop and do something for someone who needs it. They will even sit and listen to your bellyaching and help you out of a jam. Have you ever noticed this? There is your proof right there.

If you know something, it is because you need it. If you need it, it is because you put yourself in the position to need it, or were put there. If you need it, it is because you have penetrated. Penetration is very different from hopping around. This is why I say to you, show me how you gamble, how you eat, how you sleep and with whom and under what circumstances, how you drive a car, sweep a floor, make a cup of coffee, how you handle Bingo, repair a car, and I know everything about your work. I can watch someone for two minutes, not always but under the right conditions, and determine how they work.

If we cannot penetrate one thing, we cannot penetrate the Work because it requires the same amount of detail work. If we have preferences in terms of our penetration, obviously we will not succeed.

If we can penetrate one thing, we can penetrate anything. If we cannot penetrate what we are doing right now, we will not make any better penetration on the hop! It will not be any better for us this week than last week. If we cannot stick with what we are doing today to penetrate it, changing our object of penetration or changing our method, will not change our tendency to crap out in the middle.

Who has noticed in dice that some people tend to crap out? They have the tendency to crap out and just cannot roll anything but craps and sevens?

Think back how many times you have changed your direction or method, or locale, or operation entirely. How many times have you gone on the hop because you just could not handle the boredom of flatness, the same drab repetitiveness day after day? So what do you do—change? Then you have the same new repetition day after day.

Whenever we begin penetration, we are into repetitive garbage upon the slightest penetration. Tinsel is on the outside and garbage is packed all the way through. It is called the mantle effect. Just like the earth has a mantle, the outer shell of the earth is called the crust. Above the crust is the atmosphere, the tinsel.

Once we break through the crust, we find garbage, not titillating new garbage, just the same old garbage. Maybe we do not see it right away; it may take three or four times for us to see the periodicity of the garbage, and eventually, the cry springs from our lips, "Boring, boring, boring; dull, dull, dull; what a drag. Oh, no, not this again!" And so we leave the way we came in and go to the other side of the planet and try to penetrate from the other side. And the first night is exceptional, exciting, at least it is not boring, and it is utterly different from anything we have experienced before. The next night is not so different and the next night is not so different from that. Soon we begin to see that it is not only the same as itself, it is the same as the others. The inevitable cry springs from our lips, "Boring, boring, boring."

This time, cleverly, we do not hop; we reverse our path and return to the crust where we stare at the stars a while and then turn around, and it is like the first night all over again. We begin our penetration deeper and deeper until once again whining, bitching, griping, sighing, sounds escape our lips, "Take this and stuff it for a lark!"

Once again we return to the surface after having penetrated almost one-and-a-half feet below it. Of course, there is no way to mark our penetration; it is dark in there. We look at the stars, look back at the one-and-a-half foot deep hole, look back at the stars and we think to ourselves, "Maybe another planet entirely!" We float out through the Van Allen radiation belt and back through the Van Allen radiation belt for a buzz, then far out into space where we spot another planet and say, "Surely this one will be different!"

Down, down, down we plummet through the glittering atmosphere. As we plunge into the crust we once again feel that old familiar thrill that we have not experienced for three days, four hours, three minutes and seventeen seconds. But at last as we plunge through the crust down, down, down, deeper and deeper, three, four, five inches, we begin to notice that what we are passing through is somehow vaguely familiar. Yes, definitely familiar—one might even say...The End.

CHAPTER 63
ORGASM

ORGASM IS A FUSE that prevents accidental penetration into alchemical territory. The same idea of fuses can be applied to virtually anything. Most people have fuses which are set to blow at unbelievably low thresholds. There are, for instance, emotional fuses lest one should accidentally penetrate the domain of higher emotion.

Fuses blow at the level of negative emotion—at such low levels that there is an enormous safety factor. The safety factor is in thousands—not in increments of two or three times—not a five-fold or ten-fold safety factor—but thousands of times.

There are intellectual fuses that prevent accidental mentation, accidental penetration into the domain of mentations. There are sensation fuses that prevent penetration into the domain of sensing. There are organic fuses that prevent penetration into alchemical domains. There are Philadelphian fuses that prevent accidental penetration into domains of cooperation. There are jealousy fuses, envy fuses, anger fuses, boredom fuses, competition fuses and insecurity fuses—all of which prevent accidental penetration. I am telling you something you are years away from needing. I am not telling you for you. It is not for you.

These fuses are set to blow at such incredibly low levels, it would amaze you. Do you know that death, organic death, is a fuse? I am referring to death with identification, identified death, identification with the organic death, which is a fuse to prevent us from penetrating into a definite special domain which we have no business entering and for which we must use penetration to enter. If the fuse blows, we have not done our work.

If we can die before we die, in such a way that the fuse does not blow, we have earned our penetration. If we tried to pass the point of death without organic death, we would not know how. I doubt seriously if anyone knows any way of achieving a death passage short of physical death. Luckily more than one-half dozen, not quite twelve, methods which can produce death are fused with the equivalent of mirco-amp and micro-volt fuses. Whereas, what we are trying to penetrate to and beyond is in the mega-volt and milli-amp range.

Each time we pass a fuse that does not blow we can move to the next fuse and then if that fuse does not blow we can pass to the next fuse. There is a whole series of fuses, and penetration consists of penetrating a series of fuses, and when one blows we go back to the beginning. Then perhaps we can pass to the next one further than the one that turned us back.

Another way of looking at the fuses is as guardians at the gate or portal. There are fuses which blow if we are unprepared, or too prepared. Each time a fuse blows, it sends us back to the beginning. Nevertheless, this is how penetration is achieved—by blowing a fuse, going back to start again, learning how that fuse was blown, and then not blowing it the next time. We may pass that fuse, but surely we will blow the next one, and so it goes in increments.

At some point it requires an intentional, voluntary return in order to penetrate beyond this and pass further, whereas, return from the blowing of early fuses is automatic and involuntary. This is true, particularly of the fuses to which humans are set—the kundabuffer fuses—which are very low voltage fuses. Little by little, the mechanical body will become accustomed to higher and higher current, voltage and amperage. This is not just theory.

This is not impossible, it just takes solid steady work, day after day. Small hang-ups are rooted out; the whole circuit is rooted out. This precludes opening neural circuits; there is no way the headbrain can survive high voltage. It changes the function.

Do you know how an electrician typically checks to see if a circuit is operating? He licks his finger and puts it in the socket. Over the years, his body has become immune to the shocks, not completely immune, but it has built up a greater tolerance to larger and larger electrical charges, the same way that a weight-lifter builds his tolerance to lifting heavier and heavier weights.

In the same way, moving-instinctive/motor-reflexive fuses can be bypassed, shunted, so they do not blow. We would be surprised how far we may go just with the moving-instinctive/motor reflexive centrum, by not blowing fuses. Then we would be surprised how far we may go with the Emotional Centrum by not blowing fuses.

Who does not blow emotional fuses now as they have previously? Can we see how we now penetrate into mood more to some degree? Notice how our emotional fuses have been expanded and extrapolate to the future. Imagine accelerating the process and becoming able to produce virtually any mood—undreamed of moods—or moods we have never thought of before, never seen before, that our low fuses now prevent.

Now imagine the same thing in terms of mentation. Imagine mental fuses that prevent mentation which blow the same way emotional and orgasmic fuses blow, and for much the same reasons.

There are also fuses on penetration itself. Just the activity of penetration has its own fuses—impatience, activities, change of locale and many other fuses to prevent accidental penetration by the uninitiated, the unready. You can be told this, but if you are not ready to use it, it makes no difference. You will simply do what you are going to do. You are as strong as you are strong and as weak as you are weak.

Sheer perseverance itself will not penetrate, nor will cunning. Also there are no shortcuts. I have found that by taking a shortcut, I end up adding more somewhere else. This is the Law of Compensation—shortcut here, add something there. Like heading north when one is driving south. One also uses less gas driving south—it is downhill. But then you turn around and go north and use more gas—it is uphill.

This is the Law of Compensation taking effect. And if one goes too far south one will fall off onto the desk, the great oak desk in the sky. It is a plain oak desk with a blotter, an apple, sometimes two, a stack of textbooks, a flag in the corner. It is really there!

We must learn to observe ourselves and the working of our machine as a scientist would observe—which is to say, impartially and removed from personal drama.

Quite often, after blowing a fuse, not necessarily one involving a dramatic upheaval or a monstrous theatrical display, but perhaps even a very quiet fuse, with no big show, can cost us weeks, months, even years to regain that point. We do not know how long it took to arrive at that point so we do not know how far back the blown fuse will send us.

There is a method or technique of penetration in which fuses are never blown, but rather bypassed each time. This is a very dangerous method, the most dangerous. It is called the fast path, but it has the most risk.

There is a faster method in which we must realize that we simply cannot afford to blow that fuse again no matter what the provocation, simply do not. This is encoded in Jesus' teaching—kiss the other cheek or turn the other cheek—and if that does not work, offer your face—as is an eye for an eye, tooth for a tooth, nose for a nose, chin for a chin. There is also his saying, "Do unto others before they do unto you."

At some point, we realize how expensive blowing these fuses can be, and we just do not, no matter what the provocations, whether we are surprised, outraged, startled, scared or whatever, because we do not have the time to keep making it up, months in some cases. If one found oneself having backslid and having lost years of one's work, I think one would be very unhappy with oneself.

Still that is not the fast path, but it is good preparation and training for it. I am not advocating the fast path; it is too dangerous for me to recommend. One must know a great deal more than one does. We have years to go before we even become eligible to consider the fast path. The great risk with the fast path is that one may quit. One may not have the wherewithal to go all the way through it. That is complete disaster, worse than if one had never started.

CHAPTER 64
PENETRATION

TOOLS OF THE TRADE are the key; they do not come by themselves. They come with the territory; we are only given what the territory requires for the job.

It is a question of whether we are willing to pay the price, and there is not just one price, one of which is boring, boring, boring. One price is the cessation of self-indulgence. Another price is we must sell ourselves into an unknown form of slavery without receiving anything out of it for at least the rest of our lives.

Basically there is no other option—we die.

We must be scared enough to sell ourselves into slavery, smart enough to know how, to whom and for what, and under what conditions.

People sell themselves into meaningless, useless slavery many more times readily than they sell themselves into work-slavery that may do them some good. It is not my job to tell you to whom, or to what, or how to sell yourself into slavery.

I can tell you about the tools of the trade, but I cannot tell you about the trade, because it is not the same for everyone and I do not wish to influence you. I do not wish you to do what I did the way I did.

If you obtain the data, make your own mind up; do not operate on my data and on decisions I have made. If it seems that I am reluctant to direct you and give you advice, it is because I wish you to independently verify all work-data, not refer to a book some supposed authority wrote.

It is the same old problem—I tell you something, and it suggests other questions to you. Rather than pursue those, to penetrate them, you ask for immediate instant answers. If I point something out, do not look at my finger. If you do not understand that, I do not know what I can do to help.

Attention, presence, seeing the Face of God are all tools of the trade, not the job itself.

There is only one thing like death—death itself. It is only fair to mention that there are several routes we can take, faster or slower, but they are all increments of death. Anything we have ever used as a tool to produce what we consider a higher state and any exalted state we have ever experienced is "merely on the way to death."

Everyone who works for a corporation also works for themselves. Some work first and foremost, and in every possible way, for the corporation. The company man with no car of his own, no house of his own, no time of his own, with basically little relaxation. Company people, those are the Real People of the Work. Then there are those who give the company exactly what it pays for in terms of hours and duties. When they are not on the job, their life is their own. These are householders, not people of the Work. They work ***for*** the Work, not ***in*** the Work, and they also receive a set of corresponding tools for their trade, which is limited to this lifetime.

CHAPTER 65
MISSIONARY AND DOG FASHION

I DO NOT make the answers. I can only answer your questions as much as you will allow me to, and I cannot always make an answer which conforms to your beliefs or one that is pleasing to you.

Sometimes it seems there must be two positions at least for people when they are here.

Missionary and dog.

The dog feels there is no choice but to be here and the missionary feels there is something out there to accomplish.

There are also people who feel they can be here on their own terms and somehow avoid the Work.

We must continually renew our intention to remain in the Work. There is always the opportunity to walk off the job. We are always free to go.

The Beloved is always slipping behind a tree about twenty feet ahead of us, and we can never quite catch up. But if we ever manage to actually capture a leprechaun, we must remember that it is the hat we are after and not the leprechaun—only then we will have his complete attention and cooperation.

Think of a craps table at a casino as representing the Work, the dice as God, the flow of money as representing the Absolute, and the mathematical odds against winning as the force of the Void.

For some unfathomable reason which we may never understand, God has decreed that a dice roller must achieve one hundred rolls without a seven, which is a way of describing the "uncertainty principle" of quantum mechanics.

The odds are reset at every roll, regardless of the beliefs of craps players in general. Every roll of the dice returns the odds to their original level of probability.

And if somehow a hundred rolls without a seven should be achieved by some great and powerful sorcerer, or shaman, or very lucky janitor, in any case, it does not hold you there for very long.

The fascination with dice tends to falter after a few million years of play.

When we first approach anything, the excitement provokes us unconsciously to involuntarily remain with it without adding our own will.

But after a while, when it gets really boring through repetition, we must consciously and voluntarily give it life. This is when most people quit; when they first discover that in order to continue the process, they must give it blood every night.

They do not wish to give blood every day, but that is what it takes to give life to that which is in itself lifeless, a point which is well-explored in Mary Shelley's ***Frankenstein***.

This is what prayer is all about, and why the Absolute needs prayer, but seldom receives such service from human beings, who could if they were willing, provide this service to the Absolute.

The more life we give, the more surely and certainly we will die. We can "play it smart" like most people do, and dribble it all away. Then we are dragged through death slowly. Or we can face death with courage, because we are so accustomed to eternal life.

The flip side of poverty is infinite wealth. It does not matter which way the money or other gaming chips flow; they are simply a way of keeping track of how many times we have rolled the dice and not a result in themselves.

We sell ourselves into slavery for theater, for music, for art, for cartooning. It is nothing to sell yourself into slavery for the rest of your life. To ***whom***?—not a question of to whom? If we want to be a slave to the Work, however, we cannot depend on our master to support us—we must earn a living for ourselves, so we can afford to be a slave; we must pay to be a slave in the Work.

If we are going to sell ourselves into slavery, we must do it right. If we walk away after a million years of rolling dice to play blackjack because we are tired of throwing dice, blackjack will all-too-soon take on all the horrible characteristics of craps. Then as soon as we finish playing blackjack and return to the craps table, we will discover to our horror that we have wasted precious work-time at the blackjack table.

Although sometimes we leave the craps table to get a better handle on craps, we have done nothing for our work and may even have lost working capital. It is true your whole life passes by you while you are going down for the third time, in a nice way, that is.

Look at this in relation to the fast path. In using sex, sex, sex, one puts their hours in and makes their penetrations without sevening out. Sevening-out is not necessarily orgasm. It could be a break in mood, which can be as serious in very advanced Alchemical Sex as orgasm would be in early work.

Mood changes—ever so slight either way—or atmospheric changes or changes in thought all have an effect; it becomes so delicate that even a wrong move of the toes or one's breathing pattern and the changes in pattern in period or depth of breath, can throw everything completely to hell.

Embrasure, E.J. Gold, charcoal, Rives BFK, © 1990 HEI

CHAPTER 66
ALCHEMICAL ROADMAPS

AN ALCHEMICAL NOTEBOOK is a traveler's record, a log book, a map, if you wish, notating the change which has brought about a deeper internal mutation. The body is a biofeedback device indicating real change.

Changing the entries in the notebook does not produce any real results, just as if you change the hands on a clock; the time is still the same.

You've got body rust on your car, so the paint over it didn't change the rot that's going on even though it might look nice.

An alchemical notebook is simply a way of notating the corresponding changes which have taken place to a known road map. The ***Sephir Sephiroth*** is another type of road map which notates change.

All the apparent complexity of alchemy disappears when we realize that all of the alchemical notations are results, not causes, which occur in a cumulative sequence. So the alchemical sequence—which is notated in alchemical notebooks—is a road, a path, a map, if you wish, of the evolution of the being. When this occurs—when such and such an alchemical event occurs—you can be sure that this change in being has occurred to produce it unless you have acted directly upon the machine to produce that change externally and artificially.

It is possible to artificially produce what are alchemical changes in the machine without the cause, which is called the first cause or the first water. The first cause is the deep change.

The catalyst is the change in being which is then reflected in the machine which is then further capable of an advanced change, which is reflected by the being changing the machine. The machine then becomes a different machine producing a different change in being which is reflected in the machine, which produces a change in the machine, and because it is a different machine produces a different transformational effect, and so forth.

The machine is constantly changing.

It is changing because it is reflected; it reflects the change of the being, becomes a different machine producing a different change which is reflected in the machine producing a different change reflecting the machine. It is a spiraling mutually reciprocating feedback system. Once it begins, there is no stopping it.

But there can be no real change in Essence unless the machine is awake. Even an altered machine if it is not awake, will not function transformationally.

Some people feel that awakening, what is called "Enlightenment" is a huge step, but it is only a first beginning, a very small step toward work on self, and must be transcended before any serious work is to begin. Yet it is a step we must not miss or bypass.

Awakening is a little thing so subtle that it can be missed. You can be awake and not know it, but you will never fail to recognize it once you know what it is to be awake. It is a subtle change in how you exist, in your relationship. You can be asleep to your awakening. You ***can*** be asleep to your awakening. It is a subtle change.

But if the machine falls asleep, it does not stop, it simply ceases to continue. There is a difference between ceasing to continue and stopping. The process does not stop; it simply comes to a halt for the moment. For the moment, when the machine falls asleep, the alchemical process stops. But it is not stopping, it is just ceasing to continue. It does not go back, but it is cumulative. It does not regress, but it may not continue for a hundred-thousand years. It is always stabilized at each complete alchemical process; the process is stabilized. There is no reversal of it. So once begun you must finish, otherwise you live in pain.

And who says that you'll be feeling pain when you do?

There is no pain in real suffering. Real suffering can be joyous, and it is joyous. It could be called the joy of suffering.

Even evolution is sacrificed at one point. Everything—everything—eventually we must lose faith completely in absolutely everything we have come to believe in and rely upon.

Exactly what are the mechanisms by which an automobile propels itself and what are the torque valves and torque systems? What exactly are the gear ratio mechanisms? How do they work? Why does the engine rotate at a certain speed? And exactly what is the gas displacement involved? And the power's heat transfer must be taken into account. Everything about an automobile is in transfer of energy. Heat, mechanical energy, rods, pulleys, levers—you are talking about rocker arms, and if you analyze them, you will see a transfer of energy. And why must we have rocker arms? Why must there be pistons? Why must there be time and why must they fire in the way that they do, in the paticular sequence they fire in? Is there some sort of delicate balance which is maintained by the firing sequence of an engine? Of course there is.

And how is this transfer of energy accomplished through the drive train? And how do the axles transfer the energy to the wheels? And why are the wheels a particular diameter that they are? For what reason is that? And why is that ratio exact to the ratio of the gear train, and so forth. How about the weight of the automobile—we are talking about acceleration, gravity, vector analysis. As soon as you move an automobile across a plain, transversing gravity, gravitational effect, we are talking about vectors, and acceleration and deceleration. Can you drive the automobile without knowing all that?

I do not have to know how the car works in order to drive the car, but knowing something about the car helps me keep the car in good repair—to keep it running smoothly and efficiently.

Some sad alchemists do such bizarre things to alter the organic machine—to alter the body—in hopes that some sort of internal change will, as a result, take place, but this is not the way to cause Real Change.

The Popcorn Exercise as given in ***Practical Work On Self**** and as demonstrated in the video of the same name, is the beginning of the adoration exercise and can bring about Real Change.

An alchemical notebook is not a cookbook; it is a map. Can you see the difference between a cookbook and a map? One is linear, one is not linear. The cookbook you follow step-by-step, a map you can look anywhere you want to, and must know where you wish to go and even more importantly, exactly where you are now, which requires nonidentification with the machine and with its beliefs and imperatives.

What do you actually need to know about alchemy? Awakening produces transformation. Transformation is reflected in alchemical processes—alchemical results in the body. All you need to do is learn how to read the map.

So all you have to do is learn how to read the thing that says, you are here—the little red arrow that says ***"You Are Here,"*** and to move that arrow to your actual location when appropriate.

This of course means recognizing changes in the machine and in ourselves when they occur, which means having a serious degree of high impartial attention on the machine and the parts of the machine such as the mind and emotions, as well as having transcended or mostly transcended the organic machine's organic imperatives, beliefs and self-gratifications, which is to say, its automatic self-defense by lying to itself about itself.

The development of will depends completely upon the development of Conscience, which in turn depends on the development of impartiality, which itself depends upon the ability to stop lying to oneself about oneself, which is a product of self-discipline and the will to see oneself as one really is.

Most people think "conscience" refers to other human beings or to the planet or to animals or to some religious concept of good and evil or to social behavior, or to some moral judgment imposed from outside oneself. Conscience is something which arises from within the self, and which cannot be transcended or avoided.

Conscience is not about others—it is your own relationship with the Absolute.

* 1992, Gateways/I.D.H.H.B., Inc., Nevada City, CA
and Cloister Recordings Video #076

CHAPTER 67
HISTORICAL PAGAN ROOTS

THE MAJORITY of professors would be horrified if they knew what the word sabbatical originally meant. "Sabbatical" began when King's College in England allowed their teachers, who were also Priests, to take one month off during high summer solstice for the sabbat which was a month-long pagan ritual. Only later did the term come to mean a period of time taken for study at another university.

Participants prepared for the rituals of the sabbats and esbbats? By smearing ointment on their bodies—herbal ointments made with belladonna, wolfsbane, rue, mugwort, ellecampagne and henbane.

There was a war in England, over the right of succession. King Charles rode out between the two warring armies and rolled up his sleeve. On his left arm was a black garter which signified that he was the head of the thirteenth coven of the thirteen covens of England. He therefore exposed himself as head of the Wicca. Both armies promptly stopped fighting.

After this was formed the Order of the Garter in which the members originally were witches, practicing the ancient pagan rites. All members wore garters under their sleeves. The color of the garter depended on the coven to which they belonged. There were twelve covens with thirteen members each. The thirteenth coven was composed of the heads of all twelve covens and the King of England was the supreme covenmaster of all thirteen covens.

Similarly there were thirteen apostles including the Beloved disciple, the one whose name was John. That is, there was another John, just as there were two James.

Jesus Christ was known as Isa the Nazorean— Nazorean means healer. He was known as a healer and never claimed to be the Messiah or from Nazareth.

The reason this is important to you as an alchemist is so that you understand that almost nothing you think you know is true, and historical facts are the worst of all, because history is inevitably written by the winner.

Wiccans and other Pagans were branded as evil by the Catholic Church, simply so it could remain in power. It ruthlessly suppressed all competition in the same way that MicroSoft and eBay destroy all competitors, disregarding all laws regarding monopolies. In the Middle Ages, there were no laws against destroying all competition, and in modern times there might as well not be, either, because large corporations can do pretty much as they please, just as if they were a State Church.

The Inquisition was originally just that—an inquiry into the situation of heresy; it soon became a potent and dangerous political tool in much the same way that Senator Joe McCarthy applied the principles of the Inquisition to American politics in the 1950s.

Alchemy was forced into hiding by the Inquisition, and all alchemists since that time have used a variety of secret codes and encryptions to disguise their writings, not so much in fear that someone would abuse the ideas, because without discipline the ideas are useless anyway, but more because throughout history alchemy and any truly higher principles have always been ruthlessly destroyed by the reigning religious bodies as heresy.

Alchemy is a dangerous idea only in that it offers an alternative to dying like a dog, and churches prefer that their parishioners go quietly to the grave after leaving their estates to the church, and most folks are content with that arrangement.

CHAPTER 68
PSYCHE AND ESSENCE

IN ORDER to understand what happens to one during Conscious Sex it is necessary to understand the relationship between the ordinary consciousness, or the ***Psyche***, and the Superconsciousness which is the awakened subconscious, which is called ***Essence***.

It is Essence which represents the Deep Self, not the Psyche or Personality. We will begin by defining these words to see how the definition may help one to clarify and understand them.

The Essence, or Deep Self, is composed of eighteen Primordial

Habits. These are automatic programs. They are so automatic that they do not depend upon any external influences for their existence. These habits are the only part of one's consciousness and identity which survive death. That is why the Essence is also called the ***Body of Habits***.

Under optimum conditions the habits contained in the Essence should automatically create the impulses to live a conscious life, and to take only the Higher Rebirths. They should also contain the urge to awaken in each life form.

But in most individuals the habits composing the Essence have accumulated at random, thus creating impulses to take rebirth in lower forms, collect possessions, aggressively extend power, and to live in fear and ignorance. What has happened to make this come about?

Habits accumulate naturally from one's experience in time and space. Ordinarily time/space experiences should have no effect on the Body of Habits, but in order to attain this immunity one must have crystallized the Seventh Body, or Higher Being Body. If this has not occurred, the habits contained in the Essence can be replaced by other habits accumulated from time/space experiences. These time/space habits tend to be survival and pleasure-oriented.

Survival does not care how you survive. It has integrity only in the matter of survival. It provides no opportunity for the evolution of the Essence, because it has no use for conscience and compassion.

One can call this collection of unconsciously accumulated habits ***Essence, Karma, DNA,*** the ***Soul*** or the ***Transit Guide***. Through the action of this Body of Habits one is helplessly compelled to dramatize the same things over and over again, to form the same personality or psyche again and again, to relate to the same types of individuals again and again. One is doomed to endless and eternal repetition until these Basic Essence Habits are replaced by conscious habits. This cannot happen accidentally or through outside influences. Lessons Unlearned Will Be Repeated. This endless repetition of life after life is called the ***"Wheel of Karma"*** or ***"Recurrence"*** which is discussed at length in the vintage Red House video, ***The Recurrence Talk****, taped in 1971.

During periods of stress, the Essence becomes the controlling mechanism, because no other invoked presence can be present at that time.

---

* Archive Video #085-088, Cloister Recordings, Nevada City, CA

In ordinary calm periods, one is controlled by—and identifies oneself as—the psyche. The psyche is composed of habits also, but they do not survive during stress. They are the Minor Habits, created and programmed in by social and cultural conditioning. Here one finds the habits of eating, sleeping, breathing, thinking, moving, gender and social roles, memory and body perceptions and language, among others.

The psyche is the mind, plus the body, plus the nervous system. But it does not include the muscle system. The muscle system is the physical expression of the Body of Habits—the Essence.

During stress, when the psyche is forced to close down, it is this muscle system which rules the organism, acting as if it were a mind—but a very simple one.

In modern life the psyche almost always dominates the Essence, because life seems very complex, and the Essence is too simple to handle it. There is a moment during which the Essence gives control of the organism to the psyche. This is called the ***Great Moment of Self-Betrayal.***

When a period of stress occurs, the psyche closes down. Stress produces large amounts of electricity through the nervous system, and the psyche is not built to handle large voltages. So it closes down and isolates itself until the emergency is over. This protected state of the psyche is called "sporing."

Essence handles emergency conditions because it is able to function under high voltage. It is programmed to survive by copying earlier actions that worked to help it survive. The action may be wildly inappropriate now, or even harmful, but it will stupidly copy some past action that worked before, just because it worked before. It may not even have worked before, as a matter of fact. One may have been doing deep knee-bends during an earthquake and because one survived the earthquake the Body of Habits uses that action whenever the ground shakes.

If one observes oneself while under stress—severe stress—one can see why this subject should be of concern to anyone wishing to use and experience Conscious Sex.

Under ordinary conditions of life, the actions, attitudes and experience of the Essence will be anything ***but*** conscious. And yet Essence is the identity with which one will experience sex, because sex induces a high-stress state.

When one becomes aware of the existence of deep programming—the habits in the Body of Habits—one usually wishes to immediately replace them with "good" habits. But without knowing what to change and what to put in its place, one may make it even worse than before.

One may then decide to eliminate all habits. But one cannot eliminate habits. Habits ***are*** the Essence—the Deep Self. One cannot remove the self from the self.

It is valuable to alter the Essence along conscious lines, but this can only be accomplished through reaching and altering the deep levels of programming in the muscles and Movement Centrum.

Most people fear their Essence—and rightly so. They spend their lives in futile searches to avoid stress, thus enhancing the psyche and keeping it in control. But perhaps that is better than running amok.

Various forms of self-calming are used in modern cultures to prevent the accidental breakdown of cultural programming.

Of course this completely prevents the development of the Essence, because if it is not exposed, it is not open to learning or to reprogramming. Certain kinds of stress are good for replacement of habits while others are not. For example, the stress induced by drugs is a method of replacing habits, but the substitution always occurs on a random basis. Thus one may do terrible harm to the Essence. If the Essence is at all disposed to work on itself and toward its development, it is best not to tamper with it.

Essence is kept hidden beneath the veneer of the psyche because it would be hard for most people to function simply. It would also be embarrassing to be unable to read, write or talk. Essence may have shut down at a very early age, leaving one barely able to do more than open the mouth and suck milk from a nipple.

Many yogis and fakirs who suddenly give up their psyches are left in this condition.

But it is possible to pre-train the Essence to be able to function without the direction of the psyche. It is this pre-breakdown training, or Body Drills, which form the Teaching called the Sly Path. It makes possible the same thing as breaking down the ego or psyche without this preparation, but instead of being a helpless baby as a result, one is able to ***do***.

Through the intentional use of stress factors the Essence can be exposed on a more or less permanent basis. This stress is caused only by intentional struggle with the self and with one's nature. It is a battle between the higher centrums and the lower centrums, each of which have different goals.

Many people think that Buddha sat under the Bodhi tree to relax, or that meditation is a refuge from stress. This is opposite from the truth. The fact is that the Buddha sat under the Bodhi tree to wage a battle with his desires. This internal struggle is called Intentional Suffering.

Only by continuous Intentional Suffering is it possible to open the Essence and make the delicate changes necessary for conscious life. If the Essence remains buried beneath the obscuring force of the psyche, no real change in the Being is possible. The mind may change, the personality may change, basic behavior patterns may change, but there is no lasting change. Everything will be the same as before.

Even if one is willing to create stress for oneself, it usually takes the wrong form. Instead of using correct stress factors, one may prefer to believe that other more pleasurable stress factors are just as good. Thus one may use subjective art, dance or music, and self-calming meditations as stress factors. Or one may use negative stress as if it were the Method for using intentional stress factors.

Development along mental and physical lines seems like a good idea while in life, because one wishes to be successful and comfortable. For most people this kind of success is sufficient, and they do not mind the endless cycle of repetition because they do not remember it. But for some people this is not enough.

When one has learned through the Method—using intentional stress factors, one of which is Conscious Sex—to replace the automatic habits of Essence with conscious habits, one will have brought the body, mind and emotions into a usable form. Then one is ready to begin Real Work—the Crystallization of the Higher Bodies.

Dear Reader of *Alchemical Sex*,

If you have enjoyed reading this book, and have finally arrived at this last page, you have sincerely deserved a special reward for your endurance and attention.

This reward comes in the form of a promise. We at Gateways Books and Tapes have now, for almost thirty years, brought the finest spiritual and esoteric classics to you, which are otherwise very hard to find. Our promise to you is that we will continue to make available to you, our esteemed reader, a selection of the finest consciousness-related writings of our times.

For a current catalog and referral to related books and study materials, you may contact Gateways at the address below with no obligation to purchase.

Gateways Books and Tapes
P.O. Box 370-ALCH
Nevada City, CA 95959
(800) 869-0658 or (530) 272-0180
www.gatewaysbooksandtapes.com
email: info@gatewaysbooksandtapes.com

Gateways Consciousness Classics

A Partial List of Titles You Can Order

(See www.gatewaysbooksandtapes.com for complete current book list)

by Robert S. de Ropp

The Master Game: Pathways to Higher Consciousness
Self-Completion: Keys to a Meaningful Life
Warrior's Way: A Twentieth Century Odyssey

by E.J. Gold

American Book of the Dead
The Great Adventure: Talks on Death, Dying and the Bardos
The Human Biological Machine as a Transformational Apparatus
Practical Work on Self
The Hidden Work
The Seven Bodies of Man
Visions in the Stone: Journey to the Source of Hidden Knowledge
(Intro. by Robert Anton Wilson)

by John C. Lilly, M.D.

The Deep Self (due in 2003)
with E. J. Gold: *Tanks for the Memories*

by Claudio Naranjo, M.D.

Character & Neurosis: An Integrative View
The Divine Child and the Hero: Inner Meaning in Children's Literature
The Enneagram of Society (due in 2003)

by Reb Zalman Schachter-Shalomi & Howard Schwartz

The Dream Assembly

by Ka-Tzetnik 135633

Shivitti: A Vision

by Dr. Claude Needham, Ph.D.

The Original Handbook for the Recently Deceased

by Mark Olsen

The Golden Buddha Changing Masks: Essays on the Spiritual Dimensions of Acting